GEOLOGY AND REVELATION.

Sicut Augustinus docet, in hujusmodi quæstionibus duo sunt observanda. Primo quidem ut veritas Scripturæ inconcusse teneatur. Secundo, cum Scriptura Divina multipliciter exponi possit, quod nulli expositioni aliquis ita præcise inhæreat, ut si certa ratione constiterit hoc esse falsum quod aliquis sensum Scripturæ esse credebat, id nihilominus asserere præsumat; ne Scriptura ex hoc ab infidelibus derideatur, et ne eis via credendi præcludatur.

S. Thomas, *De Opere Secundæ Diei;* Summa, Pars 1, Quæst. 68, Art. 1.

As Augustine teacheth, there are two things to be observed in questions of this kind. First, that the truth of Scripture be inviolably maintained. Secondly, since Divine Scripture may be explained in many ways, that no one cling to any particular exposition with such pertinacity that, if what he supposed to be the teaching of Scripture should turn out to be plainly false, he would nevertheless presume to put it forward; lest thereby Sacred Scripture should be exposed to the derision of unbelievers, and the way of salvation should be closed to them.

Saint Thomas, *On the Work of the Second Day.*

GEOLOGY AND REVELATION:

OR THE

Ancient History of the Earth,

CONSIDERED IN THE LIGHT OF

GEOLOGICAL FACTS AND REVEALED RELIGION.

WITH ILLUSTRATIONS.

BY THE

REV. GERALD MOLLOY, D. D.,

PROFESSOR OF THEOLOGY IN THE ROYAL COLLEGE OF ST. PATRICK, MAYNOOTH.

WITH AN INTRODUCTION

To the American edition; and a chapter on COSMOGONY, [by permission] from the Manual of Geology, by Prof. J. D. DANA.

NEW YORK:

G. P. PUTNAM & SONS,

1870.

Stereotyped by LITTLE, RENNIE & CO., 645 and 647 Broadway, N. Y.

PRESS OF THE NEW YORK PRINTING COMPANY, 81, 83, and 85 Centre St., N. Y.

To the Very Reverend

CHARLES WILLIAM RUSSELL, D. D.,

PRESIDENT OF SAINT PATRICK'S COLLEGE, MAYNOOTH,

This Volume is Inscribed,

WITH EVERY SENTIMENT OF AFFECTION AND RESPECT.

PREFACE.

HE progress of modern Science has given rise to not a few objections against the truths of Revelation. And of these there is none which seems to have taken such a firm hold of the public mind in England, and, indeed, throughout Europe generally, as that which is derived from the interesting and startling discoveries of Geology. Accordingly, when I was engaged, some years ago, in explaining and defending the Evidences of Revealed Religion, I found myself brought face to face with Geological phenomena and Geological speculations.

It was plainly impossible to consider, in a candid and philosophical spirit, the argument with which I had to deal, so long as I remained ignorant of the evidence on which it was based. I resolved, therefore, to make myself familiar with the leading principles and the leading facts of Geology. And thus I was drawn insensibly into the study of this science; to which I have devoted, for some years, the greater part of my leisure hours.

Impressed with the conviction that no fact can be really at variance with Revealed Truth, I determined, in the first place, to ascertain the facts which have been brought to light by the researches of Geologists. The general principles, which might afterward appear to be clearly involved in these facts when duly classified and arranged, I was fully prepared to admit. And I hoped, in the end, to search out and discover the harmony which, I was satisfied, must exist between conclusions thus established and the Inspired Word of God.

While occupied in working out this problem for myself, it was suggested to me that others, who had not time or opportunity to pursue the same line of inquiry, would, perhaps, be glad to share in the fruits of my studies. In deference to this suggestion I consented, not without misgivings, to write a series of papers on Geology in its relations with Revealed Religion, which have appeared, from time to time, in the *Irish Ecclesiastical Record.* From the attention these papers attracted, crude and fragmentary as they were, it soon became evident that the question was not without interest for a large class of readers. And I have been led to believe that a more full and mature, but at the same time a popular, Treatise on the subject would be a welcome accession to ecclesiastical literature, and would supply a want that has long been felt. Such a Treatise I have proposed to myself in the present Volume.

In Geology I wish to disclaim, at the outset, all pretension to original researches; which my opportunities did not permit, nor the scope of my Work demand. It was not my object to enlarge the bounds of Geological knowledge; but rather to ascertain what that knowledge is, and to set it before my readers in plain and simple words. For this purpose I have had recourse to the great masters of the science: and have endeavored to gather into a systematic form the phenomena upon which they are all agreed; to sketch in outline the general theory about which there is practically no dispute; and to draw out the line of reasoning by which, as it seems to me, this theory may be most effectively demonstrated.

Exact references are given to the original authorities on all questions of importance, and on many points even of minor detail: partly that I might not seem to claim as my own what belongs to others; partly that I might consult for the convenience of those who should wish to investigate more minutely what I have but lightly touched. And here it may be well to observe, with regard to the two classic works of Sir Charles Lyell, his *Elements* and his *Principles*, which have been reproduced so many times and in so many forms, that I have uniformly referred to the latest edition of each.

The Woodcuts which illustrate the Volume will, I venture to hope, help to convey a clear and distinct impression of many natural objects which can be represented but imperfectly in words. Some of the most striking and effective are taken from the admirable Manual of Geology brought out some years ago by the Reverend Doctor Haughton, of Trinity College, Dublin. My best thanks are due to the learned author for the kindness with which he placed his Woodblocks at my disposal. I have also to express my acknowledgments to Sir Charles Lyell, who has allowed me to reproduce some of the drawings that embellish his works; and to the eminent publishers, Messrs. Bell and Daldy of London, and Mr. Nimmo of Edinburgh, who have, with great courtesy, furnished me with electrotypes of several figures from the works of Doctor Mantell and Mr. Hugh Miller.

To my colleagues in Maynooth I am much indebted for their judicious suggestions and friendly assistance during the progress of the Work. In particular I desire to testify my obligations to our distinguished Professor of Scripture, the Reverend Doctor M'Carthy, for the unwearied kindness with which he has allowed me to draw at pleasure on his profound and extensive knowledge of the Sacred Text.

G. M.

SAINT PATRICK'S COLLEGE, MAYNOOTH,
December 1st, 1869.

PREFACE TO THE AMERICAN EDITION.

DR. MOLLOY has, in the present work, made an important contribution to a department of scientific and theologic literature, which has already been enriched by the labors of several other Catholic Fathers, among whom must be mentioned CARDINAL WISEMAN,* FATHER PERRONE,† and FATHER PIANCIANI,‡ who, in Italy, maintain substantially, the same ground which, in England, has been sustained by DR. CHALMERS, DR. BUCKLAND, PYE SMITH, and HUGH MILLER, and we may now add with pleasure, by DR. MOLLOY. Names which, in the United States, find their counterparts in DR. HITCHCOCK, PROF. SILLIMAN, PROF. A. GUYOT, DR. THOMPSON, and J. D. DANA.

Reviewing the progress of opinion touching the relations of Science to Revealed Religion, it is noteworthy that while many Protestant theologians and writers on both sides of the Atlantic have, until a recent period, treated the discoveries of science, and especially of Geology, so far as they affect theological dogmas, in a manner, if not of contempt, at least of distrust or unfairness: on the contrary, the Romanist writers who have discussed these themes, have done so, generally, in a spirit of broad catholicity well calculated to command the respect it merits. They have shown no sensitiveness or timidity lest, perchance, their exegesis might be disturbed by candidly admitting the changes demanded by the discoveries of Science.

* Twelve Lectures on the Connection between Science and Revealed Religion, by NICHOLAS WISEMAN, D.D., Principal of the English College, and Professor in the University of Rome. Andover: Gould & Newman, 1837.

† Prelectiones Theologicæ.

‡ Cosmogonia Naturale comparata Col Genesi.

The author's discussion of the principles of Geology evinces much familiarity both with the science and what is equally important, the necessities of the unscientific reader. He has presented, in the second part of his book, an interesting review, infused by copious quotations from the Christian Fathers, from the time of St. Augustine, showing that long before Geology had any existence as a science, and of course, when the discussions and doubts it has excited were unknown, the essential points respecting Time and the order of Creation had received careful attention from devout thinkers, and that the conclusions at which they arrived, on purely theological grounds, were, in most cases, much the same as those which the best writers of our time deduce from Geological evidence.

It is now thirty-five years since (1835) CARDINAL, then DR. WISEMAN, delivered in Rome, before the English College, of which he was the head, his Lectures, already referred to, on the connection between Science and Religion, in the fifth and sixth of which he considers more particularly the Geological argument. The spirit of these lectures was a just rebuke to the narrow bigotry of such writers as MR. CROLY, FAIRHOLM, and GRANVILLE PENN, as well as certain American theologians, who, by means of arrogance and denunciation, sought to silence the voice of truth, as proclaimed in the language of discovery, announcing the nature and the extent of those changes in life and in physical development which are recorded in the Genesis of the Rocks, because they conceived these immutable truths must of necessity conflict with the Genesis of Moses; the real conflict being only with their narrow interpretations. With rare moral courage DR. WISEMAN grappled with the great questions discussed so well in his lectures, at a time when there prevailed, with reference to such themes, a very wide-spread distrust, even among men of moderate opinions. In fact, the candor and courtesy displayed by DR. WISEMAN in his lectures, presents an enviable contrast to the acrimony of many theologians, and worthy of all praise, and in harmony with the learning and good taste which characterize his writings.

DR. MOLLOY is a worthy disciple of the same school, and

we are glad to find in him the same candor and liberality which it is certainly to be hoped he will receive at the hands of those who may differ from him. His geological arguments and illustrations are very naturally drawn, chiefly from British authorities. It is evident that the condition of opinion upon these matters among religious teachers and readers in Great Britain is less advanced than it is in this country or in continental Europe. Our author has obviously but little familiarity with the American literature of this subject. The similarity in some parts of his book both in thought and style with the writings on this subject of the late PROFESSOR SILLIMAN, of Yale College, is quite noticeable. He has obviously not seen the writings of DR. HITCHCOCK, of GUYOT, of DANA, and of other American writers. We have therefore by the kind permission of the author reproduced in this edition the chapter on COSMOGONY from PROFESSOR DANA'S *Manual of Geology.** The views set forth, in a very condensed form, in this chapter, embrace also the ideas of PROFESSOR ARNOLD GUYOT, of Princeton, as presented by him in his unpublished lecture upon the same subject.

American readers will remember also that PROFESSOR DANA has discussed this subject much more at length in a series of papers published in the *Bibliotheca Sacra*,† in a review of DR. TAYLER LEWIS'S *Six Days of Creation.*‡ It is greatly to be desired that PROFESSOR DANA should soon make a revised edition of his various writings upon this subject, a work which would be received with interest on both sides of the Atlantic.

We do not propose here to present the bibliography of this subject with any completeness, but we desire to mention, to those who have not seen it, a little volume of excellent spirit by DR. JOS. P. THOMPSON, of New York, entitled *Man in Genesis*

* A Manual of Geology; treating of the Principles of the science with special reference to American Geological History, etc., by JAMES D. DANA, M. A., LL. D., etc., 8vo, pp. 998. Philadelphia: Thos. Bliss & Co.

† January and July, 1856, and April and July, 1857, covering in all 219 pages, 8vo.

‡ The Six Days of Creation, or the Scriptural Cosmology; with the Ancient Idea of Time Worlds in Distinction from Worlds in Space, by TAYLER LEWIS, Professor of Greek in Union College. 12mo, pp. 407. Schenectady, 1855.

and Geology,* which discusses chiefly the relations of man tc creation, in seven lectures, the first of which is an "Outline of Creation in Genesis." Even as we write another small volume on this subject comes to hand under the title of *Chemical History of the Six Days of Creation*,† by MR. JOHN PHIN, which also contains the substance of a series of lectures delivered by the author, who handles his theme in a spirit equally reverential and scientific, and well calculated to do good.

Those who desire to know the best exposition of this subject at the hands of a modern theologian will read the first part of DR. LANGE'S *Genesis, or the First Book of Moses*,‡ in DR. TAYLER LEWIS'S translation, pp. 159–177. The candid and scholarly spirit of the learned authors of this work indicates a marked change in discussions of this nature when compared with similar literature of the last generation.

These few suggestions, chiefly on the American literature of this subject, are offered in the belief that some readers may be glad to know where to turn for similar discussions, while DR. MOLLOY will certainly not misinterpret our kindly intentions in suggesting to him some contemporary sources of information to most of which he very probably had no means of access when his excellent work was prepared.

JULY, 1870.

* Man in Genesis and Geology; or, the Bible account of Man's Creation tested by Scientific Theories of his Origin and Antiquity, by JOSEPH P. THOMPSON, D.D., LL.D. New York, 12mo, pp. 149. 1870.

† The Chemical History of the Six Days of Creation, by JOHN PHIN, editor of the Technologist. American News Company, New York, pp. 95, 12mo, 1870.

‡ Genesis, or the First Book of Moses, together with a General Theological and Homitetical Introduction to the Old Testament, by JOHN PETER LANGE, D. D., Professor in Ordinary of Theology in the University of Bonn. Translated from the German, with additions by Professor TAYLER LEWIS, LL. D., Schenectady, New York, and A. GOSMAN, D. D., Lawrenceville, N. J. New York: Charles Scribner & Co., 654 Broadway. 1868. 8vo, pp. 665.

CONTENTS.

INTRODUCTORY CHAPTER.

PART I.

GEOLOGICAL THEORY AND THE EVIDENCE BY WHICH IT IS SUPPORTED.

CHAPTER I.

THEORY OF GEOLOGISTS.

CHAPTER II.

THEORY OF DENUDATION ILLUSTRATED BY FACTS.

CHAPTER VI.

STRATIFIED ROCKS OF MECHANICAL ORIGIN—FURTHER ILLUSTRATIONS.

CHAPTER VII.

STRATIFIED ROCKS OF CHEMICAL ORIGIN.

CHAPTER VIII.

STRATIFIED ROCKS OF ORGANIC ORIGIN—ILLUSTRATIONS FROM ANIMAL LIFE.

CHAPTER IX.

STRATIFIED ROCKS OF ORGANIC ORIGIN—ILLUSTRATIONS FROM VEGETABLE LIFE.

CHAPTER XVI.

SUBTERRANEAN HEAT—ITS POWERS ILLUSTRATED BY EARTHQUAKES.

CHAPTER XVII.

SUBTERRANEAN HEAT—ITS POWERS ILLUSTRATED BY UNDULATIONS OF THE EARTH'S CRUST.

PART II.

THE ANTIQUITY OF THE EARTH CONSIDERED IN RELATION TO THE HISTORY OF GENESIS.

CHAPTER XVIII.

STATEMENT OF THE QUESTION AND EXPOSITION OF THE AUTHOR'S VIEW.

CHAPTER XIX.

FIRST HYPOTHESIS;—AN INTERVAL OF INDEFINITE DURATION BETWEEN THE CREATION OF THE WORLD AND THE FIRST MOSAIC DAY.

CHAPTER XX.

SECOND HYPOTHESIS;—THE DAYS OF CREATION LONG PERIODS OF TIME.

CHAPTER XXI.

APPLICATION OF THE SECOND HYPOTHESIS TO THE MOSAIC HISTORY OF CREATION—CONCLUSION.

LIST OF ILLUSTRATIONS.

LIST OF TABLES.

GEOLOGY AND REVELATION.

INTRODUCTORY CHAPTER.

Scope of the work explained—Geology looked on with suspicion by Christians—Hailed with triumph by Unbelievers—No contradiction possible between the works of Nature and the Word of God—Author not jealous of progress in Geological Discoveries—Points of contact between Geology and Revelation—The question stated—The answer—Division of the work.

MONG the various pursuits that engage the human mind, there are few so attractive as Geology, none so important as Revelation. Each of these two studies has an interest peculiar to itself. The one is chiefly concerned about the world in which we are living: the other about the world to which we are hastening. Geology leads us down into the depths of the Earth, and there, unfolding to our view a long series of strange unwritten records impressed on lasting monuments by the hand of Nature, it proceeds to trace back the history of our Globe through myriads of ages into the distant past. Revelation, on the other hand, comes to us from above; and setting forth the far more wonderful records of God's dealings with man, holds out the hope of another world "everlasting in

* 2 Cor. vi. 1.

the heavens"* which shall still remain when this earth and all the works that are therein shall have melted away with fervent heat.*

But, it may be asked, why should two such incongruous topics be set down for discussion side by side? To answer this question is to explain the scope and design of the present work. We are not going to write a Manual of Geology; nor yet a Treatise on Revelation. Taken separately, these two subjects have been handled with eminent skill and ability; the one by the votaries of Science, the other by the friends of Theology. It is our purpose to consider them not so much in themselves as in their mutual relations: to compare the conclusions of Geology with the truths of Revelation; and to inquire if it be possible to accept the one and yet not to abandon the other.

An uneasy apprehension has long prevailed among devout Christians, and a declared conviction among a large class of unbelievers, that the discoveries of Geology are at variance with the facts recorded in the Book of Genesis. Now, the historical narrative of Genesis lies at the very foundation of all Revealed Religion. Hence the science of Geology, has come to be looked on with suspicion by the simple-minded faithful, and to be hailed with joy, as a new and powerful auxiliary, by that infidel party which, in these latter days, has assumed a position so bold and defiant. It is now confidently asserted that we cannot uphold the teaching of Revelation, unless we shut our eyes to the evidence of Geology; and that we cannot pursue the study of Geology, if we are not prepared to renounce our belief in the doctrines of Revelation.

Yet surely this cannot be. Truth cannot be at variance with truth. If God has recorded the history of our Globe, as Geologists maintain, on imperishable monuments within the Crust of the Earth, we may be quite sure He has not

* 2 Pet. iii. 10.

contradicted that Record in His Written Word. There may be for a time, indeed, a conflict between the student of Nature and the student of Revelation. Each is liable to error when he undertakes to interpret the record that is placed in his hands. Many a brilliant Geological theory, received at first with unbounded applause, has been dissipated by the progress of discovery even within the lifetime of its author. On the other hand, it cannot be denied that Theologians have sometimes imputed to the Bible that which the Bible does not teach. Learned and pious men—Protestants and Catholics alike—once believed that the Book of Joshua represents the succession of day and night as produced by the revolution of the Sun around the Earth: whereas it is now considered quite plain that the Book of Joshua, properly understood, teaches nothing of the kind; but that the Inspired Writer, in describing a wonderful phenomenon of Nature, simply employs the language of men according to the established usage of his time. We need not wonder, therefore, that a conflict of opinion should sometimes arise between the Geologist and the Theologian; but a conflict there cannot be between the story which God has described on His works and the story He has recorded in His Written Word.

Though we come forward, therefore, among those whose duty and whose glory it is to uphold Revelation, we are by no means jealous of the wonderful ardor, and we may add, the wonderful success, with which the study of Geology has been lately pursued. We have too much confidence in the truth of our cause to apprehend that it can suffer in any way from the progress of Natural Science. It is our conviction, rather, that the more thoroughly the works of Nature are understood, the more perfectly they will be found to harmonize with the truths of Revelation. We are not afraid, therefore, to venture into the realms of Geology and to come face to face with its discoveries. Too long, perhaps, has this interesting and popular science been neglected by those who are ranged under the banner of Religion. Let it be ours to show that the study of God's works is not incompatible with the belief in God's Word; and that it is quite possible to investigate the ancient history of the world we inhabit without forfeiting our right to a better.

The points of contact between Geology and Revelation are chiefly these two:—First, the Antiquity of the Earth; Secondly, the Antiquity of the Human Race. In the present Volume we shall confine our attention to the Antiquity of the Earth. The subject that offers itself for discussion may be stated in a few words. Geologists maintain that the Crust of the Earth has been slowly built up by means of a long series of operations which would require hundreds of thousands, perhaps millions of years for their accomplishment: whereas the Bible narrative, it is alleged, allows but the short lapse of six or eight thousand years from the creation of the world to the present time. The Geological record, then, seems to contradict the Mosaic; and the question is, how this apparent contradiction is to be explained.

Some have ventured to solve the problem by rejecting the historical narrative of the Bible: others by ignoring the plain facts of Geology. But there is a third class of writers, including many names of the highest eminence and authority, who contend that we may admit the extreme Antiquity of our Globe, which Geology so imperatively demands, without compromising in the smallest degree the truthfulness of the Mosaic story. They say that the Chronology of the Bible stops short with Adam, and does not go back to the beginning of the world. By means of the data which the Bible supplies we may calculate, at least roughly, the lapse of time from the Creation of Adam to the Birth of Christ. But from the first beginning of all created things, when God made the Heavens and the Earth, to the close of the Sixth Day when Adam was introduced upon the scene, that is an interval which, in the Bible narrative, is left altogether undefined and uncertain. This is the view which we hope to develop and to illustrate in the course of the following pages.

Our task naturally divides itself into two parts. First, it will be our duty to consider the received theory of Geology, and to examine in detail some of the interesting and wonderful phenomena on which it is founded. This course of investigation, while it is plainly indispensable for the intelligent appreciation of our subject, cannot fail at the same time to unfold many new and striking views of the Power, and the Goodness, and the Providence of God. "For the invisible things of Him from the creation of the world are clearly seen, being understood by the things that are made; even His eternal Power and Godhead."*

In the Second Part we shall consider the Antiquity of the Earth in reference to the History of Genesis. It will be our purpose to show that, as far as the Bible narrative is concerned, an interval of countless ages may have elapsed between the first creation of the Heavens and the Earth and the beginning of the Six Mosaic Days. Furthermore, we shall contend that, without any prejudice to the Sacred History, we may suppose these Days themselves to have been, not days in the ordinary sense of the word, but long and indefinite Periods of Time. If we succeed in establishing these views, it will be obvious to infer that, while the Bible enables us to determine, at least by approximation, the Age of the Human Race, it allows time without limit for the past history of the Earth.

* Rom. i. 18.

PART I.

GEOLOGICAL THEORY AND THE EVIDENCE BY WHICH IT IS SUPPORTED.

CHAPTER I.

THEORY OF GEOLOGISTS.

Geology defined—Facts and Theories—Recent progress of Geology—Stratification of Rocks—Aqueous Rocks; of Mechanical Origin—of Chemical Origin—of Organic Origin—Igneous Rocks, Plutonic and Volcanic—Metamorphic Rocks—Summary of the Rocks that compose the Crust of the Earth—Relative order of position—Internal condition of the Globe—Movements of the Earth's Crust—Subterranean disturbing force—Uplifting and bending of Strata—Denudation and its Causes—Fossil Remains—Their Value in Geological Theory.

HE object of Geology is to examine and record the appearances presented by the Crust of the Earth; and by the aid of these appearances, to trace out the long series of events by which it has been brought into its present condition. Geology, therefore, like all other natural sciences, is made up partly of fact, and partly of theory. It belongs to the Geologist first to investigate the phenomena which the Crust of the Earth exhibits to the eye. For this purpose he descends into the mine and the quarry; he visits the lofty cliff by the sea-shore, the deep ravine on

the mountain side, the cutting of a railway ; in a word, every spot where a section of the Earth's Crust is exposed to view, either by the action of Nature or by the hand of man. He then retires into the silence of his closet, with his note-book and his specimens ; and there, having arranged and classified the various phenomena which he has already examined with his eyes in the outer world, he proceeds to make his deductions, and to build up his theory. He seeks to explain how materials, so diverse in their composition, have come to be piled up together, with such admirable order, and yet with such endless variety; and how the solid rocks have come to be the repository of petrified trees and plants and bones and shells, which seem, as it were, to start up from their graves, and to tell strange stories of a bygone world.

In the early days of Geology there were comparatively few who devoted themselves with patient industry to the collection and classification of facts : while the number was legion of those who, with a very meagre knowledge of facts, set themselves to build up systems. A vast multitude of different and conflicting theories were, in this way, brought into existence, and attracted for a time much public attention, each one being vehemently defended by its friends and as vehemently assailed by its enemies. These theories resting on no solid foundation, could not hold their ground against the advancing tide of new discoveries. They flourished for a brief space, and then gave way to others scarcely more substantial, which were destined in their turn to be likewise rejected and forgotten. Thus it came to pass, from the manifest instability of its principles, that Geology was long held in light repute, and practical men set little store by its boasted discoveries and startling revelations.

But it would be unjust and unphilosophical to condemn the modern theory of Geologists because of their past errors. We must judge of this science, not according to what it once was in the feebleness of its infancy, but according to what it now is in the growing strength of its mature years. It seems to be in the nature of things that groundless speculations and wild conjectures go before, and sober Science follows in their wake. The visionary dreams of the Alchemist led the way to the science of Chemistry, and the idle fancies of the Astrologist have given place to the marvellous discoveries of Astronomy. So, too, amidst the confused mass of conflicting arguments and opinions, by which the phenomena of Geology were for a long time enveloped and obscured, the seeds of a new science were slowly germinating. New facts were eagerly sought after to support or to impugn the favorite theory of the hour; and though theory after theory passed away, yet the facts remained. In course of time this accumulation of facts became broad and deep and solid enough to form a sound basis for inductive reasoning; and thus almost within our own days Geology may be fairly said to have assumed the rank and dignity of a science.

During the last quarter of a century it has been studied with a more ardent enthusiasm than, perhaps, any other science in England, in France, in Germany, and in America. It has been studied, too, upon better principles than before: less attention has been paid to the building up of theories, and far more pains and labor have been expended on the careful investigation of natural phenomena. There are still, no doubt, different schools of Geologists which are divided among themselves as regards many important details of theory; but there are some general conclusions upon which all Geologists are substantially agreed, and which, they assure us, are established by evidence that is absolutely irresistible. It is to these conclusions we wish to invite the attention of our readers; for they bear very closely on the question of the Antiquity of the Earth.

Geologists tell us, then, that the materials of which the

Earth's Crust is composed, are not heaped together in a confused mass, but are disposed with evident marks of definite and systematic arrangement. This is an important truth, of which many examples are familiar to us all, though perhaps we do not all attend to their significance. Thus in a quarry, we see commonly enough first a bed of limestone, then above that a bed of gravel, and higher still a bed of clay : and even the limestone itself is not usually a compact mass, but is arranged in successive layers, something like the successive courses of masonry in a building. Now it appears that a very large proportion of the Earth's Crust is made up in this way of successive layers, or *strata*, as they are called by Geologists. These *strata* are composed of various substances, such as clay, chalk, sand, lime, and coal; and they present everywhere the same general appearances. They are known under the common name of Aqueous Rocks,* because it is believed that they were originally formed under water; and here it is that the professors of Geology first come into collision with the popular notions that formerly prevailed.

They hold that these stratified rocks were not arranged as we see them now, when the Earth first came from the hands

* It may be useful once for all to inform the reader that the term *Rock* is employed by Geologists in a technical sense. It is applied to every large mass of mineral matter that goes to form the Crust of the Earth, whether it be hard and strong, or soft and plastic. Thus, for example, gravel and clay, coal and slate, are called *Rocks*, just as well as limestone and granite. "Our older writers endeavored to avoid offering such violence to our language, by speaking of the component materials of the Earth as consisting of rocks and *soils*. But there is often so insensible a passage from a soft and incoherent state to that of stone, that Geologists of all countries have found it indispensable to have one technical term to include both, and in this sense we find *roche* applied in French, *rocca* in Italian, and *felsart* in German. The beginner, however, must constantly bear in mind, that the term rock by no means implies that a mineral mass is in an indurated or stony condition."—Lyell's Elements of Geology, p. 4.

of its Creator, but have been formed, during the lapse of unnumbered ages, by the operation of natural causes. Nay more, they have divided the rocks into sundry classes, and they undertake to explain the particular process by which each several variety has been produced. First in order and importance are those which derive their existence from the mechanical force of moving water. The materials of which they are composed first existed in the form of minute particles, which were transported by the action of water from one place to another; then they were spread out over a given surface, just as we now see layers of sand, or mud, or gravel deposited near the mouths of rivers, or in the estuaries of the sea, or even upon the land itself during temporary inundations. Lastly, after a long interval came the slow but certain process of consolidation. The fine sand was cemented together and became sandstone; the loose gravel by a similar process was transformed into a solid mass, known by the name of Conglomerate or Pudding-stone; while the soft mud by simple pressure was converted into a kind of slaty clay, called Shale. Thus from age to age Nature was ever building up new strata, and consolidating the old.

Next in order are the Aqueous Rocks, which owe their origin to the agency of chemical laws. To this class belong many of our limestone formations. Large quantities of carbonate of lime are held in solution by water charged with carbonic acid gas: when the carbonic acid, in course of time, passes off, the carbonate of lime can no longer be held in solution, and it is accordingly precipitated in a solid form to the bottom. In this manner was formed that peculiar kind of limestone called Travertine, which abounds in Italy, and which is well known to all who have visited Rome, as the stone of which the Coliseum was built. A still more familiar example, on a small scale, is seen in the case of Stalactites and Stalagmites. Water saturated with carbonic acid trickles down the sides, or drops from the roof of a limestone cavern. In its course it dissolves carbonate of lime, and holds it in solution; afterward, reaching the floor of the cavern, it slowly evaporates and leaves behind it a thin sheet of limestone which is called a Stalagmite; while the icicle-like pendants that are formed by a similar process, on the roof of the cavern, are called Stalactites.

There is a third class of Aqueous Rocks which are supposed to be made up almost exclusively of the fragmentary remains of plants and animals, and are therefore called Organic. The well-known coral reefs, so dreaded by the sailor in tropical seas, are believed to be nothing more than a mass of stony skeletons belonging to the minute marine animalcules known among zoologists as Polyps or Zoophytes. These little creatures, existing together in countless multitudes, extract carbonate of lime from the waters of the ocean in which they dwell, and by the action of their living organs, convert it into a solid frame or skeleton, which is called coral. From generation to generation the same process has been going on during the long succession of Geological ages; and huge masses of coral rock, hundreds of miles in length, have thus been slowly built up from fathomless depths of the ocean to within a few feet of its surface. Our vast coal formations, on the other hand, afford a ready example of rocks which are chiefly composed of vegetable remains.

So much for the Aqueous or Stratified Rocks. Geology next brings before us another and a very different group, of which the origin is ascribed to fire, and which are consequently designated by the title of Igneous Rocks. In their general appearance they are chiefly distinguished from the former by the absence of regular stratification; but they are, nevertheless, intersected by numerous planes of division, or joints, as they are called, and thus divided into blocks of various size and form. Geologists believe that these rocks were at one time reduced to a molten state by the action of intense heat, and afterward allowed slowly to cool and to crystallize. They are divided into two classes, the Plutonic and the Volcanic. The Plutonic Rocks are chiefly granite of some kind or another; and though they now often appear at the surface, they are supposed to have been produced originally at a considerable depth within the crust of the Earth, "or sometimes, perhaps, under a certain weight of incumbent ocean."* The Volcanic Rocks have been formed at or near the surface of the Earth, and, as the name implies, they are usually ejected, in a state of fusion, from the fissures of an active volcano; though not unfrequently they assume the more imposing form of basaltic columns, as at the Giant's Causeway in Ireland, or on the island of Staffa near the coast of Argyleshire in Scotland.

One group of rocks yet remains to be noticed. They have been called by various names at different times, but are now generally designated by the term Metamorphic. In some respects they resemble the Aqueous Rocks, while, in others, they are more nearly allied to the Igneous. Like the former, they are stratified in their outward arrangement; like the latter, they are more or less crystalline in their internal texture. As to their origin, we are told that they were first deposited under water, like the Aqueous Rocks, and that afterward their internal structure was altered by the agency of subterranean heat. Hence the name Metamorphic, first suggested by Sir Charles Lyell, which conveys the idea that these rocks have undergone a *change of form*. To this group belong many varieties of slate, and also the far-famed statuary marble of Italy.

Our readers will perceive from this brief outline that,

* Lyell's Elements of Geology, p. 7.

if we follow the theory of Geologists, the rocks which compose the Crust of the Earth may be conveniently divided, according to their origin, into three leading groups, the Aqueous, the Igneous, and the Metamorphic. The Aqueous are formed under water, either by the mechanical force of the water itself when in motion, or by the agency of chemical laws, or by the intervention of organic life. Hence they are naturally subdivided into three classes, the Mechanical, the Chemical, the Organic. The Igneous Rocks are produced by heat, being first melted and then allowed to cool. When this process takes place under great pressure in the depths of the Earth, the result is granite ; and the granite Rocks are called Plutonic : when near the surface, through the agency of a volcano, the Rocks so formed are called Volcanic. Lastly, the Metamorphic Rocks are nothing else than Aqueous Rocks, of which the texture has been altered by the action of intense heat.

As regards the relative order of position amongst these various classes of rocks, the lowest place seems uniformly to belong to the granitic or Plutonic group. It is true that the granite will often appear at the surface of the Earth ; but wherever there is a series of rocks piled one above the other, the granite will always be the lowest. This assertion is based on two broad facts ; first, whenever we get to the bottom of the other rocks, they are always found to rest on granite ; and secondly, no other rock has ever yet been found beneath it. From this circumstance granite is conceived to be the solid foundation of the Earth's Crust, and so is often called fundamental granite. Above the granite the Aqueous Rocks have been slowly spread out layer by layer during the long lapse of ages, now in this part of the world, now in that, according as each in its turn was exposed to the action of water. The Volcanic Rocks do not occur in any fixed order of succession. They are distributed irregularly over almost every country of the globe, occurring sometimes in the form of cone-shaped mountains, sometimes in the form of stately pillars, and sometimes in the form of massive solid walls, called Dykes, forced right through the softer Aqueous Rocks, which were deposited on the surface of the Earth before the eruption. As to the Metamorphic Rocks, which are supposed to owe their peculiar character to the contact of molten mineral matter, wherever they occur, they are found in the immediate neighborhood of some Igneous Rock.

The condition of the Earth beneath its thin external crust has never been the subject of direct observation; for Geologists have never yet been able to penetrate below the granite rocks. Nevertheless, this subject has been often discussed, and has offered a wide field for philosophical speculation. Upon one point all are agreed, that within the Crust of the Earth an intense heat very generally prevails;—a heat so intense that it would be quite sufficient, acting under ordinary circumstances, to reduce all known rocks to a state of igneous fusion. Hence it was a common opinion among the older Geologists that the condition of our globe is that of a vast central nucleus composed of molten mineral, and covered over with a comparatively thin external shell of solid rock. The most eminent Geologists, however, of the present day, hesitate to accept this opinion. They observe: (1) That we have not yet learned what the material is of which the interior of the Earth is composed; therefore we cannot tell for certain what degree of heat is sufficient to reduce that material to a liquid state. (2) It is uncertain how far the immense pressure at great depths may operate to keep matter in a solid state, even when raised to a very high degree of temperature. (3) There are certain astronomical and physical difficulties involved in this theory, which have not yet been fully cleared up. Modern Geologists, therefore, proceeding with more caution than their predecessors, while they regard the opinion as probable, refuse to set it down as conclusively demonstrated. But, that a very high temperature prevails in the interior of our globe, is a conclusion, they say, which is established by abundant evidence, and which may be regarded as morally certain.

It may be asked how the various strata of Aqueous Rocks, which constitute the chief portion of the Earth's Crust, have been lifted up above the level of the sea; for, according to our theory, they were all first deposited under water. This is a question that must inevitably occur to the mind of every reader, and Geologists are ready with an answer. They tell us that from the earliest ages the Crust of the Earth has been subject to disturbance and dislocation. At various times and in various places it was upheaved, and what had been before the bed of the ocean became dry land; again it sunk below its former level, and what had been before dry land became the bed of the ocean. Thus, in the former case a new stratum which had been deposited at the bottom of the sea, with all its varied remains of a bygone age, was converted for a season into the surface of the Earth, and became the theatre of animal and vegetable life: while in the latter case, the old surface of the Earth with its countless tribes of animals and plants,—its *fauna* and *flora* as they are called,—was submerged beneath the waters, there to receive in its turn the broken up fragments of a former world, deposited in the form of mud, or sand, or pebbles, or minute particles of lime. Nor is this all; it is but a single link in the chain of Geological chronology. We are asked to believe that, in many parts of the globe, this upward and downward movement has been going on alternately for unnumbered ages; so that the very same spot which was first the bed of the ocean, was afterward dry land, then the bottom of an estuary or inland lake, then perhaps once more the floor of the sea, and then dry land again: and furthermore we are assured that, while it remained in each one of these various conditions, thousands and thousands of years may have rolled away.

But from what source does that mighty power come which can thus upheave the solid Earth, and banish the ocean from its bed? We are told in reply that this giant power dwells in the interior of the Earth itself, and is no other than the subterranean heat of which we have already spoken. This vast internal fire acts with unequal force upon different parts of the shell or Crust of the Earth, uplifting it in one place, and in another allowing it to subside. Now it is violent and convulsive, bursting asunder the solid rocks, and shaking the foundations of the hills: again it is gentle and harmless, upheaving vast continents with a scarcely perceptible undulation, not unlike the long, silent swell of the ocean. So it has been from the beginning, and so it is found to be even now, in this last age of the Geological Calendar. For even within historic times mountains have been suddenly upheaved from the level plain; and many parts of the Earth's Crust have been subject to a slow, wave-like movement, rising here and subsiding there, at the rate of perhaps a few feet in a century. Sometimes, too, the fiery liquid itself has burst its barriers, and poured its destructive streams of molten rock far down into the peaceful, smiling valleys.

This theory of an internal disturbing force, which from time to time produces elevations and depressions of the Earth's Crust, serves to explain another phenomenon, that cannot fail to have struck even the least observant eye. The Aqueous Rocks of mechanical formation are said to have been composed of minute fragments, which were first held suspended in water, and afterward fell to the bottom. If this be true, it follows that these rocks, in the first period of their existence, must have been arranged in beds parallel to the horizon, or nearly so. But we now find them, as everybody knows, in a great variety of positions: sometimes they are parallel to the horizon, sometimes inclined to it, sometimes at right angles to it; sometimes, too, they are broken right across, sometimes curved and twisted after a very fantastic fashion. Now, all these appearances are the natural results of an upheaving force acting irregularly from below on the solid shell of the Earth. When the subterranean fire is brought to bear equally at the same time on a broad extent of surface, then the overlying strata are bodily lifted up, and preserve their horizontal position. But when the whole force acts with local intensity on a very contracted area, then, at that particular spot, the rocks above will be tilted up, and their position entirely changed. Sometimes they will be only bent and crushed together, sometimes dislocated and turned over; sometimes, perhaps, a mountain will be formed, and the rocks before parallel to the horizon, will afterward remain parallel to the slopes of the mountain.

There is another process known by the name of Denudation, which we cannot pass over in silence, for it occupies a very important place in the Natural History of our globe. Since time first began Denudation has been ever going on at the surface of the Earth, and it has left its mark more or less distinctly upon every group of rocks, from the lowest to the highest. It includes all the various operations by which the old existing rocks are broken up into fragments, or ground into powder, or worn away by friction, or dissolved by chemical action, and then transported from their former site to become the elements of new strata. Hence the name Denudation; since by these operations the former surface of the Earth is carried away and a surface before covered is *laid bare.* The amount of destruction effected by this process in each successive age is always equal to the bulk of Aqueous Rocks formed within the same time. This will be at once understood when we remember that the Aqueous Rocks are produced, for the most part, by the deposition of sediment; and sediment is nothing else than the fragments, more or less minute, of pre-existing rocks. What is deposited on the bed of the ocean has been taken from the surface of the land; and the new strata are built up from the ruins of the old. When we see a great building of stone towering aloft to the sky, we are certain that somewhere else on the Earth a quarry has been opened, and that the amount of excavation in the quarry is exactly represented by the bulk of solid masonry in the building. Just in the same way, the mass of Aqueous Rocks is at once the monument and the measure of previous Denudation.

The process of Denudation is the work of many and various natural causes. Heat and cold, rain, hail, and snow, chemical affinities, the atmosphere itself, all have a share in it; but the largest share belongs to the mechanical action of moving water. Every little rill that flows down the mountain side is charged with finely-powdered sediment which it is ever wearing away from the surface of its own bed. Every great stream, besides the immense quantities of mud and sand which in times of flood it carries along in its turbulent course, has its channel strewn over with pebbles at which it never ceases to work, rounding off the angles and polishing the surfaces; and these pebbles, what are they but the fragments of old rocks and the elements of new,—the rubble-stone of Nature's edifice on its way from the quarry to the building? Then there are those mighty rivers, such as the Amazon, the Orinoco, the Mississippi, the Nile, the Ganges, discharging into the sea day by day their vast freight of mineral matter, millions of cubic feet in bulk, and thousands upon thousands of tons in weight. Often this ponderous volume of mud or sand is carried far out to sea by the action of currents, but sometimes it is deposited near the shore, forming what is called a Delta, and exhibiting an admirable example of stratified rock in the earliest stage of its existence. Lastly, we have to notice the giant power of the great ocean itself, acting with untiring energies on the coasts of continents and islands all over the world, excavating and undermining cliffs, rolling huge rocks hither and thither, and spreading out the divided fragments in a new order at the bottom of the sea.

To apprehend fully the magnitude of the effects which may fairly be ascribed to this last-mentioned power, we must remember that, according to Geological theory, almost every portion of the Earth's Crust has been more than once lifted up above the surface of the ocean, and afterward depressed below it. It is believed that this alternate rising and sinking was effected very often, perhaps most commonly, not by sudden convulsions, but rather by slow or gradual movements. Now, during this process, as the land was emerging from the waters or sinking beneath them, new surfaces would be presented in each succeeding century to the force of the ocean currents and the erosive action of the breakers; and it is not difficult to conceive that the accumulated ruins produced, in a long lapse of time, by destructive agents so powerful, so untiring, so universal, may have readily furnished the materials for a very large proportion of the Aqueous Rocks now in existence.

Hitherto we have considered the Crust of the Earth as a great structure slowly reared up by the hand of Nature; we have spoken of the Rocks that compose it, of their origin and history, of the order in which they are disposed, and of the various agencies that have been at work to mould them into their present form and feature. We have now to contemplate this marvellous structure under a new aspect; for we are told by Geologists that it is a vast sepulchre, within which lie entombed the remains of life that has long since passed away. Each series of strata is but a new range of tombs; and each tomb has a story of its own. Here a gigantic monster is disclosed to view, compared to which the largest beast that now roams through the forest is puny in form and contemptible in strength: there, within a narrow space, millions of minute animal frames are found closely compacted together, each so small that its existence can be detected only by the aid of a powerful microscope. In one place whole skeletons are found almost entire, embedded in the bosom of the solid rock; in another, we have a boundless profusion of bones and shells; and again in another, neither the skeleton itself appears, nor yet its scattered bones, but simply the imprint of footsteps once left upon the sandy beach, and still remaining engraved on the stone into which the fine sand has been converted chiefly by the agency of pressure. There is no scarcity of relics in this wonderful charnel-house of Nature. For half a century the work of plunder has been going on without relaxation or remorse; the tombs have been yielding up their dead; every city in the civilized world has filled its museums, and the cabinets of private collectors are overflowing: but the spoils that have hitherto been carried away seem to bear a very small proportion to those which yet remain behind.

These remains of animals and plants embedded in the Crust of the Earth are called Fossils; and Geologists maintain that the Fossils preserved in each group of strata represent the animals and plants that flourished on the surface of the Earth, or in the waters of the ocean, when that group of strata was in process of formation. There they lived, and there they died, and there they were buried, in the sand, or the shingle, or the mud that came down from the waters above. Their descendants, however, still lived on, and new forms of life were called into being by the voice of the Omnipotent Creator, making, as it were, a connecting link between the new age of the world that was coming in and the old one that was passing away. But they, too, died and found a tomb beneath the waters; for Nature, with unexhausted energies, was still busy collecting materials from the old rocks, and building up the new. And so that age passed away like the former, and another came; and every age was represented by its own group of strata; and each group of strata was, in its turn, covered over with a new deposit; and the tombs were all sealed up, with their countless legions of dead, their massive monuments of stone, their strange hieroglyphic inscriptions. At length came the last stage of the world's history, and man appeared upon the scene; and it is his privilege to descend into this wonderful sepulchre, and to wander about amidst the monuments, and to strive to read the inscriptions. In our own days more especially, eager and enthusiastic students are abroad over the whole face of the globe, and are gathering together from every country the Fossil Remains of extinct worlds. By the aid of Natural History they seek to assign to each its own proper place in the ranks of creation; to trace the rise, the progress, and the extinction of every species in its turn; and even to describe the nature and the character of all the various forms of life that have dwelt upon the Earth from the beginning.

Such is the theory of Geology as expounded at the present day by its most able and popular advocates. We have passed over a multitude of minor details that we might not weary our readers, and we have kept aloof from disputed points that we might not get entangled in a purely scientific controversy. Our object has simply been to gather together into a systematic form those more general conclusions which, however startling they may seem to practical men of the world, and even to many of those whose minds have been accustomed to the pursuit of science in other departments, are nevertheless regarded as certain by all who have devoted their lives to the study of Geology. It now remains to investigate the facts on which these conclusions are based, and to consider the line of argument by which so many able and earnest men have been led to accept them. In this vast field of inquiry we shall chiefly direct our attention to those points that bear upon the Antiquity of the Earth; and in attempting to bring home to our readers the nature and the force of Geological reasoning, we shall confine ourselves altogether to simple and familiar illustrations.

CHAPTER II.

THEORY OF DENUDATION ILLUSTRATED BY FACTS.

Principle of reasoning common to all the physical sciences—This principle applicable to Geology—Carbonic acid an agent of denudation—Vast quantity of lime dissolved by the waters of the Rhine and borne away to the German ocean—Disintegration of rocks by frost—Professor Tyndall on the Matterhorn—Running water—Its erosive power—An active and unceasing agent of denudation—Mineral sediment carried out to sea by the Ganges and other great rivers—Solid rocks undermined and worn away—Falls of the Clyde at Lanark—Excavating power of rivers in Auvergne and Sicily—Falls of Niagara—Transporting power of running water—Floods in Scotland—Inundation in the valley of Bagnes in Switzerland.

IN the physical sciences it is a common principle of reasoning to account for the phenomena that come before us in nature, by the operation of natural causes which we know to exist. Nay, this principle seems to be almost an instinct of our nature, which guides even the least philosophical amidst us, in the common affairs of life. When we stand amongst the ruins of an ancient castle, we feel quite certain that we have before us, not alone the monument of Time's destroying power, but also the monument of human skill and labor in days gone by. We entertain no doubt that ages ago the sound of the mason's hammer was heard upon these walls, now crowned with ivy ; that these moss-grown stones were once hewn fresh in the quarry, and piled up one upon another by human hands ; and that the building itself was designed by human skill, and intended for the purposes of human habitation and defence. Or, if we see a footprint in the sand, we conclude that a living foot has been there ; and from the character of the traces it has left, we judge what was the species of animal to which it belonged, whether man, or bird, or beast. It is true that God is Omnipotent. He might, if it had so pleased Him, have built the old castle at the creation of the world, and allowed it to crumble slowly into ruins : or he might have built it yesterday, and made a ruin begin to be where no castle had stood before ; and covered the stones with moss, and mantled the walls in ivy. And as to the footprint in the sand, it were as easy for Him to make the impress there, as to make the foot that left the impress. All this is true : but yet if any one were to argue in this style against us, he would fail to shake our convictions ; we should still unhesitatingly believe that human hands once built the castle, and that a living foot once trod the shore.

Now, this principle of reasoning is the foundation on which the ablest modern Geologists claim to build their science. The untiring hand of Nature is ever busy around us : they ask us to come and look at her works, and to judge of what she has done in past ages, by that which she is now doing before our eyes. She is still, they say, building up her strata all over the globe, of limestone, and sandstone, and clay ; she is still lifting up in one place the bed of the ocean, and in another submerging the dry land ; she is still bursting open the Crust of the Earth by the action of internal fire, disturbing and tilting up the horizontal strata ; she is still upheaving her mountains and scooping out her valleys. All these operations are open to our inspection ; we may go forth and study them for ourselves : we may examine the works that are wrought, and we may discover, too, the causes by which they are produced. And if it should appear that a very close analogy exists between these works that are now coming into existence, and the long series of works that are piled up in the Crust of the Earth, it is surely not unreasonable to refer the latter class of phenomena to the action of the same natural causes which we know to have produced the former.

It cannot be denied that this argument is deserving of a fair and candid consideration. Let us proceed, then, to examine how far it is founded on fact, and how far it can be justly applied to the various heads of Geological theory. We will commence with the origin and history of Stratified Rocks; for this constitutes, in a manner, the framework on which the whole system of Geology is supported and held together. It is alleged that the elements of which Stratified Rocks are composed are but the broken fragments and minute atoms of pre-existing rocks, carried off by the agents of Denudation, and spread out over some distant area in regular beds or layers; which, in progress of ages, were slowly consolidated into rocks of various quality and texture. With the view of testing this theory by the light of the principle just explained, we purpose, in the first place, to exhibit some examples of the many forms in which the process of Denudation is going on at the present day all over the world; and afterward, to show that out of the materials thus obtained Stratified Rocks of every description—Mechanical, Chemical, Organic—are being regularly built up in sundry places; and that these correspond in every essential feature with the Stratified Rocks in the Crust of the Earth.

Among the chemical agents of Denudation, there is none more widely diffused than Carbonic acid gas. It is everywhere given out by dead animal and vegetable matter during the process of putrefaction; it is plentifully evolved from springs in every country; and it is emitted in enormous quantities from the earth in all volcanic districts, as well those in which the volcanoes are now extinct as those in which they are active. Now, it is well known from observation, that carbonic acid has the property of decomposing many of the hardest rocks, especially those in which felspar is an ingredient. This phenomenon is exhibited on a large scale in the ancient volcanic district of Auvergne, in central France. The carbonic acid, which is abundantly evolved from the earth, penetrates the crevices and pores of the solid granite, which being unable to resist its decomposing action, is rapidly crumbling to pieces. This mysterious decay of hard rock has been happily called by Dolomieu, "la maladie du granite."*

Again, all the water which flows over the surface of the land is highly charged with carbonic acid. The rain imbibes it in falling through the atmosphere; and the rivers receive still further accessions from the earth as they pursue their course to the sea. In this combination we discover a powerful agent of Denudation; for limestone rock will be dissolved by water which is impregnated with carbonic acid. Thus all the rivers and streams in the world, when they flow through a limestone channel, are constantly dissolving the solid rock and bearing away the elements of which it is composed. A single example will be sufficient to show the magnitude of the results which are thus produced. It has been calculated by Bischof, a celebrated German chemist, that the carbonate of lime which is carried each year to the sea by the waters of the Rhine, is sufficient for the formation of 32,000,000,000 of oyster shells; or, to view the matter in another light, it would be sufficient to produce a stratum of limestone one foot thick, and four square miles in extent.† If such be the yearly produce of

* See Lyell's Principles of Geology, vol. i., pp. 411–413.

† See Jukes, The Student's Manual of Geology, p. 125.

one river, how great must be the accumulated effects of all the rivers in the world since our planet first came from the hand of its Creator!

Passing from the chemical to the mechanical agents of Denudation, it is worth while to notice the immense power which is often generated by the agency of frost, especially in those countries that are subject to great vicissitudes of heat and cold. During a thaw, water finds its way into the clefts and joints by which all rocks are traversed, and when it is afterward converted into ice, it expands with a mechanical force that is almost irresistible. The hardest rocks are burst asunder, great blocks are detached from the mountain side, and sent rolling down its slopes, or tumbling over crags and precipices, until at length they come to rest in shattered fragments at the bottom of the valley. In this condition they await but the coming of the winter's torrent to be borne still further on their long journey to the sea.

The fearful havoc done in this way by the alternate action of sun and frost contributes in no small degree to the fantastic and picturesque forms assumed by the mountain peaks of Switzerland. Huge masses of rock have been literally hewn away, until nothing has remained behind but those splintered obelisks and tapering pinnacles so familiar to the eye amidst the sublime scenery of the Alps. Indeed one of the greatest perils encountered by the adventurous spirits whose ambition it is to rival one another in the danger of their exploits, and to climb whatever was before regarded as inaccessible, arises from the enormous fragments of rock which are rent almost unceasingly from the overhanging crags and hurled into the abysses below them. The following incident related by Professor Tyndall is very much to the point. "We had gathered up our things, and bent to the work before us, when suddenly an explosion occurred overhead. Looking aloft, in mid-air was seen a solid shot from the Matterhorn describing its proper parabola through the air. It split to pieces as it hit one of the rock-towers below, and its fragments came down in a kind of spray, which fell wide of us, but still near enough to compel a sharp look out. Two or three such explosions occurred afterward, but we crept along the back fin of the mountain, from which the falling boulders were speedily deflected right and left."

This occurred in 1862, on the occasion of an unsuccessful attempt to reach the highest peak of the Matterhorn. Six years later, when Professor Tyndall at length actually accomplished the object on which he seems to have set his heart, he found the work of destruction still going on. "We were now," he says in his narrative, "beside a snow-gully, which was cut by a deep furrow along its centre, and otherwise scarred by the descent of stones. Here each man arranged his bundle and himself so as to cross the gully in the minimum of time. The passage was safely made, a few flying shingle only coming down upon us. But danger declared itself where it was not expected. Joseph Maquignas led the way up the rocks. I was next, Pierre Maquignas next, and last of all the porters. Suddenly a yell issued from the leader: 'Cachez vous!' I crouched instinctively against the rock, which formed a by no means perfect shelter, when a boulder buzzed past me through the air, smote the rocks below me, and with a savage hum flew down to the lower glacier."*

Even in our own country, every one is familiar with the efficacy of frozen water in producing landslips. The rain which soaks into the ground in winter, is converted into ice when frost sets in; and upon steep slopes or precipices, its expansive power bursts open the earth, and causes large masses of stones and clay to tumble headlong to the bottom.

But moving water constitutes the most powerful, and, at

* Professor Tyndall, Odds and Ends of Alpine Life.

the same time, the most universal agent of Denudation. And it is chiefly to the effects of moving water that we mean to direct attention; because its action is more striking to the eye, and more easily understood by the general reader. Every one is aware that the waters of the ocean are constantly passing off by evaporation into the higher regions of the atmosphere, and are there condensed into clouds. These clouds in course of time descend upon all parts of the earth, but especially on the high and mountainous districts. Then rivulets are formed which flow smoothly down the gentle slopes of the undulating country, or plunge headlong over the rocky mountain cliffs; and the rivulets uniting form streams, and the streams, receiving new tributaries as they advance, become rivers; and the rivers flow on to the sea, and discharge each day and each hour their enormous volumes of water back again into the ocean from which they came. Thus all the water of the world is constantly in motion, ever hurrying on, as it were, in one unending round of duty. This is the teaching of daily experience and observation. And we may add, it is the teaching of Sacred Scripture as well. The Wise Man said long ago: "All the rivers run into the sea, yet the sea doth not overflow: unto the place from whence the rivers come, thither they return to flow again."*

Now, the power of this moving water is a mighty widespread agent of change in the physical condition of the globe. For wherever water is in motion over the surface of the land, whether it be a rippling stream, or a mountain torrent, or a majestic river, it is surely wearing away the channel through which it flows, and carrying along in its course particles of clay, or sand, or gravel. This subject is illustrated with great force and great simplicity by Mr. Page. "Every person," he says, "must have observed

* Ecclesiastes, i. 7

the rivers in his own district, how they become muddy and turbid during floods of rain, and how their swollen currents eat away the banks, deepen the channels, and sweep away the sand and gravel down to some lower level. And if, during this turbid state, he will have the curiosity to lift a gallon of the water, and allow it to settle, he will be astonished at the amount of sediment or solid matter that falls to the bottom. Now, let him multiply this gallon by the number of gallons daily carried down by the river, and this day by years and centuries, and he will arrive at some faint idea of the quantity of matter worn from the land by rivers, and deposited by them in the ocean. In the same way as one river grinds and cuts for itself a channel, so does every stream and rill and current of water. The rain as it falls washes away what the winds and frosts have loosened; the rill takes it up, and, mingling it with its own burden, gives it to the stream; the stream takes it up and carries it to the river, and the river bears it to the ocean."*

When the current is feeble, the greater part of this earthy material is thrown down upon the way, and forms a stratum of alluvial soil in the bed of the river, and also in the adjoining lowlands, during the time of temporary floods. But when several streams unite, then the carrying power of the current is enormously increased: huge stones are rolled along, and dashed one against another, and broken into fragments, and the fragments are rounded by friction, and become pebbles, and the pebbles become gravel, and the gravel, mud; and the mud is carried on to the mouth of the river, and there falling to the bottom, it forms a tongue of land which is called a delta; or else perhaps it chances to meet with some great ocean current, and then it begins a new journey, and is borne far away to be deposited in the profound and tranquil depths of the sea. It is not,

* Page, Advanced Text-Book of Geology, p. 55.

however, mineral matter alone that is transported by the action of rivers. Trees that once were growing on the banks of the stream, and the bones of animals, and human remains, and works of art, are seen floating down with the current, and are found embedded in the sand and mud of the delta at the river's mouth.

These are some of the actual realities which all may witness, who will go and study for themselves the history of this wonderful element, from the time when it first soars aloft as vapor to the sky, until it returns to the bosom of its parent ocean laden with the spoils of the land. To some of our readers, perhaps, results of this kind may appear insignificant, when considered in relation to the enormous bulk of the stratified rocks. But it should be remembered that the force of which we speak is unceasing in its operation over the whole surface of the earth; and even though the work were small which is accomplished in each successive year, the accumulated effects produced in a lengthened period of time must be immensely great. Besides, it would be a very serious error to form our ideas on this subject, as many would seem to do, from the examples which are to be found within the narrow limits of our own island. We should rather seek for our illustrations among those mighty rivers that drain the vast continents of the world, and exhibit the erosive and transporting power of running water on the grandest scale.

It happens, fortunately for our purpose, that an attempt has been made by scientific men to compute the amount of matter discharged into the sea, by some particular rivers within a given time. For such a computation it is necessary, in the first place, to calculate the volume of water that passes down the channel during that time; and then, by repeated experiments, to ascertain the average proportion of earthy matter which is held suspended in the water. This has been done with the greatest care by the Rev. Mr.

Everest, in the case of the river Ganges; and it appears that during the rainy season, which lasts four months every year, from June to September, about 6,000,000,000 cubic feet of mud are carried along by the stream past the town of Ghazepoor, near which the observations were made. Now this enormous bulk of mineral matter would be sufficient to form a stratum of rock one foot in height, and two hundred and eighteen square miles in extent. Or, to adopt the computation of Sir Charles Lyell, the amount which passes by every day is equal to that which might be transported by 2000 Indiamen, each freighted with a cargo of mud 1400 tons in weight. And it is important to remember that this estimate represents but a portion of the sediment which passes into the sea through the channel of the Ganges; for the observations of Mr. Everest were taken at a point which is 500 miles from the sea, and at which the river has not yet received the contributions of its largest tributaries.

We are able, therefore, with some degree of confidence, to estimate the amount of Denudation which is every year effected by the Ganges. And, although the same calculations have not yet been applied with equal care to other great rivers, there is no reason to suppose that the Ganges is an exception. It is asserted on good grounds that the Brahmapootra, which unites with the Ganges close to the Bay of Bengal, carries with it an equal amount of earthy sediment. According to Sir Charles Lyell, the quantity of solid matter brought down each year by the Mississippi amounts to 3,702,758,400 cubic feet. And it is said that 48,000,000 cubic feet of earth are *daily* discharged into the sea by the Yellow River in China, called by the natives the Hoang Ho.* Thus year after year the waste of the land is

* See on this subject, Lyell's Principles of Geology, vol. i., p. 458, and pp. 480–3; Jukes, Manual of Geology, pp. 105–11; Page, Advanced Text-Book of Geology, pp. 52–56.

carried away by rivers, to be spread out over wide areas of the ocean, and perhaps to furnish the materials of future continents.

The effects of running water in wearing away and transporting masses of solid rock are not less deserving of our notice. Every one who has followed the course of a great river when it flows through a rocky channel, must have observed large blocks projecting from the cliffs above, which, having been undermined by the action of the water, seem ready to tumble headlong into the stream; and others lying below, which had fallen before; and others again which had been already carried a considerable distance by the winter's torrent. Even where the rocks are not displaced, they are gradually being worn away, partly by the friction of the water, but much more by the grinding action of the gravel which the water holds in suspension. Not only is the surface of the rocks thus rounded and polished, but large circular pits, called *pot-holes*, are formed by the whirling waters of an eddy carrying round and round a few grains of hard sand.

At the falls of the Clyde near Lanark in Scotland, these various phenomena may be seen to great advantage. Good illustrations are to be found also in many volcanic regions. Some of the larger streams in Auvergne have in course of time forced their way through the solid lava rock, cutting out for themselves channels broad and deep. In Sicily too, we are told, the river Simeto, whose course was blocked up by a current of lava about the beginning of the seventeenth century, has since that time eaten its way through this compact and hardened mass, and now flows on to the sea through a rocky passage forty feet in depth and from fifty to several hundred feet in width.*

But there is no part of the world yet explored where these effects are exhibited on the same gigantic scale as at the far-

* Lyell, Principles of Geology, vol. i., pp. 356–7.

famed Falls of Niagara. The massive limestone rock from which the waters are precipitated is slowly but certainly disappearing. An enormous volume of water, more than a third of a mile in breadth, plunges in a single bound over a sheer precipice of one hundred and sixty-five feet. The soft slaty rocks upon which the limestone rests are soon eaten away by the action of the spray which rises from the pool below; and then the overhanging cliffs, left without any support, topple over, and are carried off by the torrent. The position of the Falls, therefore, is not stationary, but is receding by very sensible degrees in the direction of Lake Erie, from which the river flows. Speaking of this phenomenon, Sir Charles Lyell observes with much show of reason: "The idea of perpetual and progressive waste is constantly present to the mind of every beholder: and as that part of the chasm which has been the work of the last hundred and fifty years resembles precisely in depth, width, and character the rest of the gorge, which extends seven miles below, it is most natural to infer, that the entire ravine has been hollowed out in the same manner, by the recession of the cataract. It must at least be conceded, that the river supplies an adequate cause for executing the whole task thus assigned to it, provided we grant sufficient time for its completion."*

With a view to enable our readers to understand more fully the prodigious force which rivers have been known to exert in the transportation of rocks, it may be useful to draw attention to one or two principles of physical science. First, we have the well-known law of Archimedes, that *a solid body immersed in a liquid loses a part of its weight equal to the weight of the liquid displaced.* Now solid rock as compared with water, bulk for bulk, is rarely more than three times, and often not more than twice as heavy. Conse-

* Principles of Geology, vol. i., p. 360.

quently, according to this law, almost all rocks will lose a third of their weight, and many will lose one-half, when immersed in water. Again, it has been established that *the power of water to move bodies that are in it increases as the sixth power of the velocity of the current.* Hence, if the velocity of a current is increased *two-fold*, its moving power will be increased *sixty-four fold;* if the velocity is increased *three-fold*, the moving power will be increased *seven hundred and twenty fold;* and so on.

From these principles it follows, first, that a much smaller power is required to move a block of stone lying in the bed of a river, than if it were lying on the surface of the land; and secondly, that a very slight increase in the velocity of a current effects a very great increase in its moving power. We need not wonder, then, when we hear of the enormous masses of rocks and trees and mason-work which are carried away even by small rivers in times of flood.*

Here are a few examples. In August, 1829, a fragment of sandstone, fourteen feet long, three feet wide, and one foot thick, was carried by the river Nairn, in Scotland, a distance of two hundred yards. On the same occasion the river Dee swept away a bridge of five arches, built of solid granite, which had stood uninjured for twenty years; the whole mass of masonry sunk into the bed of the stream and was seen no more. And the river Don, as we are assured on the authority of Mr. Farquharson, forced a mass of stones four or five hundred tons in weight up a steep inclined plane, leaving them in a great rectangular heap on the summit. A small rivulet called the College, in Northumberland, when swollen by a flood in August, 1827, "tore away from the abutment of a mill-dam a large block of greenstone-porphyry weighing nearly two tons, and trans-

* See Jukes, Manual of Geology, pp. 108–10; Hopkins, Presidential Address to the Geological Society of London, 1852, p. xxvii.

ported it to the distance of a quarter of a mile."* But it is needless to multiply examples of phenomena which are occurring every day around us, and of which many among our readers have probably been eye-witnesses.

The transporting power of rivers must not always be estimated by the bulk and velocity of the current; for it is often greatly increased by some accidental obstruction, which for a time blocks up the channel through which the river flows. An instructive illustration is afforded by the river Dranse, which flows through the valley of Bagnes, in Switzerland, and empties itself into the Rhone above the lake of Geneva. In the year 1818 the avalanches which fell down from the mountain side formed a barrier across the valley, and thus effectually blocked up the course of the stream. The upper part of the valley was, in consequence, soon converted into a lake which gradually increased in size as the season advanced. When summer came, and the melting of the snows began, the ice barrier suddenly gave way with a tremendous crash, and the lake was emptied in half an hour. The mass of water, thus in a moment disengaged, burst with destructive violence over the lower valley, sweeping away rocks, forests, houses, bridges, and cultivated lands. Thousands of trees were torn up by the roots, fragments of granite as large as houses were rolled along, and the whole flood presented the appearance of a moving mass of ruins.

* For these facts see Lyell, Principles of Geology, vol. i., pp. 349, 350; Quarterly Journal of Science, No. XIII., New Series; The English Cyclopædia, Natural History Division, Alluvium.

CHAPTER III.

THEORY OF DENUDATION—FURTHER ILLUSTRATIONS.

The breakers of the ocean—Caverns and fairy bridges of Kilkee—Italy and Sicily—The Shetland Islands—East and south coast of Britain—Tracts of land swallowed up by the sea—Island of Heligoland—Northstrand—Tides and currents—South Atlantic current—Equatorial current—The Gulf Stream—Its course described—Examples of its power as an agent of transport.

HILE the rain, the rivers, and the streams, are thus wasting away the mountains and plains of the interior country, the waves of the sea are exerting a power no less destructive on the coasts of islands and of continents. The breakers dashing against the foot of a lofty cliff, dissolve and decompose and wear away the lower strata; and the overhanging rocks, thus undermined, fall down in course of time by their own weight. With the next returning wave these rocks are themselves hurled back against the cliff; and so, as some one has happily remarked, the land would seem to supply a powerful artillery for its own destruction. The effects of the breakers are often very unequal, even on the same line of cliffs. Some parts of the rock are more yielding than others, or perhaps they are more exposed to the action of the waves, or perhaps they are divided by larger joints and more freely admit the destructive element. These parts will be the first

to give way, while the harder and less exposed rock will be left standing: and in this way forms the most capricious and fantastic are produced.

No finer examples could be wished for than those which are seen in the neighborhood of Kilkee, and along the promontory of Loop Head, in the county of Clare. Sometimes the ground is undermined with caverns, into which, when the tide is coming in, the waves of the Atlantic rush with resistless force, making new additions each day to the accumulated ruins of ages. Sometimes lofty pinnacles of rock are left standing in the midst of the waters, like giant sentinels stationed there by Nature to guard the coast. In one or two instances these isolated fragments are connected with the main land by natural arches of rock, which are called *fairy bridges* by the people; but more commonly they appear as rocky islets, and answer exactly to the poet's description—

"The roaring tides
The passage broke that land from land divides;
And where the lands retired the rushing ocean rides."

It is interesting to observe in passing, that, in the original verses of the Æneid, of which these lines are Dryden's translation, Virgil has recorded a belief which prevailed in his time, and which, upon scientific grounds, is now regarded as highly probable by Geologists, that the island of Sicily had been once connected by land with Italy, and was separated from it by the action of the waves:

"Hæc loca, vi quondam et vasta convulsa ruina,
Tantum ævi longinqua valet mutare vetustas!
Dissiluisse ferunt, quum protenus utraque tellus
Una foret; venit medio vi pontus et undis
Hesperium Siculo latus abscidit, arvaque et urbes
Litore deductas angusto interluit æsta."

Æneid, iii., 414–19.

But whatever may be thought of this opinion thus rendered immortal by the genius of the poet, we shall not stop to discuss its merits. For in the present stage of our argument, it is our object to deal, not with vague and uncertain traditions, nor even with philosophical speculations, but rather with the facts which are actually going on in nature, and which any one of our readers may examine for himself. With this object in view, we shall take a few examples from the Eastern and Southern coasts of Great Britain, which have been carefully explored by scientific men for the purpose of observing and recording the amount of destruction accomplished by the waves within recent times.

Fig. 1.—Granitic rocks to the south of Hillswick Ness, Shetland. From Lyell's Principles of Geology.

The Shetland Islands, exposed to the whole fury of the Atlantic, present many phenomena not unlike those of Kilkee and Loop Head, but upon a far grander scale. Whole islands have been swept away by the resistless power of the waters, and of others nothing remains but massive pillars of hard rock, which have been well described as rising up "like the ruins of Palmyra in the desert of the ocean."

Passing to the mainland, it is recorded that in the year 1795 a village in Kincardineshire was carried away in a single night, and the sea advanced a hundred and fifty yards inland, where it has ever since maintained its ground. In England, almost the whole coast of Yorkshire is undergoing constant dilapidation. On the south side of Flamborough Head the cliffs are receding at an average rate of two yards and a quarter in the year, for a distance of thirty-six miles along the coast. This would amount to a mile since the Norman Conquest, and to more than two miles since the occupation of York by the Romans. It is not surprising, therefore, to learn that many spots marked in the old maps of the country as the sites of towns or villages, are now sandbanks in the sea. Even places of historic name have not been spared. The town of Ravenspur, from which, in 1332, Edward Baliol sailed for the invasion of Scotland, and at which Henry the Fourth landed in 1399, to claim the throne of England, has long since been swallowed up by the devouring element.

On the coast of Norfolk it was calculated, at the beginning of the present century, that the mean loss of the land was something less than one yard in the year. The inn at Sherringham was built on this calculation in 1805, and it was expected to stand for seventy years. But unfortunately the actual advance of the sea exceeded the calculation. Sir Charles Lyell, who visited this spot in 1829, relates that during the five preceding years seventeen yards of the cliff had been swept away, and nothing but a small garden was then left between the building and the sea. The same distinguished writer tells us that in the harbor of this town there was at that time water sufficient to float a frigate where forty-eight years before had stood a cliff fifty feet in height with houses built upon it. And remarking upon these facts, he says, that "if once in half a century an equal amount of change were produced suddenly by the momentary shock of an earthquake, history would be filled with records of such wonderful revolutions of the earth's surface; but if the conversion of high land into deep sea be gradual, it excites only local attention."

In the neighborhood of Dunwich, once the most considerable seaport on the coast of Suffolk, the cliffs have been wasting away from an early period of history. "Two tracts of land which had been taxed in the time of King Edward the Confessor, are mentioned in the Conqueror's survey, made but a few years afterward, as having been devoured by the sea." And the memory of other losses in the town itself—including a monastery, several churches, the town-hall, the jail, and many hundred houses—together with the dates of their occurrence, is faithfully preserved in authentic records. In 1740 the sea reached the churchyard of Saint Nicholas and Saint Francis, so that the graves, the coffins, and the skeletons, were exposed to view on the face of the cliffs. Since that time the coffins, and the tombstones, and the churchyard itself, have disappeared beneath the waves. Nothing now remains of this once flourishing and populous city but the name alone, which is still attached to a little village of about twenty houses. The spot on which the Church of Reculver stands, near the mouth of the Thames, was a mile inland in the reign of Henry the Eighth; in the year 1834 it was overhanging the sea; and it would long ago have been demolished, but for an artificial causeway of stones constructed with a view to break the force of the waves. It is estimated that the land on the northeast coast of Kent is receding at the rate of about two feet in the year. The promontory of Beachy Head in Sussex is also rapidly falling away. In the year 1813 an enormous mass of chalk, three hundred feet in length and eighty in breadth, came down with a tremendous crash; and slips of the same kind have often occurred, both before and since.

To these examples from Great Britain we may add one or two from the German Ocean. Seven islands have completely disappeared within a very narrow area since the time of Pliny; for he counted twenty-three between Texel and the mouth of the Eider, whereas now there are but sixteen. The island of Heligoland, at the mouth of the Elbe, has been for ages subject to great dilapidation. Within the last five hundred years three-fourths of it have been carried away; and since 1770 the fragment that remains has been divided into two parts by a channel which is at present navigable for large ships. A still more remarkable instance of destruction effected by the waves of the sea occurred in the island of Northstrand, on the coast of Schleswig. Previous to the thirteenth century it was attached to the mainland, forming a part of the continent of Europe, and was a highly cultivated and populous district about ten miles long, and from six to eight broad. In the year 1240 it was cut off from the coast of Schleswig by an inroad of the sea, and it gradually wasted away up to the seventeenth century, when its entire circumference was sixteen geographical miles. Even then the industrious inhabitants,—about nine thousand in number,—endeavored to save what remained of their territory by the erection of lofty dykes; but on the eleventh of October, 1634, the whole island was overwhelmed by another invasion of the sea, in which 6000 people perished, and 50,000 head of cattle. Three small islets are all that now remain of this once fertile district.*

The breakers of the ocean receive no small aid in their

* For these facts illustrating the destructive action of the waves of the sea we are chiefly indebted to the following authorities: Hibbert, Description of the Shetland Isles; Phillips, Rivers, Mountains, and Sea-coast of Yorkshire; Geology of Yorkshire, by the same author; Pennant's Arctic Zoology, vol. i.; Lyell's Principles of Geology, vol. i., chapters xx. and xxi.; Gardner's History of the Borough of Dunwich; the English Cyclopædia, Alluvium.

work of destruction from the action of tides and currents which co-operate with the winds to keep the waters of the sea in constant motion. And though the winds may sleep for a time, the tides and currents are always actively at work, and never for a moment cease to wear away the land. But they are even more powerful auxiliaries as agents of transport. If it were not for them, the ruins which fall from the rocks to-day would to-morrow form a barrier against the waves, and the work of destruction would cease. But Nature has ordained it otherwise. When the tide advances, it rolls the broken fragments toward the land, and when it recedes, it carries them back to the deep; and so by unceasing friction these fragments are worn away to pebbles, and then, being more easily transported, they are carried off to sea and deposited in the bed of the ocean: or else, perhaps, they are cast up on the sloping shore, to form what is so familiar to us all under the name of a shingle-beach.

This is a subject on which it is needless to enlarge. Every one knows that the tides have the power of transporting solid matter; though most of us, perhaps, do not fully appreciate the magnitude of their accumulated effects, working as they do with untiring energies upon the coasts of islands and continents all over the world. It is not, however, so generally known that the ocean is traversed in all directions by powerful currents, which, from their regularity, their permanence, and their extent, have been aptly called the rivers of the ocean. We do not mean here to inquire into the causes of these currents, upon which the progress of physical science has thrown considerable light: neither can we hope to describe even the principal currents that prevail over the vast tracts of water which constitute about three-fourths of the entire surface of our globe. We shall content ourselves with tracing the course of one great system, which may serve to give some idea of their general character and enormous power.

This system would seem to have its origin with a stream that flows from the Indian Ocean toward the southwest, and then doubling the Cape of Good Hope, turns northward along the African coast. It is here called the South Atlantic Current. When it encounters the shores of Guinea, it is diverted to the west, and stretches across the Atlantic, traversing forty degrees of longitude until it reaches the projecting promontory of Brazil in South America. In this part of its course it is known as the Equatorial Current, because it follows pretty nearly the line of the Equator: it varies in breadth from two hundred to five hundred miles, and it travels at the mean rate of thirty miles a day, though sometimes its velocity is increased to seventy or eighty. Next, under the name of the Guyana Current, it pursues a northwesterly direction, following the line of the coast; and passing close to the island of Trinidad, becomes diffused, and almost seems to be lost, in the Caribbean Sea. Nevertheless, it again issues with renewed energy from the Gulf of Mexico, and rushing through the Straits of Florida at the rate of four and five miles an hour, it issues once more into the broad waters of the Atlantic. From this out it is called the Gulf Stream, and is well known to all who are concerned in Transatlantic navigation; for it sensibly accelerates the speed of vessels which are bound from America to Europe, and sensibly retards those sailing from Europe to America.

The Gulf Stream, however, does not set out on its Transatlantic voyage directly that it issues from the Straits of Florida. It keeps at first a northeasterly course, following the outline of the American continent, passing by New York and Nova Scotia, and brushing the southern extremity of the great Newfoundland Bank. Then taking leave of the land, it sweeps right across the Atlantic. After a time it seems to divide into two branches, one inclining to the south, and losing itself among the Azores, the other bending toward the north, washing the shores of Ireland, Scotland, Norway, and reaching even to the frozen regions of Spitzbergen. The breadth of the Gulf Stream, when it issues from the Straits of Florida, is about fifty miles, but it afterward increases to three hundred. Its color is a dark indigo blue, which, contrasting sharply with the green waters of the Atlantic, forms a line of junction distinctly visible for some hundreds of miles: afterward, when this boundary line is no longer sensible to the eye, it is easily ascertained by the thermometer; for the temperature of the Gulf Stream is everywhere from eight to ten degrees higher than that of the surrounding ocean.*

We leave our readers to infer from this brief description how immense must be the power of transport which belongs to such currents as these. They sweep along the shores of continents, and carry away the accumulated fragments of rock, which had first been rent from the cliffs by the waves of the sea, and then borne out to a little distance by the tides: they pass by the mouths of great rivers, and receiving the spoils of many a fertile and populous country, and the ruins of many an inaccessible mountain ridge, they hurry off to deposit this vast and varied freight in the deep abysses of the ocean. There is one circumstance, however, which we ought not to pass over in silence; for it is of especial importance to the Geologist, and might easily escape the notice of the general reader. It is a well ascertained fact that plants and fruits and other objects from the West Indian Islands are annually washed ashore by the Gulf Stream on the northwestern coasts of Europe. The mast of a man-of-war burnt at Jamaica was after some months found stranded on one of the Western Islands of

* Rennell's Investigation of the Currents in the Atlantic Ocean; Maury's Physical Geography of the Sea, chapters ii. and iii.; Humboldt's Cosmos; The English Cyclopædia, Atlantic Ocean; Lyell's Principles of Geology, vol. i., chapter xx.

Scotland ;* and General Sabine tells us that when he was in Norway, in the year 1823, casks of palm-oil were picked up on the shore near the North Cape, which belonged to a vessel that had been wrecked the previous year at Cape Lopez on the African coast.† It seems most probable that these casks of oil must first have crossed the Atlantic from east to west in the Equatorial Current, then described the circuit of the West Indian Islands, and finally coming in with the Gulf Stream, recrossed the Atlantic, performing altogether a journey of more than eight thousand miles. From these facts it is clear that, by the agency of ocean currents, the productions of one country may be carried to another that is far distant. And Geologists do not fail to make use of this important conclusion when they find the animal and vegetable remains of different climates associated together in the same strata of the Earth.

* Mantell's Wonders of Geology, p. 70.

† In his notes to the translation of Humboldt's Cosmos, p. xcvii.

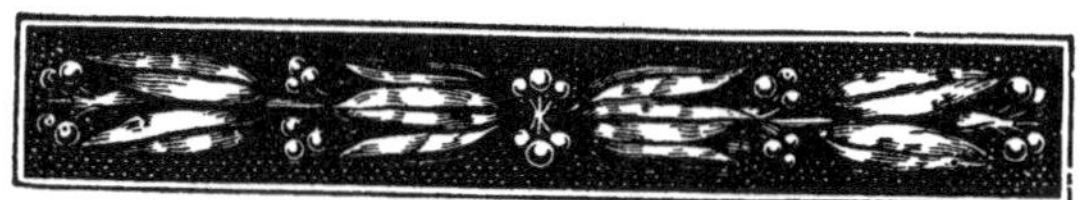

CHAPTER IV.

THEORY OF DENUDATION—CONCLUDED.

Glaciers—Their nature and composition—Their unceasing motion—Powerful agents of denudation—Icebergs—Their number and size—Erratic blocks and loose gravel spread out over mountains, plains, and valleys, at the bottom of the sea—Characteristic marks of moving ice—Evidence of ancient glacial action—Illustrations from the Alps—From the mountains of the Jura—Theory applied to northern Europe—To Scotland, Wales, and Ireland—The fact of denudation established—Summary of the evidence—This fact the first step in geological theory.

HE next agent of Denudation to which we invite the attention of our readers, is one of which our own country affords us no example, but which may be seen in full operation amidst the wild and impressive scenery of Switzerland. And we know not how we can better introduce the subject than by the solemn address of a great poet, in whom an ardent love of nature was blended with a deep sense of religion. As he stood in the midst of the snow-clad mountains that shut in the valley of Chamouni, his spirit, "expanded by the genius of the spot," soared away from the scenes before him to the Great Invisible Author of all that is beautiful and sublime in nature, and he poured forth that well-known hymn of praise and worship in which he thus apostrophizes the massive glaciers of Mont Blanc :—

"Ye ice-falls! ye that from the mountain's brow
Adown enormous ravines slope amain—
Torrents, methinks, that heard a mighty voice,
And stopped at once amid their maddest plunge!
Motionless torrents! silent cataracts!
Who made you glorious as the gates of Heaven
Beneath the keen full moon? Who bade the sun
Clothe you with rainbows? Who with living flowers
Of loveliest blue, spread garlands at your feet?
God! let the torrents, like a shout of nations,
Answer! and let the ice-plains echo, God!
God! sing ye meadow-streams with gladsome voice!
Ye pine-groves, with your soft and soul-like sounds!
And they too have a voice, yon piles of snow,
And in their perilous fall shall thunder, God!"*

A Glacier is an enormous mass of solid ice filling up a valley, and stretching from the eternal snows which crown the summits of the mountains, down to the smiling corn-fields and rich pastures of the plains. It is constantly fed by the accumulated snows of winter, which, slipping and rolling down the slopes of the mountains, lodge in the valleys below, and are there converted into ice. For it must be remembered that the Glacier properly so called does not commonly extend much higher than 9000 feet above the level of the sea. Beyond that elevation the compact and massive ice gradually passes into frozen snow, called by the French Nevé, and by the Germans Firn. The change which takes place in the condition of the snow as it descends into the valley is chiefly owing to these two circumstances: first, it is closely compacted together by the weight of the snowy masses pressing down upon it from above; and secondly, in the summer months it is thawed upon the surface during the day by the heat of the sun, and frozen again at

* A Hymn before Sunrise in the Vale of Chamouni, by Samuel Taylor Coleridge.

night. On a small scale this process is practically familiar to every school-boy. When he makes a snow-ball he is practically converting a mass of snow into ice, and that by a series of operations very closely resembling those which Nature employs in the manufacture of a Glacier.

In Switzerland the Glacier is often two or three miles in breadth, from twenty to thirty miles in length, and five or six hundred feet in depth. Though so vast in its bulk and so solid in its character, it is not, as might be supposed, a fixed, immovable mass. On the contrary, it is moving incessantly, but slowly, down the valley which it occupies, at the rate of several inches—sometimes one or two feet, and even more—in the day. In Greenland a Glacier explored by Doctor Hayes, in his expedition to the North Pole, was found to move for a whole year at the average rate of a hundred feet a day. It may be thought, perhaps, that this fact requires further confirmation; but at all events it is certain that the language of the poet, when he addreesss the Glaciers as "motionless torrents," though it conveys an accurate and beautiful idea of the appearance they present to the eye, is not rigorously true in a scientific sense. Indeed, it is just because the Glaciers are not motionless that they serve as instruments of Denudation.

Their agency in this respect "consists partly in their power of transporting gravel, sand, and huge stones, to great distances, and partly in the smoothing, polishing, and scoring of their rocky channels, and the boundary walls of the valleys through which they pass. At the foot of every steep cliff or precipice in high Alpine regions, a sloping heap is seen of rocky fragments detached by the alternate action of frost and thaw. If these loose masses, instead of accumulating on a stationary base, happen to fall upon a Glacier, they will move along with it, and, in place of a single heap, they will form in the course of years a long stream of blocks. If a Glacier be twenty miles long, and its annual progression about five hundred feet, it will require about two centuries for a block thus lodged upon its surface to travel down from the higher to the lower regions, or to the extremity of the icy mass. This terminal point usually remains unchanged from year to year, although every part of the ice is in motion, because the liquefaction by heat is just sufficient to balance the onward movement of the Glacier, which may be compared to an endless file of soldiers, pouring into a breach, and shot down as fast as they advance.

"The stones carried along on the ice are called in Switzerland the *moraines* of the Glacier. There is always one line of blocks on each side or edge of the icy stream, and often several in the middle, where they are arranged in long ridges or mounds of snow and ice, often several yards high. The reason of their projecting above the general level, is the non-liquefaction of the ice in those parts of the surface of the Glacier which are protected from the rays of the sun, or the action of the wind, by the covering of the earth, sand, and stones. The cause of *medial moraines* was first explained by Agassiz, who referred them to the confluence of tributary Glaciers. Upon the union of two streams of ice, the right lateral moraine of one of the streams comes in contact with the left lateral moraine of the other, and they afterward move on together, in the centre, if the confluent Glaciers are equal in size, or nearer to one side if unequal.

"Fragments of stone and sand which fall through crevasses in the ice, and get interposed between the moving Glacier and the fundamental rock, are pushed along so as to have their angles more or less worn off, and many of them are entirely ground down into mud. Some blocks are pushed along between the ice and the steep boundary rocks of the valley, and these, like the rocky channel at the bottom of the valley, often become smoothed and polished, and scored with parallel furrows, or with lines and scratches produced by hard minerals, such as crystals of quartz, which act like the diamond upon glass. The effect is perfectly different from that caused by the action of water, or a muddy torrent forcing along heavy stones; for these not being held like fragments of rock in ice, and not being pushed along under great pressure, cannot scoop out long rectilinear furrows or grooves parallel to each other. The discovery of such markings at various heights far above the surface of existing Glaciers, and for miles beyond their present terminations, affords geological evidence of the former extension of the ice beyond its present limits in Switzerland and other countries."*

Fig. 2.—Iceberg seen in mid-ocean 1400 miles from any known land.

Sometimes, however, it happens, especially in extreme northern and southern latitudes, that the glacier valley leads down to the sea. In such cases, huge masses of ice are floated off, and, with their ponderous burden of gravel,

* Lyell's Principles of Geology, vol. i., pp. 374–5.

mud, and rocks, are carried away by currents toward the equator. Immense numbers of these floating islands of ice, or Icebergs, as they are called, are seen by mariners drifting along in the Northern and Southern oceans. In 1822 Scoresby counted five hundred between the latitudes 69° and 70° N., many of which measured a mile in circumference, and rose two hundred feet above the surface of the sea.* The annexed drawing, copied by kind permission of the author from Sir Charles Lyell's Principles of Geology, affords a good idea of the appearance that such Icebergs present to the eye. The one represented in the foreground was supposed to reach a height of nearly three hundred feet, and was observed with many others floating about in the Southern Ocean at a distance of 1400 miles from any known land. An angular mass of rock was visible on the surface. The part exposed was twelve feet high and from five to six broad: but it was conjectured, from the color of the surrounding ice, that the greater part of the stone was concealed from view.

How enormous must be the magnitude of those ponderous masses may be learned from the fact that the bulk of ice below the level of the water is about eight times as great as that above: and in point of fact, Captain Sir John Ross saw several of them aground in Baffin's Bay, where the water was 1500 feet deep. It has been calculated that the beds of earth and stones which they carry along cannot be less than from 50,000 to 100,000 tons in weight. Sir Charles Lyell, writing in 1865 from the results of the latest investigations on this subject, says: "Many had supposed that the magnitude commonly attributed to icebergs by unscientific navigators was exaggerated; but now it appears that the popular estimate of their dimensions has rather fallen within than beyond the truth. Many of them, carefully

* Voyage in 1822, p. 233.

measured by the officers of the French exploring expedition of the Astrolabe, were between 100 and 225 feet high above water, and from two to five miles in length. Captain d'Urville ascertained one of them, which he saw floating, to be *thirteen miles long*, and a hundred feet high, with walls perfectly vertical."*

They have been known to drift from Baffin's Bay to the Azores, and from the South Pole to the Cape of Good Hope.† As they approach the milder climate of the temperate zones, the ice gradually melts away, and thus the moraines of arctic and antarctic glaciers are deposited at the bottom of the deep sea. In this way, submarine mountains and valleys and table-lands are strewn over with scattered blocks of foreign rocks, and gravel, and mud, which have been transported hundreds of miles across the unfathomable abysses of the ocean.

Though we are chiefly concerned with Glaciers and Icebergs as agents of Denudation, yet we cannot pass away from the subject without referring to the Geological theory of an ancient Glacial Period. This little digression from the main purport of our present argument will not be unacceptable, we hope, to our readers. The theory is in itself interesting and ingenious; and it offers an admirable illustration of the kind of reasoning by which Geologists are guided in their speculations.

It is well known that the action of moving ice leaves a very peculiar and characteristic impress on the surface of the rocks, and even on the general aspect of the country over which it passes. This is no mystery of science, but a plain fact which any one that chooses may observe for himself. Every Glacier carries along in its course a vast quantity of loose gravel, hard sand, and large angular

* Elements of Geology, pp. 145, 146.

† Captain Horsburg, On Icebergs in Low Latitudes. Phil. Trans., 1830.

stones. A considerable proportion of these materials in course of time fall through crevasses in the ice, and become firmly embedded in the under surface of the Glacier. Then, as the moving mass slowly descends the valley, they are shoved along under enormous pressure, and the surface of

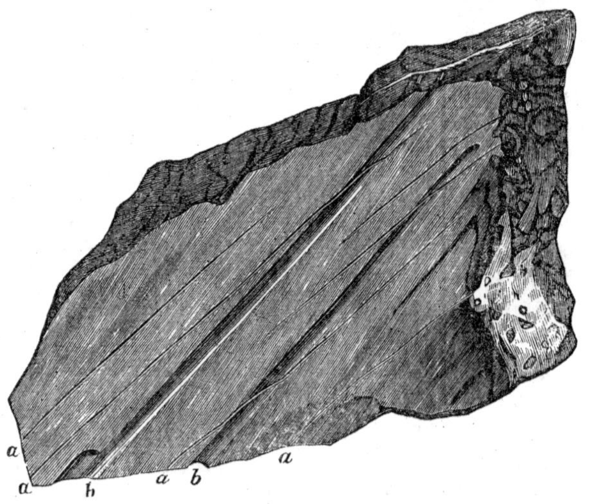

Fig. 3.—Block of Limestone furrowed, scratched, and polished, from the Glacier of Rosenlaui, Switzerland. (Lyell.)

aa, White streaks or scratches. *bb*, Furrows.

the rocks beneath is furrowed, scratched, and polished, in a remarkable and unmistakable manner. The furrows and scratches are rectilinear and parallel to an extent never seen in the marks produced by any other natural agency: and they always coincide more or less in their direction with the general course of the valley. A reciprocal action often takes place: the large blocks of stone, frozen into the under surface of the Glacier, are themselves scored and polished by friction against the floor and sides of the valley.

Similar effects are produced by Icebergs; not of course when drifting about in the deep sea, but when they come into contact with a gently-shelving coast and grate along the bottom. These mountains of ice, laden with the débris of the land, are often carried along with the velocity of from two to three miles an hour; and before their enormous momentum can be entirely destroyed, an extensive surface of rock must have been rounded, grooved, and scarred, pretty much in the same way as by the action of a Glacier. There can be no failure of the grinding materials. During the process of melting, the Iceberg is constantly turning over according as the centre of gravity shifts its position; and thus a new part of its surface, with fresh angular blocks of stone, together with fresh masses of sand and gravel, is constantly brought into contact with the floor of the ocean. And this is not mere theory. All these phenomena may be witnessed any day on the shores of Baffin's Bay and Hudson's Bay, and along the coast of Labrador.

Again, the evidence of glacial action may be discovered in the materials themselves which have been transported by ice. Many of the large erratic blocks, after having travelled immense distances, exhibit the same sharp angular appearance as if they had only just fallen down from the cliff on the mountain side. By this circumstance they are at once distinguished from blocks of stone transported by running water; for in these the angles are sure to be rounded off by friction. Sometimes, too, they are deposited not only far away from the same rock, but in regions where no rock of the same kind exists. In the case of Icebergs, they are not unfrequently carried many hundreds of miles before being dropped into the depths of the ocean, and, in the course of their long journey, borne over the lofty ridges of submarine mountain chains.

Furthermore, it often happens that a Glacier shrinks backward up the valley, and sometimes even disappears altogether. When the melting of the ice at the lower extremity exactly balances its onward progress, then the Glacier seems stationary to the eye, and occupies from year to year the same position. But, when a number of hot seasons follow one another in immediate succession, the ice is melted more rapidly than the Glacier advances, and in consequence it gradually becomes shorter, and seems to the eye to recede toward the upper parts of the valley. In this case the long lines of moraines, which before had rested on the ice, are left spread out on the plains or deposited on the slopes of the mountain. Immense blocks of stone are by this means frequently set down on the summits of lofty crags, and in such like positions to which they could not be brought by any other natural agency. These Perched Blocks, as they are called, and also those long regular mounds of earth and stones abound in several of the Swiss valleys, and constitute a very striking feature of Alpine scenery.

Now, it appears that all these various characteristic marks of glacial operations can be distinctly traced in many countries where the action of moving ice has been unknown within the period of history. And on this fact is founded the Geological theory of an ancient Glacial Period. We are confidently assured that a great part of Northern Europe, including even our own islands, not to speak of America and other countries as well in the northern as in the southern hemisphere, were, in some far distant age, the scene of those same phenomena which are witnessed at the present day amid the solemn grandeur of the Alps, and in the frozen wastes of the Arctic regions. In that age enormous Glaciers moved slowly downward from the snow-clad heights over innumerable valleys now rich with the fruits of the earth; ponderous Icebergs floated over wide areas of the ocean, where now the dry land appears; and vast piles of promiscuous rubbish, with great angular blocks of stone, were deposited on the slopes and crests of submarine mountains that now tower hundreds of feet above the level of the sea.

To illustrate this theory, we would begin with a country where the vestiges of glacial operations in past times may be studied side by side with the glacial phenomena of the present day. In Switzerland it needs but little skill to discern many marks and tokens of moving ice where moving ice is no longer found. In descending, for example, the valley of the Hasli or the valley of the Rhone, the intelligent traveller can hardly fail to observe how the rocks all around are scarred and furrowed, precisely after the same fashion as the rocks in the higher parts of the same valleys are now being scarred and furrowed by the Glacier of the Aar and the Glacier of the Rhone. At intervals, too, may be seen long mounds of unstratified gravel and mud, with large fragments of rock, in every way resembling the terminal moraines now daily accumulating at the extremities of existing Glaciers. When these facts are once distinctly brought home to the mind, it is impossible to resist the conclusion that several of the Alpine Glaciers once extended far beyond their present limits down the valleys of Switzerland.

If we proceed a little distance to the mountains of the Jura, now wholly devoid of Glaciers, we shall find that the same glacial phenomena with which we have become so familiar in the Alps, are still everywhere presented to the eye. And we feel instinctively impelled to pursue the same line of inductive reasoning. Moving ice, we know from abundant observation, is capable of producing these effects : nor have we ever seen effects of this kind produced by any other cause : nay, there is no other natural agent known that is capable of producing such effects : it is therefore reasonable to infer that moving ice was the cause of these effects ; and that, in some bygone age, great masses of ice moved slowly over the valleys of the Jura as they now move slowly over the valleys of the Alps.

Another circumstance may here be noticed which is well worthy of consideration. The Alps are composed of granite, gneiss, and such like crystalline rocks: the Jura, of limestone and various other formations, altogether different from those of the Alps. Now, scattered loosely over the valleys of the Jura, and perched upon its lofty crests, we find immense angular blocks—some of them as large as cottages—of the Alpine rocks. The question naturally arises, how have they been transported to their present site. Certainly not by the action of water; for in that case the projecting angles would have been rounded off, and the sharp edges worn away. But the work might have been easily accomplished by the power of moving ice, and could not have been accomplished by any other natural agency with which we are acquainted. Thus we are led to conclude that the Glaciers of the Alps must, by some means or another, have once made their way northward across the great valley of Switzerland, fifty miles wide, and deposited their ponderous burdens of gravel, sand, and erratic blocks on the mountains of the Jura.

It would carry us too far from our present purpose to draw out this theory in all its details. But we cannot forbear briefly to touch upon some of the bold and startling conclusions to which it has led. The Geologist having, by patient and varied exercise, in the regions of existing Glaciers, trained his eye and his judgment in the observation of those phenomena that mark the action of moving ice, soon begins to discover that they are not wanting in other countries. They are not to be found, indeed, beneath the burning sun of Africa, nor on the borders of the Mediterranean Sea. But as he travels northward they begin by degrees to appear; and when at length he reaches the shores of the Baltic, they are spread out profusely before him as they were in the bosom of the Alps. All this had puzzled Geologists for years; but the clue has been found at last. What is going on to-day in Switzerland, and in Greenland, and on the shores of Labrador, must have been going on, ages ago, in Germany, and in Denmark, and on the shores of the Baltic. We may argue from the effect to the cause. Here are the moraines, the erratics, the perched blocks, and the surfaces of rock furrowed and scratched with ice: at some past time there must have been the moving Glaciers and the floating Icebergs.

Following out this line of argument, and applying it to countries nearer home, Geologists have come to the conclusion that the Grampian Hills in Scotland, the mountains of Kerry in Ireland, the Snowdonian heights in Wales, and many other ranges of hills in these islands, were in former times subjected to the action of moving ice. Nay, it is contended, with much show of reason, that these islands must have been, for a considerable time, in great part submerged beneath the sea, and traversed by floating Icebergs. When large erratic blocks are found in the immediate neighborhood of the formation from which they have been derived, then it is easy to explain their origin and to trace their course. But it often happens that the nearest rock of the same mineral composition, and therefore, the nearest rock from which they can possibly have been derived, is separated from the site which they now occupy by a lofty chain of mountains. By what means, then, have they been transported hither? Not by moving water, for their sharp edges and projecting angles are still preserved. Not by Glaciers; for a Glacier cannot climb a steep mountain ridge. It would seem, indeed, that in the present geographical distribution of land and water, there is no natural cause which could carry them from the parent rocks to their present position. But if we suppose that in some long past age of the world, Great Britain and Ireland were submerged beneath the sea, and that Icebergs floated in the waters above, the problem is solved at once. The fragments of far distant rocks frozen into the Icebergs might then have been carried over the summits of what are now lofty mountains, and as the ice melted away, might have been deposited all along their slopes and even on their highest crests.

The presence of marine shells, belonging chiefly to species which now exist only in the arctic seas, affords a strong confirmation of this hypothesis. For they are found intimately associated with the erratic blocks, not merely in valleys, to which the sea might be supposed to have had access in times of extraordinary flood, but upon lofty mountains at a height of five hundred, six hundred, and even thirteen hundred feet above the level of the sea. There is no difficulty in accounting for this phenomenon if we suppose the country to have been at one time submerged, and the glacial drift in which the shells are found embedded to have been deposited by Icebergs on the floor of the ocean. If we refuse to make this supposition the difficulty is simply insurmountable.*

But it is somewhat beside our purpose to wander so far into the region of theory and speculation. Our main object in these chapters has been to establish the fact that Denudation is actually taking place to an almost incredible extent, in the present age of the world. For this purpose we have enumerated the principal agents by which this process is carried on; and we have endeavored to show from the authenticated researches of travellers and scientific men that they have been at work within the period of history, and are still at work around us. Our summary is, indeed,

* Agassiz, Etudes sur les Glaciers; Tyndall, Glaciers of the Alps; also Heat as a mode of Motion, by the same Author; Lyell, Principles of Geology, vol. i., chapter xvi.; Elements of Geology, chapters xi., xii.; Wallace, Ice Marks in North Wales, in the Quarterly Journal of Science, No. xiii.

brief; but it is still sufficient to demonstrate that, even during the present age, the whole surface of the Globe has been ever in a constant state of change; that mountain heights have been worn away, and valleys have been scooped out, and lofty cliffs have disappeared, and bold headlands have beer rent in twain, and rocks and earths have day by day been broken up and dissolved and decomposed, by the never ceasing operation of natural causes; and that the broken fragments are at every moment moving along over the surface of the land or through the depths of the sea.

Now Geologists tell us that these are the raw materials of a new building which is going on in these latter times under the guiding hand of Nature. Indeed, they say it is not so much a new building as the uppermost story of an old building. If we descend into the Crust of the Earth we may trace this building even from the foundations, which are laid upon the solid granite, up through each successive stage of limestone, and sandstone, slate, conglomerate, and clay, until we come to the surface, where new strata, composed of the same elements, and exhibiting the same general characteristics, are slowly growing up before our eyes. Thus will the idea gradually steal upon the mind, that the works of ages long gone by are reproduced once again in our own days, and that we may study the history of the past in the mirror of the present which nature holds up to our view.

This is the branch of Geological argument upon which we are now about to enter. We have visited Nature, as it were, in her quarry, and we have seen how she collects her materials, how she fashions them to her purpose, how she transports them to the place for which they are designed. If it be true, as alleged, that with these materials she is actually engaged, at the present moment, in building upon the existing surface of our Globe a new series of stratified rocks, which are the exact counterpart of those beneath, this fact affords at least a very strong presumption in favor of one very important principle in the theory of Geologists. Let us, then, follow the course of her operations and judge for ourselves.

CHAPTER V.

STRATIFIED ROCKS OF MECHANICAL ORIGIN—THEORY DEVELOPED AND ILLUSTRATED.

Formation of stratified rocks ascribed to the agency of natural causes—This theory supported by facts—The argument stated—Examples of mechanical rocks—Materials of which they are composed—Origin and history of these materials traced out—Process of deposition—Process of consolidation—Instances of consolidation by pressure—Consolidation perfected by natural cements—Curious illustrations—Consolidation of sandstone in Cornwall—Arrangement of strata explained by intermittent action of the agents of Denudation.

HE Stratification of Rocks is one of the most remarkable features which the Crust of the Earth presents to our notice; and the principles by which this phenomenon is explained belong to the very foundation of Geological theory. It is now universally agreed that the successive layers or strata, which constitute such a very large proportion of the Earth's Crust, and which cannot fail to attract the notice even of the most careless observer, have been slowly built up during a long series of ages by the action of natural causes. In support of this bold and comprehensive theory, geologists appeal to the operations which are going on in nature at the present day, or which have been observed and recorded within historic times. There is a vast machinery, they say, even now at work all over the world, breaking up the rocks that appear at the surface of the Earth, transporting the materials to different sites, and there constructing new strata, just the counterpart of those which we see piled up one above the other, wherever a section of the Earth's Crust is exposed to view. It is given to us, therefore, on the one hand to contemplate the finished work as it exists in the Crust of the Earth, and on the other, to examine the work still in progress upon its surface; and if both are found to agree in all their most remarkable characteristics, it is not unreasonable to infer that the one was produced in bygone ages by the very same causes that are now busy in the production of the other.

In the examination of this argument we first turned our attention to the numerous and powerful agents that are now employed in the breaking up and transporting of existing rocks. It was impossible within our narrow limits to enumerate them all. But we selected those which are at the same time the most familiar in their operations, and the most striking in their results:—mighty rivers discharging daily and hourly into the sea the accumulated spoils of vast continents; the breakers of the ocean dashing with unceasing energy against all the cliffs and coasts of the world; the tides and currents of the sea taking up the ruins which the breakers have made, and carrying them far away to the lonely depths of the ocean; the frozen rain bursting massive rocks asunder with its expansive force, and sending the fragments over lofty cliffs and steep precipices to become the prey of roaring mountain torrents, or perhaps, more fortunate, to find a place of tranquil rest on the bosom of the glittering Glacier; then this wondrous Glacier itself, a moving sea of ice, bearing along its ponderous burden from the summits of lofty mountains far down into the smiling plains, and meanwhile, with tremendous power, grinding, and furrowing, and wearing away the floor of the valley, and leaving behind it an impress which even time cannot efface; and lastly, the massive Icebergs which stud the northern and southern seas, drifting along like floating islands above the fathomless abysses of the ocean, and scattering their huge boulders over the surface of submarine mountains and valleys.

All these phenomena have been learned from actual and repeated observation. They are not philosophical speculations, but ascertained facts. We cannot doubt, therefore, that the work of demolition is going on; it remains for us now to inquire about the work of reconstruction.

The reader will remember that Geologists divide the stratified rocks into three distinct classes, Mechanical, Chemical, and Organic. This distinction, they say, is founded on the actual operations of Nature. From a close examination of the natural agents now at work in the world, it appears that some strata are being formed chiefly by the action of mechanical force; others chiefly by the influence of chemical laws; and others again chiefly by the intervention of organic life. Thus we have three distinct classes of rock at present coming into existence, each exhibiting its own peculiar characteristics, and each, moreover, having its counterpart among the strata that compose the Crust of the Earth. We shall now proceed to set forth some of the evidence that may be advanced in favor of these important conclusions, beginning with those rocks that are called Mechanical.

And first it is important to have, at least, a general idea of the appearance which Mechanical Rocks present to the eye. We shall take three familiar examples, Conglomerate, Sandstone, and Clay. Conglomerate, or Pudding-stone as it is sometimes called, is composed of pebbles, gravel, and sand, more or less compacted together, and generally forming a hard and solid mass. The various materials of which it is composed, though united in the one rock, nevertheless retain their own external forms, and may be distinctly recognized even by the unpractised eye. Sandstone, as the name implies, is made up of grains of sand closely compressed and cemented together. The quality and appearance of this rock vary very much according to the size and character of its constituent particles. Often the grains of sand are as large as peas, or even larger; sometimes they are so minute that they cannot be distinguished without the aid of a lens. For the most part they consist of quartz, with grains of limestone intermixed; and they are usually rounded, as if by the action of running water. Clay is a rather vague and general term, now commonly employed to denote any finely-divided mineral matter which contains from ten to thirty per cent. of Alumina, and is thereby rendered plastic, and capable, when softened with water, of being moulded like paste with the hand. It occurs in many different forms among the strata of the Earth, according to the different minerals that enter into its composition and the different influences to which it has been subjected. Marl and Loam may be taken as well-known illustrations: the former is a clay in which there is a large proportion of calcareous matter; the latter is a mixture of clay and sand. Sometimes by pressure clay is condensed into a kind of slaty rock called Shale, which has the property of being easily split up into an immense number of thin plates or laminæ.

It should be remembered that there is not always a perfect uniformity in the structure of these rocks. In Conglomerate, for example, the pebbles may be as large as cannon balls, or they may be only the size of walnuts. So, too, we have every variety of fineness and coarseness in the quality of Sandstone. Again, both Conglomerate and Sandstone are often largely adulterated with clay, and on the other hand, clay will sometimes contain more than its usual proportion of sand or lime. Lastly, these materials are in one place compacted into hard and solid rock, in another they are found in a loose and incoherent condition.

But amidst all these varieties of form and texture, the rocks we have been describing generally preserve their peculiar characteristics, and with a little experience can be easily recognized. They are found to constitute a very large part, perhaps we might say the larger part, of the stratified rocks in every country that has hitherto been explored by Geologists. Wherever we go we are met by the same familiar appearances;—beds of Conglomerate, Sandstone, Clay, Marl, Shale, recurring again and again through a series of many hundred strata, sometimes in one order, and sometimes in another; sometimes without any formation of a different kind intervening, and sometimes alternating with limestone or other rocks of which we shall speak hereafter.

Such is the general character and appearance of those strata which are known among Geologists as Aqueous Rocks of Mechanical origin. Now, it must at once strike the reader, that these rocks are made up of just those very materials—the same both in kind and in form—that we have already shown to be daily prepared and fashioned by a vast and complex machinery in the great workshop of Nature. He will remember how enormous blocks are detached from the mountain side, or from the cliffs on the seashore, and broken up into fragments; how the fragments in time become pebbles, sand, and mud; and how these are caught up by rivers, tides, and currents, and carried far away to sea. Here we have certainly all the materials that are necessary for the building up of Conglomerate, Sandstone, and Shale. We have seen how they are prepared by the hand of Nature, how they are moulded into shape, how they are transported from place to place. Let us now pursue the sequel of their history, and follow them on to the end.

It is plain they cannot remain forever suspended in water; sooner or later they must fall to the bottom. Yet they will not all fall together. For though all are carried downward by the one force of gravity, those materials that are smaller and lighter will be more impeded by the resistance of the water. The pebbles and coarse gravel will be the first to reach the bottom, then the sand, and last of all the fine, impalpable mud. Thus, as the current sweeps along in its course, the sediment which it bears away from the land will be in a manner sorted, and three distinct layers of different materials will be deposited in the bed of the ocean;—first, nearest to the shore, a layer of pebbles and coarse gravel, then a layer of sand, and last of all a layer of fine mud or clay. This is the first step in the construction of stratified rock. To complete the work nothing more is necessary than the consolidation of these loose and incoherent materials. If this could be accomplished, then we should have a solid stratum of Conglomerate, a solid stratum of Sandstone, and a solid stratum of Shale formed in the bed of the ocean.

With regard to this operation, however, we cannot hope for the advantage we have hitherto enjoyed, of actual observation. The process of consolidation, if it take place at all, is going on in the depths of the Sea. But though it is thus removed beyond the reach of our senses, it is not beyond the reach of our intelligence. We may borrow the torch of Science, and search even into the hidden recesses of Nature's secret laboratory.

In the first place, a partial consolidation of clay and sand, and even of gravel, may take place under the influence of pressure alone. Many of us are familiar with this truth, but few, perhaps, are aware how extensively it is illustrated in the practical arts of life. Here are some curious and interesting examples. The minute fragments of coal which are produced by the friction of larger blocks against one another, and which may be obtained abundantly in the neighborhood of every coal mine, are now manufactured into a solid patent fuel by the simple process of forcible compression. Again, the dust and rubble of black lead, formerly cast aside as useless, are now carefully collected, and by no other force than pressure are converted into a solid mass, fit to be employed in the manufacture of lead-pencils. "The graphite, or black lead of commerce," says Sir Charles Lyell, "having become very scarce, Mr. Brockedon contrived a method by which the dust of the purer portions of the mineral found in Borrowdale might be recomposed into a mass as dense and as compact as native graphite. The powder of graphite is first carefully prepared and freed from air, and placed under a powerful press on a strong steel die, with air-tight fittings. It is then struck several blows, each of a power of a thousand tons; after which operation the powder is so perfectly solidified that it can be cut for pencils, and exhibits, when broken, the same texture as native graphite."* An instance yet more to our purpose occurs in the experiments made to try the force of gunpowder. Leathern bags filled with sand are put into the mortar that is to receive the cannon-ball at a distance of fifty feet from the mouth of the gun; and the sand is often compressed by the percussion of the ball into a solid mass of Sandstone.† Now the deposits of which we are speaking cannot fail to be subjected to a very powerful and a very constant compressing force. For, since the process of deposition is always going on, the matter which is deposited to-day will to-morrow be covered with a new layer, and in the course of ages it may lie beneath an immense pile of mineral matter, hundreds or even thousands of feet in thickness.

But in fact there is another and more important agent

* Elements of Geology, p. 38.

† Mantell, Wonders of Geology, vol. i., p. 102.

at work. When the harder and more compact blocks of Conglomerate and Sandstone are subjected to a close analysis in the laboratory of the chemist, it is found that they are strongly cemented together, sometimes by a solution of lime filling up the interstices between the grains or pebbles, sometimes by a solution of silica, sometimes by a solution of iron. Now this discovery affords a useful clue when we come to study the present operations of Nature. It is to the agency of a mineral cement we must look for the perfect consolidation of Mechanical Rocks. Let us see if such a cement can be found.

It is well known that the water of rivers, lakes, and springs, is more or less charged with carbonic acid gas; and therefore, when it comes in contact with limestone, it dissolves a portion of the lime and holds it in solution. Hence it follows that in every part of the world there exists an abundant store of calcareous cement. Again, our readers must have observed the brownish, rusty color sometimes produced by streams on the surface of rocks and herbage. This is the result of the iron with which the streams are impregnated: and we are informed by scientific inquirers that water containing a solution of iron prevails very generally in almost all countries. The solution of silica in water is not so common; because pure silica cannot be dissolved by water except at a very high temperature. Nevertheless, it has been clearly demonstrated by observation, that silica, where it occurs in certain combinations with other mineral substances, may be dissolved readily enough: for instance, in the decomposition of felspar, and of all rocks in which felspar is an ingredient, silica is carried off in a state of solution.* And since these rocks are very numerous, and distributed over every part of the earth, we may fairly conclude that a solution of silica exists very abundantly in nature.

* Lyell, Elements of Geology, p. 42; also Principles, vol. i., p. 410.

Now when we bear in mind that we have on the one hand in the Crust of the Earth, solid strata of Conglomerate and Sandstone, exhibiting the evident operation of these mineral cements; and on the other hand, near the surface, the loose materials of Conglomerate and Sandstone as if ready to be cemented, and close at hand the cementing mineral itself in a convenient form, it is not unreasonable to assume that the process should actually take place; —that water highly charged with iron, or lime, or silica, should filter through the loose gravel and sand, depositing its mineral cement as it passes along, and converting the newly-formed strata into compact and solid rock.

But this conclusion does not rest upon antecedent probability alone. We have proof unquestionable that a process such as we have described is actually going on. In the dredging of the river Thames large masses of solid Conglomerate are found from time to time, firmly compacted together by a ferruginous cement. And there is internal evidence that the process of solidification has been effected by natural causes within historic times; for it happens not unfrequently that Roman coins and fragments of pottery are found embedded in the solid block of stone. Similar discoveries were made in deepening the bed of the river Dove in Derbyshire, about the year 1832. Thousands of silver coins were found about ten feet under the surface, firmly cemented into a hard Conglomerate. Several of these coins bear dates of the thirteenth and fourteenth centuries; and therefore the pebbles which form the rock must have been deposited and converted into a solid mass since that time. But we must not suppose that so long an interval is necessary for the consolidation of rocks. In the early part of the present century a vessel called the Thetis was wrecked off cape Frio on the coast of Brazil. A few months afterward, when an attempt was successfully made to recover the dollars and other treasures which had gone to the bottom with the wreck, they were found completely enveloped in solid masses of quartzose Sandstone. The materials of the newly-formed stone were in this case manifestly derived from the granite rocks of the Brazilian coast.*

In many parts of the Mediterranean, and along its shores, this process is known to be going on with equal rapidity. "The new-formed strata of Asia Minor," writes Sir Charles Lyell, "consists of stone, not of loose, incoherent materials. Almost all the streamlets and rivers, like many of those in Tuscany and the south of Italy, hold abundance of carbonate of lime in solution, and precipitate Travertine, or sometimes bind together the sand and gravel into solid Sandstones and Conglomerates; every delta and sandbar thus acquires solidity, which often prevents streams from forcing their way through them, so that their mouths are constantly changing their position."† In the Museum at Montpelier is exhibited a cannon embedded in a crystalline calcareous rock which was taken up from the bed of the Mediterranean near the mouth of the Rhone.‡

To these examples of the solidification of rock within recent times we are tempted to add one more, taken from a Memoir published by the late Dr. Paris in the Transactions of the Royal Geological Society of Cornwall. "A sandstone occurs in various parts of the northern coast of Cornwall, which affords a most instructive example of a recent formation, since we here actually detect Nature at work in converting loose sand into solid rock. A very considerable portion of the northern coast of Cornwall is covered with calcareous sand, consisting of minute particles of comminuted shells, which in some places has accumulated in quantities so great, as to have formed hills of from forty

* Mantell's Wonders of Geology, pp. 70, 81, 82, 83.

† Lyell, Principles of Geology, vol. i., p. 431.

‡ Id, ib., p. 429.

to fifty feet in elevation. In digging into these sand-hills, or upon the occasional removal of some part of them by the winds, the remains of houses may be seen; and in places where the churchyards have been overwhelmed, a great number of human bones may be found. The sand is supposed to have been originally brought from the sea by hurricanes, probably at a remote period. It first appears in a state of slight but increasing aggregation on several parts of the shore in the Bay of St. Ives; but on approaching the Gwythian River it becomes more extensive and indurated. . . . It is around the promontory of New Kaye that the most extensive formation of Sandstone takes place. Here it may be seen in different stages of induration, from a state in which it is too friable to be detached from the rock on which it reposes, to a hardness so considerable that it requires a very violent blow from a sledge to break it. Buildings are constructed of it; the church of Cranstock is entirely built with it; and it is also employed for various articles of domestic and agricultural uses."

No reasonable doubt can therefore remain that the loose beds of gravel, sand, and clay, which, as we have already seen, are deposited from day to day, and from year to year, and from century to century, beneath the waters of the ocean, may be converted in the course of time by natural agents into solid rocks of Conglomerate, of Sandstone, and of Shale. But this is not enough. It yet remains for us to explain how these solid rocks come to be arranged in a series of distinct layers or strata. The reader will remember that the supply of materials in any given area of the ocean is not fixed and continuous, but, on the contrary, variable and intermittent. During the periodical rains within the tropics, and during the melting of the snows in high latitudes or in mountain regions, the rivers become enormously swollen, and carry down a far greater quantity of sediment than at other seasons. The waste of cliffs, too, by the action of the waves, is much greater in winter than in summer. Thus, while at one season a particular river or current may be comparatively free from sediment, at another it will carry along in its turbid course an almost incredible freight of mineral matter. We have a notable example in the case of the Ganges. The bulk of earthy matter which this river discharges into the sea during the four months of rain, averages about 50,000,000 of cubic feet per day; whereas the daily discharge during the three months of hot weather is considerably less than one hundredth part of that amount.*

Besides this variety in the quantity of materials carried, there is also a great variety in the velocity both of rivers and of currents; and therefore they will not always carry the same materials to the same distance; for the less rapid the stream, the sooner will the sediment fall to the bottom. We may add that currents, as is well known, often change their direction from various causes, and thus at different times they will carry the waste of the land to different parts of the ocean.

From these considerations two conclusions may be fairly deduced: First, that the process of deposition may often go on very rapidly for a time over a given area, and then altogether cease, and after an interval begin again. In this way time may be allowed for one deposit to acquire more or less consistency before the next is superimposed; and thus a succession of distinct beds will be produced. Secondly, we may infer that the same precise materials will not always be deposited over the same area; at one time it will be sand, at another gravel, at another clay, at another

* The figures given by Sir Charles Lyell, and derived from the observations of Mr. Everest, are these: total discharge during the four months of rain, 6,082,041,600 cubic feet; total discharge during the three months of hot weather, 38,154,240 cubic feet.—Principles of Geology, vol. i., p. 481.

some combination of these or other mineral substances. And thus it may happen that the strata deposited in successive periods of time shall not only be distinct one from the other, but composed of different materials;—that there shall be, in fact, as we so often see that there are, beds of Conglomerate, Sandstone, Clay, Marl, and other rocks, succeeding one another in every variety of order.

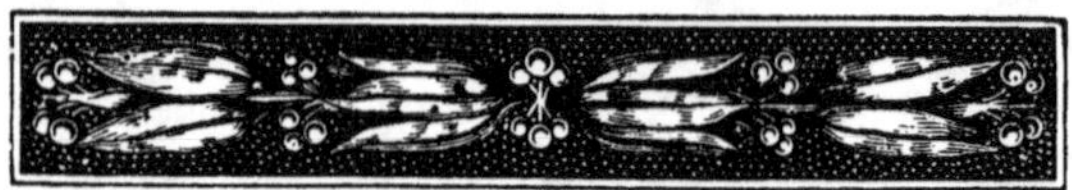

CHAPTER VI.

STRATIFIED ROCKS OF MECHANICAL ORIGIN—FURTHER ILLUSTRATIONS.

Impossible to witness the formation of stratified rocks in the depths of the ocean—On a small scale examples are exhibited by rivers and lakes—Alluvial plains—Their extraordinary fertility—Great basin of the Nile—Experiments of the Royal Society—The Mississippi and the Orinoco—Some rivers fill up their own channels—Case of the river Po—Artificial embankments—Large tract of alluvial soil deposited by the Rhone in the Lake of Geneva—Deltas—The delta of the Ganges and Brahmapootra—Delta of the Nile.

THE argument set forth in the last chapter is simple, ingenious, and persuasive. Nay, we must fairly confess that to us it seems conclusive. We do not mean to say that it amounts to a rigorous demonstration. But it affords at least a strong presumption that the process of deposition, the process of consolidation, and the process of stratification, are going on to a vast extent beneath the waters of the ocean; and that, in these latter ages of the world's history, Aqueous Rocks are slowly growing up under the influence of natural causes, which resemble in every important feature those that are now attracting so much attention within the Crust of the Earth. We are therefore prepared to accept this conclusion, if it be not found at variance with any well-established fact, or with any known and certain truth. But in matters of physical science the evidence of our senses is, after all, the most satisfactory argument. And our readers, no doubt, would like to witness, if possible, with their eyes, the building up of Stratified Rocks. Now, though it is not given to us to see this process in all its colossal magnitude as it goes on within the depths of the mighty ocean, it is yet possible to behold it exhibited, as it were, in miniature, in certain cases where the sediment of rivers is deposited within reach of observation.

Every one is familiar with the fact that many rivers overflow their banks at certain seasons, and spread themselves out over a wide area, sometimes reaching to the foot of the hills that bound the valleys through which they flow. This is the origin of those Alluvial Plains so remarkable for their surpassing richness and fertility. In each successive year a thin film of sediment is deposited on the surface of the land ; and thus in the course of ages a soil is formed capable of producing, season after season, the most luxuriant crops without manifesting any symptoms of exhaustion. The soil of the Alluvial Plain near St. Louis, on the Mississippi, is thus spoken of by a modern traveller : "As to the quality of the land, any given number of crops might be grown off it. Corn has been raised on it for a hundred years together—as far back as the settlement is known. To inquire about the system of farming in the West is not productive of information which would be of service on the continent of Europe. There is no system : the farmer scratches the ground and throws in the seed, and his bountiful harvests come up year after year without further thought or trouble. Thousands of centuries have made the soil for him, and it defies him to make too heavy demands upon it. It gives him all he asks, and is never known to disappoint or fail." *

The great basin of the Nile offers an admirable example

* From a Special Correspondent, in the Times Newspaper, December 7, 1866.

of an Alluvial Plain on a scale of considerable magnitude. Even in the days of Herodotus, Egypt was regarded as the "gift of the Nile:" and the correctness of this opinion has been placed beyond all reasonable doubt by the investigations of modern science. The river bears along in its current, especially during the flood season, a large quantity of fine earthy sediment obtained by the process of Denudation from the mountains of central Africa. Once a year, between the months of July and November, it overflows its banks, and this sediment is deposited on the adjoining plains. Thus a new layer of rich soil is spread out every year over the existing surface; and the whole country is, in a manner, growing upward at the average rate, according to a rough estimate, of about six inches in the century. Near Cairo, where excavations have been made, the successive layers of annual deposit are distinctly visible to the eye. And it is worthy of remark that, although each one of these is no thicker than a sheet of paste-board, the stratum of alluvial soil which overlies the sands of the desert, and which to all appearance has come into existence by the very same process, is often forty, fifty, and even sixty feet in depth.

A series of interesting observations and experiments have been recently made under the auspices of the Royal Society, which afford some useful information on this subject. The colossal statue of Rameses, near Memphis, was found to be partly embedded in a stratum of mud which had gradually accumulated around it. Upon sinking a shaft, it was discovered that from the present surface of the plain to the base of the pedestal is a distance of nearly ten feet. Now, Rameses flourished, according to Lepsius, about one thousand three hundred and sixty years before the Christian Era; and therefore, since that time, or within a space of 3200 years, it is pretty clear that a thickness of ten feet has been added at this spot to the Alluvial Plain of the Nile.

It is hard to resist the conclusion that the next stratum of ten feet as we proceed downward, which, in every respect, resembles the first, must have been produced in the same way by natural causes; and so on till we reach the barren sand of the desert, which is here just forty-two feet below the present level of the plain.*

It should seem, therefore, that Egypt is nothing more than a great Alluvial Plain, slowly built up in the long lapse of ages, by the annual inundations of the Nile. Vast tracts of the same kind are to be found in other parts of the world. The Mississippi, which drains about one-seventh of the whole North American continent, has formed an Alluvial Plain more than a thousand miles in length, and from thirty to eighty in breadth. And in South America, the Orinoco once a year spreads out its swollen and turbid waters over an area not unfrequently seventy miles broad; leaving behind, when it subsides, a substantial layer of muddy sediment to enrich the soil.† It would be easy to accumulate examples. But we shall be content with having referred the reader to the Great Basin of the Nile, which affords special opportunities for the study of alluvial phenomena; being illustrated at once by the historical monuments of remote antiquity and the scientific researches of recent times.

There is another process by which Alluvial Plains are formed. It often happens that a river fills up the channel in which it has been moving for years, and is forced to shift its course and seek a new passage to the sea. In progress of time this channel is filled up like the former and deserted, and then a third, and then a fourth. At each change a new stratum is formed, almost always distinguished for its extraordinary fertility. This phenomenon is chiefly

* Horner, Alluvial Land of Egypt, Phil. Trans., part I., for 1855; Lyell, Principles of Geology, vol. i., pp. 431–9.

† The English Cyclopædia, Alluvium.

to be looked for when an extensive and almost level plain lies between some lofty range of mountains and the sea. In such a case, the river which bears away the waste of the mountains, will move onward in its course with a sluggish current, and will, of necessity, deposit the greater part of its burden on the way. There is scarcely a country in the world that does not abound in formations of this kind; and we could point to many notable instances in which herds of cattle are now grazing on the very spot where, within quite recent times, the turbid waters of some great stream flowed sullenly along.

The river Po, which receives through a thousand mountain torrents an enormous quantity of mineral sediment from the Alps, affords an instructive example. Since the beginning of the fifteenth century it has many times changed its course, often committing great devastations, and always leaving behind unmistakable traces of its movements. Several towns that once stood on the left bank of the river are now on the right. In some instances parish churches and religious houses were pulled down when the devouring stream was seen slowly to approach, and then rebuilt with the same materials at a greater distance. An old channel may be easily recognized at the present day near Cremona, which bears the name of Po Morto, and another called Po Vecchio, in the territory of Parma.

It may be interesting to our readers to learn that these movements have been checked in modern times. By a system of artificial embankment the waters of the river are now confined within definite and narrow limits: thus the velocity of the current is increased and a very considerable portion of the sediment is carried on to the sea. Nevertheless, much is still deposited in the bed of the river, which is, in consequence, raised higher and higher each successive year. Hence it has become necessary, in order to prevent inundations, to add every season to the height of the embankments, so that the river now presents the appearance of an enormous aqueduct, of which some idea may be formed from the fact that, in the neighborhood of Ferrara, the surface of the stream is higher than the roofs of the houses. This system of embankment is carried on very extensively in Northern Italy to check the overflowing of rivers, and to prevent them from changing their courses. It is as old as the time of Dante, who tells us that the inhabitants of Padua erected barriers along the Brenta when the snows began to melt and the season of the floods was approaching,

> "Per difender lor ville e lor castelli,
> Anzi che Chiarentana il caldo senta."
>
> *Inferno*, Canto xv.

As a river sometimes fills up its own channel, so too may it fill up a lake through which it flows, and convert it likewise into a great Alluvial Plain. Thus it is said several extensive lakes have been transformed into dry land in modern times near Parma, Piacenza, and Cremona. Elsewhere the process may be seen in actual operation. The Rhone when it enters the lake of Geneva is a turbid discolored stream ; the natural consequence of the immense quantity of earthy sediment with which it is charged. But as it slowly moves along, the sediment falls to the bottom, and when, at length, "by Leman's waters washed," it emerges at the town of Geneva, and shoots beneath the magnificent bridge that joins the opposite shores, it has already assumed that beautiful azure blue which travellers love to gaze on, and poets love to sing. The sediment left behind goes to form a great alluvial tract which is slowly but steadily advancing into the lake. An ancient town called Port Vallais, which, eight centuries ago, stood at the water's edge, is now a mile and a half inland. And if the world were to last long enough, and the natural agents at present in operation were to remain unchanged, the time would come, we can scarcely doubt, when the whole lake of Geneva would have been converted into an Alluvial Plain of vast extent and inexhaustible fertility.

This last example leads us on to the phenomenon of Deltas, which afford, perhaps, the best opportunity of observing the actual formation of stratified rocks. Some large rivers, as we have already seen, enter the sea with such extreme velocity as to bear away their sediment to a distance of several hundred miles from the land. But in other cases the onward rush of the stream is much sooner arrested, and the sediment, if it be not caught up by ocean currents, is deposited near the mouth of the river, and forms a triangular tract of alluvial land. This kind of deposit is called a Delta, from the resemblance it bears to the letter (Δ) of that name in the Greek Alphabet. The apex of the triangle points up the stream, the base is toward the sea. Hence, when a Delta is formed the river naturally divides into two branches, one flowing to the right, the other to the left. In progress of time new channels are almost always made, and the great stream empties itself into the sea by many mouths.

The Delta formed in the Bay of Bengal by the two great rivers of India, the Ganges and the Brahmapootra, offers an illustration of this phenomenon on a scale of unusual magnitude. Indeed, strictly speaking, it is not one Delta only, but rather two Deltas lying side by side; the one deriving its origin from the Ganges, the other from the Brahmapootra. This double Delta extends its base for two hundred and fifty miles along the Bay of Bengal, and stretches inward into the continent of India to an almost equal distance. Here, then, is a vast tract of country manifestly composed of earthy sediment, obtained by the process of Denudation from the Himalayan mountains, and afterward transported to its present site by the agency of moving water. But the deposition of earthy matter does not suddenly come to an end when we reach the present line of the coast. The sea is visibly discolored by the sediment far beyond the actual base of the Delta; and a sloping bank of mud is found to stretch beneath the waters of the Bay to a distance of a hundred miles.

Even within the short period of a man's life the domain of dry land is often visibly enlarged. Sandbanks are first formed in some of those numerous winding channels through which the two rivers find their way to the sea. The sandbanks, receiving fresh accessions during each succeeding flood, in a short time become islands; and the islands have been known, in a few years, to attain a superficial extent of many square miles. Then begins to appear a wild and luxuriant vegetation—reeds, long grass, shrubs, and trees; and those impenetrable thickets are formed, to which the buffalo, the rhinoceros, and the tiger soon resort for shelter. A very extensive tract of this kind, adjoining the sea-coast, and known as the Sunderbunds, is said to be as large as the principality of Wales.

The Delta of the Nile, though not quite one-half as large as the Delta of the Ganges, presents nevertheless some features of peculiar interest. In many places where a vertical section is exposed to view, the phenomenon of stratification may be distinctly recognized. The upper part of the deposit belonging to each year is composed of earth of a lighter color than the lower part; and the whole forms a distinct layer of hardened clay, which may be easily separated from those above and below. This formation, therefore, corresponds exactly with those strata of shale which we so often meet with in the Crust of the Earth. Again, many of the old channels through which the Nile made its way to the sea in ancient times, have been since filled up and converted into solid land. The two extreme arms of the river, which formerly enclosed the Delta, were two hundred miles apart where they entered the Mediterranean. But these channels are now Alluvial Plains, and the base of the Delta is but ninety miles in length. Hence, though the quantity of land which has been formed by the sediment of the Nile is much greater now than it formerly was, the size of the Delta properly so called has not been increased but diminished.

If we turn to the great continent of America, we are met by results not less striking and important. The Delta of the Mississippi is two hundred miles in length, and one hundred and forty in breadth. This vast stratum of mud is between five and six hundred feet thick, and covers an area twelve thousand square miles in extent. Each year it receives from the great *Father of Rivers* a new accession of sediment which is computed at 3,700,000,000 of cubic feet. And besides this annual deposit of inorganic matter, we must not omit from our estimate the countless trees of various species and of gigantic size, which are torn up by the floods, carried along by the impetuous stream, and buried at last with the bones of animals, and works of human art, and other spoils of the land, in the mud of the Delta at the river's mouth.*

* Lyell, Principles of Geology, vol. i., chapters XVIII., XIX.

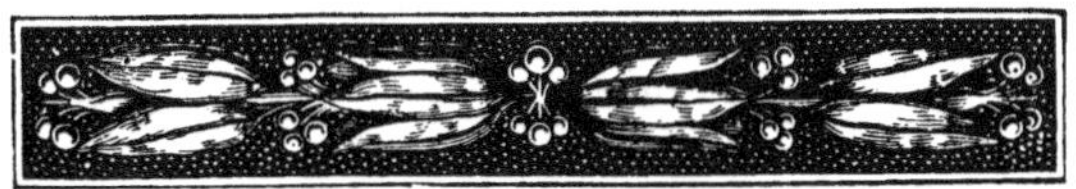

CHAPTER VII.

STRATIFIED ROCKS OF CHEMICAL ORIGIN.

Chemical agency employed in the formation of mechanical rock—But some rocks produced almost exclusively by the action of chemical laws—Difference between a mixture and a solution—A saturated solution—Stalactites and Stalagmites—Fantastic columns in limestone caverns—The grotto of Antiparos in the Grecian Archipelago—Wyer's cave in the Blue Mountains of America—Travertine rock in Italy—Growth of limestone in the Solfatara Lake near Tivoli—Incrustations of the Anio—Formation of travertine at the baths of San Filippo and San Vignone.

HE Aqueous Rocks of which we have spoken in the last two chapters are called by Geologists Mechanical; inasmuch as they owe their existence chiefly to the agency of Mechanical force. It should be observed, however, that a very considerable share in the production of these rocks must be ascribed, not unfrequently, to Chemical influence. Chemical action helps to prepare the materials of which they are composed; and Chemical action likewise furnishes the calcareous, siliceous, and other mineral cements by which they are, in a great measure, consolidated. There is, however, a second class of Aqueous Rocks which are produced almost exclusively by the operation of Chemical laws, and which we have accordingly denominated Stratified Rocks of Chemical Origin. It is of these that we purpose to speak in the present chapter. They constitute a much smaller propor-

tion of the Earth's Crust than either the Mechanical or the Organic Rocks. But the history of their formation is curious and instructive. We shall confine ourselves to one or two simple and familiar illustrations.

In the course of these illustrations we shall have a good deal to say about Carbonate of Lime in a state of solution; and it may perhaps be useful to explain, first of all, what is meant by a solution, in the technical language of Chemistry. If a spoonful of salt is put into a tumbler of water, the particles of salt, after a little time, cease to cohere together, and become so diffused through the water as to be no longer visible to the eye, although their presence in every part may be easily discerned by the taste. The salt is then said to be *dissolved*, and the water in which it is dissolved is called a *solution* of salt. It is important to distinguish the case of a solution from the case of a mere mechanical mixture. If, instead of the salt, we were to put into the tumbler of water a spoonful of very fine sand, then we should have a *mixture* but not a *solution*. By stirring briskly the contents of the tumbler we might, indeed, effect a very close union between the particles of water and the particles of sand: but this union would be altogether different in kind from the union that was observed in the former case between the particles of water and the particles of salt. First, the sand would remain visible to the eye, making the water turbid and discolored; whereas the salt entirely disappeared, leaving the water limpid and transparent as before. Again, if the water be allowed to rest, the sand will in time fall to the bottom, whereas the salt will not.

But there is a limit to the capacity of water for holding salt in solution. If spoonful after spoonful be added, it will be found, when a certain point has been reached, that the water can at length dissolve no more. It is then called a *saturated solution* of salt. If, in this case, a portion of the water were to pass away by evaporation, it is clear, we should have the same quantity of salt as before, in a smaller quantity of water. The consequence would be that *all* the salt could not then be held in solution, and some of it would fall to the bottom ; or, in chemical language, a precipitate of salt would be formed on the bottom of the tumbler. Now, according to the theory of Geologists, many rocks, hundreds of feet thick, and solid enough to form the walls of our palaces, our churches, and our castles, have been produced in the Crust of the Earth by just such a process as this. In support of their theory we are about to show that the process is actually going on in our own time, and is open to the examination of all who may desire to study it for themselves.

We shall begin with the formation of Stalactites and Stalagmites. The mode in which these singular masses of rock are brought into existence is very clearly explained, and the picturesque appearance they so often present to the eye is very graphically described, by Dr. Mantell, in his Wonders of Geology, from which the following passages are taken :—"One of the most common appearances in limestone caverns is the formation of what are called Stalactites, from a Greek word signifying distillation or dropping. Whenever water filters through a limestone rock it dissolves a portion of it; and on reaching any opening, such as a cavern, oozes from the sides or roof, and forms a drop, the moisture of which is soon evaporated by the air, and a small circular plate or ring of calcareous matter remains; another drop succeeds in the same place, and adds, from the same cause, a fresh coat of incrustation. In time, these successive additions produce a long, irregular, conical projection from the roof, which is generally hollow, and is continually being increased by the fresh accession of water, loaded with calcareous or chalky matter: this is deposited on the outside of the Stalactite already formed, and, trickling down, adds to its length by subsiding to the point, and evaporating as before; precisely in the same manner as, during frosty weather, icicles are formed on the edges of the eaves of a roof. When the supply of water holding lime in solution is too rapid to allow of its evaporation at the bottom of the Stalactite, it drops on the floor of the cave, and drying up gradually, forms in like manner a Stalactite rising upward from the ground, instead of hanging from the roof; this is called for the sake of distinction Stalagmite.

"It frequently happens, where these processes are uninterrupted, that a Stalactite hanging from the roof, and a Stalagmite formed immediately under it from the superabundant water, increase until they unite, and thus constitute a natural pillar, apparently supporting the roof of the grotto. It is to the grotesque forms assumed by Stalactites and these natural columns, that caverns owe the interesting appearances described in such glowing terms by those who witness them for the first time. One of the most beautiful stalactitic caverns in England is at Clapham, near Ingleborough. In the Cheddar Cliffs, Somersetshire, there has been discovered a similar cave richly incrusted with sparry concretions. There are others in Derbyshire.

"The grotto of Antiparos in the Grecian Archipelago, not far from Paros, has long been celebrated. The sides and roof of its principal cavity are covered with immense incrustations of calcareous spar, which form either Stalactites depending from above or irregular pillars rising from the floor. Several perfect columns reaching to the ceiling have been formed and others are still in progress, by the union of the Stalactite from above with the Stalagmite below. These, being composed of matter slowly deposited, have assumed the most fantastic shapes; while the pure, white, and glittering spar beautifully catches and reflects the light of the torches of the visitors to this subterranean palace, in a manner which causes all astonishment to cease at the romantic tales told of the place—of its caves of diamonds and of its ruby walls; the simple truth, when deprived of all exaggeration, being sufficient to excite admiration and awe.

"Sometimes a linear fissure in the roof, by the direction it gives to the dropping of the lapidifying water, forms a perfectly transparent curtain or partition. A remarkable instance of this kind occurs in a cavern in North America called Wyer's Cave. This cave is situated in a ridge of limestone hills running parallel to the Blue Mountains. A narrow and rugged fissure leads to a large cavern, where the most grotesque figures, formed by the percolation of water through beds of limestone, present themselves, while the eye, glancing onward, watches the dim and distant glimmers of the lights of the guides—some in the recess below, and others in the galleries above. Passing from these recesses, the passage conducts to a flight of steps that leads into a large cavern of irregular form and of great beauty. Its dimensions are about thirty feet by fifty. Here the incrustations hang just like a sheet of water that was frozen as it fell; there they rise into a beautiful stalactite pillar; and yonder compose an elevated seat, surrounded by sparry pinnacles. Beyond this room is another more irregular, but more beautiful; for besides having sparry ornaments in common with the others, the roof overhead is of the most admirable and singular formation. It is entirely covered with Stalactites, which are suspended from it like inverted pinnacles; and they are of the finest material, and most beautifully shaped and embossed. In another apartment an immense sheet of transparent Stalactite, which extends from the floor to the roof, emits, when struck, deep and mellow sounds like those of a muffled drum.

"Farther on is another vaulted chamber, which is one hundred feet long, thirty-six wide, and twenty-six high. Its walls are filled with grotesque concretions. The effect of the lights placed by the guides at various elevations, and leaving hidden more than they reveal, is extremely fine. At the extremity of another range of apartments, a magnificent hall, two hundred and fifty feet long, and thirty-three feet high, suddenly appears. Here is a splendid sheet of rock-work running up the centre of the room, and giving it the aspect of two separate and noble galleries. This partition rises twenty feet above the floor, and leaves the fine span of the arched roof untouched. There is here a beautiful concretion, which has the form and drapery of a gigantic statue; and the whole place is filled with stalagmitical masses of the most varied and grotesque character. The fine perspective of this room, four times the length of an ordinary church, and the amazing vaulted roof spreading overhead, without any support of pillar or column, produce a most striking effect. In another apartment, which has an altitude of fifty feet, there is at one end an elevated recess ornamented with a group of pendant Stalactites of unusual size and singular beauty. They are as large as the pipes of a full-sized organ, and ranged with great regularity: when struck they emit mellow sounds of various keys, not unlike the tones of musical glasses. The length of this extraordinary group of caverns is not less than one thousand six hundred feet."

In the case of Stalactites and Stalagmites the actual formation of limestone by the influence of Chemical action is brought home forcibly to the mind, and, in a manner, made palpable to the senses. We shall now pass to other examples in which the process is scarcely less open to observation, and in which the limestone assumes a somewhat more massive and rock-like form. Every one who has been in Italy is familiar with the limestone rock called Travertine. It is seen in the ancient walls and the venerable temples of Pæstum, which have withstood unharmed the wasting hand of time for upward of twenty centuries. In Rome, too, this stone is associated in our minds as well with the enduring monuments of antiquity, as with the imposing splendor of Christian art. The Coliseum, the most stupendous of ruins, and St. Peter's, the most sublime of temples, are built of Travertine. In fact it seems to have been, in every age, the chief building stone employed in the architecture of the Eternal City; and the quarries from which it was taken in ancient times may still be seen at Ponte Lucano, near Tivoli. Now it is an interesting fact, that close to this very spot, at the Solfatara lake on the one side, and at Tivoli itself on the other, the formation of Travertine is going on in our own time, by the precipitation of lime from a state of solution.

The Solfatara lake, situated about fourteen miles from Rome, on the road to Tivoli, is supplied with an unfailing stream of tepid water, impregnated with carbonic acid gas and saturated with carbonate of lime. The amount of carbonate of lime which the water is capable of holding in solution depends chiefly on three things: first, on the presence of carbonic acid; secondly, on the high temperature of the water; and thirdly, on its quantity. Now the carbonic acid is ever rising in bubbles to the surface and passing away; the temperature of the water is lowered by contact with the cooler atmosphere; and its quantity is diminished by evaporation. Thus the capacity which the water at first had for holding the carbonate of lime in solution is notably diminished, and a part of the lime is precipitated to the bottom in a solid form, or clings to the vegetable matter with which it comes in contact.

A very simple and interesting experiment, made in the early part of the present century by Sir Humphrey Davy, will illustrate the rapidity with which the formation of solid stone is even now taking place. In the month of May he fixed a stick in the bed of the lake, and left it standing until the following April, when he found that it was covered with an incrustation of limestone several inches thick.* In precisely the same way new layers of Travertine are annually deposited in the bed of the lake, and incrusted on its rocky margin ; and so the lake itself is becoming smaller and smaller from year to year. We are told that in the middle of the seventeenth century it was a mile in circuit, and now it is a little more than a quarter of a mile.† Here, therefore, we have an immense mass of compact limestone rock, built up by natural agents within the last two centuries.

At Tivoli, about four miles beyond the Solfatara, and two miles from the quarries of Ponte Lucano, phenomena of the same kind are exhibited. The waters of the Anio, which are saturated with carbonate of lime, form incrustations of Travertine on the banks of the river ; and at the celebrated falls, where the whole volume of the stream leaps at a bound from a height of three hundred and twenty feet, the most beautiful stalactites are formed by the foam.

The formation of Travertine is going on with no less activity in other parts of the Italian Peninsula. At the baths of San Filippo, in Tuscany, there are three warm springs which contain a very large amount of mineral matter in solution. The water which supplies the baths falls into a pond, where it has been known to deposit a solid stratum of rock *thirty feet thick* in twenty years. In the same neighborhood are the mineral baths of San Vignone. The source from which the water flows is situated on the summit of a hill not more than a few hundred yards from the high road between Sienna and Rome ; and so rapid is the formation of stone, that half a foot of solid Travertine is deposited every year in the pipe that conducts the water to the baths. At this spot we have a very good illustration of the argument we are now considering. As

* Consolations in Travel, p. 127.

† Handbook of Rome and its Environs : Murray, 1858, p. 325.

the stream of water flows down the slopes of the hill, a thin layer of Travertine rock is produced on the surface of the earth, almost before our eyes; and so it was previous to our own time, and so it has been for ages, as history and tradition testify. The quantity produced in each year and in each century is comparatively small, but we can have no doubt that it *has* been produced by the means described. Now, beneath the surface of the Earth, immediately below these modern formations, of which we have so clearly ascertained the origin, we find strata of the same kind, composed of the same materials, and arranged in the same way, layer resting upon layer, down to a depth of two hundred feet: and the Geologist accounts for the formation of the one according to the same laws which he has seen at work in the production of the other.*

* Lyell, Principles of Geology, vol. i., 400–3.

CHAPTER VIII.

STRATIFIED ROCKS OF ORGANIC ORIGIN—ILLUSTRATIONS FROM ANIMAL LIFE.

Nature of organic rocks—Carbonate of lime extracted from the sea by the intervention of minute animalcules—Chalk rock—Its vast extent—Supposed to be of organic origin—A stratum of the same kind now growing up on the floor of the Atlantic ocean—Coral reefs and islands—Their general appearance—Their geographical distribution—Their organic origin—Structure of the zoophyte—Various illustrations—Agency of the zoophyte in the construction of coral rock—How the sunken reef is converted into an island and peopled with plants and animals—Difficulty proposed and considered—Hypothesis of Mr. Darwin—Coral limestone in the solid crust of the earth.

E now pass to the third division of Aqueous Rocks, those, namely, which are believed to have come into existence chiefly through the agency of animal and vegetable life, and are therefore called Organic. The study of these rocks has been prosecuted with no inconsiderable ardor during the last thirty years; and the facts which have been brought to light are certainly amongst the most curious and interesting in the whole range of physical science. Indeed we are convinced that a simple narrative of the researches which have recently been made upon this subject, and the discoveries to which these researches have led, would be no less attractive, and scarcely less wonderful, than a fairy tale. But it is not for us to wander at large over this vast and tempting field of inquiry. We

must be content with one or two examples, which may help to illustrate the process of inductive reasoning upon which the general principles of geological science are founded.

It is argued, then, that the present operations of Nature afford the best key for the interpretation of her works in bygone times. We observe various beds of rocks now in course of formation on the surface of the Earth; and within the Crust of the Earth we discover corresponding strata of the self-same rock already complete, and laid by, as it were, in Nature's storehouse. Side by side, therefore, we may study and compare the finished work and the work that is yet in progress; and if, on a close examination, they are found to agree in all essential characters, we have doubtless a strong presumption, that the same causes which are now producing the one, must in former times have produced the other. This line of argument we have already considered in reference to those two classes of Aqueous Rocks, which are said to be respectively of Mechanical and of Chemical origin. We now proceed to show that it is no less applicable to those which are called Organic. And although we may not hope to unfold all the secret wonders of Nature's laboratory, that have come to light in recent times, yet we may afford a passing glimpse at her operations, which can scarcely fail to be interesting and instructive.

We have shown how strata of solid rock are sometimes formed in lakes by the precipitation of lime from a state of solution. Now this process cannot take place in the sea; for though lime is present in the sea, the quantity of carbonic acid with which it is there associated, is far more than sufficient to render its precipitation impossible.* But Nature has another contrivance for gathering together the solid elements of her building. The depths of the ocean are teeming with life; and countless tribes of minute

* Jukes, Manual of Geology, p. 127.

animals are furnished with the power of extracting the lime from the waters they inhabit, and of reproducing it under a new form. Sometimes, through this mysterious operation of organic life, the lime is converted into a calcareous shell, like that of the oyster; sometimes into a stony skeleton, as in the case of the numerous families of coral-producing animalcules. After death the soft, fleshy substance of these animals melts away and disappears; but the limestone shells and skeletons remain, accumulating during the long course of ages to an almost incredible extent. And, if we are to believe Geologists, out of these accumulated materials, sometimes preserving their original form and structure, sometimes altered more or less by chemical action, sometimes broken up into fragments by mechanical force, has been produced a very large proportion of the limestone rocks which occur so abundantly in the Crust of the Earth.

No better illustration can be found than the white earthy limestone, familiar to every one under the name of chalk. An undulating stratum of Chalk Rock, attaining not unfrequently a thickness of one thousand feet, may be said, speaking roughly, to underlie the southeastern half of England. Sometimes it appears at the surface: sometimes it dips downward, and forms a kind of great basin, over which are regularly spread out various other groups of Stratified Rocks. On the southern coast it rises to a height of several hundred feet above the level of the sea in a line of perpendicular cliffs, conspicuous from a distance by their dazzling whiteness. But the White Chalk of England is only an insignificant part of a great rock-formation, which may be traced over extensive areas throughout all Europe, from Ireland to the Crimea, from the Baltic Sea to the Bay of Biscay; and which everywhere preserves in a remarkable degree the same mineral character, and presents to the eye the same general appearance.

Now it had often been suggested by Geologists that this

wide-spread formation derived its existence chiefly from the accumulated remains of organic life. For in many instances the broken shells of minute animalcules could be distinctly observed to constitute a part of the rock. And even where the organic structure could not be so clearly traced, the carbonate of lime composing the Chalk presented just that appearance which would naturally result from the decomposition of such shells. This theory, however, was long put forward with diffidence and received with incredulity. Even scientific men found it hard to persuade themselves that a solid rock of such great extent and thickness could have been the work of agents apparently so insignificant. But it has been confirmed and illustrated in a very interesting and unexpected manner within the last few years.

When the project of connecting Europe and America by a telegraph cable was first set on foot, it became necessary to ascertain, as far as possible, the general configuration of the ocean bottom and the exact nature of the bed on which the cable was to lie. Accordingly in the year 1857 an expedition was fitted out for this purpose under the command of Captain Dayman; and a careful series of soundings was taken between Valentia, on the West Coast of Kerry, and Trinity Bay on the shores of Newfoundland. It was found that the floor of the ocean between Ireland and America is a vast irregular plain, and that by far the greater part is covered over with a kind of soft mud or ooze. Samples of this ooze were scooped up, even at the most profound depths, by means of an ingenious apparatus attached to the sounding-lines, and brought undisturbed to the surface. Afterward they were carried home to England and submitted for examination to Professor Huxley. The result has been to show that the materials of a limestone rock, resembling in every essential feature the White Chalk of Europe, are being spread out at the present day over an area of immense extent on the floor of the Atlantic Ocean.

With the permission of our readers we shall allow Professor Huxley, as far as may be, to tell his own story.* As to the ocean floor itself, "It is," he says, "a prodigious plain—one of the widest and most even plains in the world. If the sea were drained off, you might drive a wagon all the way from Valentia to Trinity Bay. And, except upon one sharp incline about two hundred miles from Valentia, I am not quite sure that it would even be necessary to put the skid on, so gentle are the ascents and descents upon that long route. From Valentia the road would lie down hill for about two hundred miles to the point at which the bottom is now covered by 1700 fathoms of sea-water. Then would come the central plain, more than a thousand miles wide, the inequalities of the surface of which would be hardly perceptible, though the depth of water upon it now varies from 10,000 to 15,000 feet; and there are places in which Mont Blanc might be sunk without showing its peak above water. Beyond this the ascent on the American side commences, and gradually leads for about three hundred miles, to the Newfoundland shore."

The central plain here described, which has been since found to extend many hundred miles north and south of the cable line, is covered almost everywhere by that soft, mealy sort of mud of which we have already spoken; and this, it is now confidently believed, is nothing else than a stratum of Chalk Rock in an early stage of formation. When thoroughly dried it assumes a whitish color, and exhibits a texture which even to the superficial observer appears closely to resemble fine chalk. Nay, we are told that if so disposed, one may take a bit of it in his fingers and write with it upon a blackboard. Like chalk, too, when chemically analyzed it is found to be almost pure carbonate of lime.

* See his Lecture On a Piece of Chalk, delivered during the Meeting of the British Association at Norwich, 1868.

But there is a yet more striking analogy between the mud of the Atlantic and the White Chalk of Europe. Both have been submitted to the magnifying power of the Microscope; and, after an examination conducted with scrupulous care, a wonderful and almost startling identity of mineral, or rather we should say of organic, composition has been established between them. To the naked eye Chalk is simply a soft, earthy sort of stone. But when a thin transparent slice is placed under the Microscope, the general mass is found to be made up of very minute particles, in which are embedded a vast number of other bodies possessing a well-defined form and structure. These are of various sizes, but on a rough average may be said not to exceed a hundredth of an inch in diameter. Hundreds of thousands of them are sometimes contained in a cubic inch of Chalk, together with countless millions of the more minute granules.

Professor Huxley succeeded in separating these bodies from the mass of granules in which they were embedded, and by examining them apart, he has ascertained still more fully their exact structure and composition. "Each one of them," he says, "is a beautifully constructed calcareous fabric, made up of a number of chambers communicating freely with one another. They are of various forms. One of the commonest is something like a badly-grown raspberry, being formed of a number of nearly globular chambers of different sizes congregated together. It is called Globigerina; and some specimens of Chalk consist of little else than Globigerinæ and granules."

Previous to 1857 the Globigerinæ of the Chalk were a matter of no small controversy among Geologists and Naturalists. Some contended that they were the organic remains—the shells or skeletons—of ancient animalcules. Others were disposed to regard them simply as aggregations of lime, which, so to speak, chanced to assume the form of these little chambered bodies; though it was not easy to explain, on this hypothesis, how these chance concretions, however much they varied in size, preserved over the whole of Europe the same exact form and structure. But the controversy is now at an end. The specimens of the Atlantic ooze brought home by Captain Dayman, when examined under the higher powers of the Microscope, are found, like Chalk, to be composed almost entirely of Globigerinæ. And that no doubt may remain as to their organic origin, a portion of the fleshy integument of the little animalcules is seen, in many cases, still adhering to the calcareous skeleton.

"Globigerinæ of every size," we are told, "from the smallest to the largest, are associated together in the Atlantic mud, and the chambers of many are filled by a soft animal matter. This soft substance is, in fact, the remains of the creature to which the Globigerina shell, or rather skeleton, owes its existence—and which is an animal of the simplest imaginable description. It is, in fact, a mere particle of living jelly, without defined parts of any kind—without a mouth, nerves, muscles, or distinct organs; and only manifesting its vitality to ordinary observation by thrusting out and retracting, from all parts of its surface, long filamentous processes which serve for arms and legs. Yet this amorphous particle, devoid of everything which, in the higher animals we call organs, is capable of feeding, growing, and multiplying; of separating from the ocean the small proportion of carbonate of lime which is dissolved in sea-water; and of building up that substance into a skeleton for itself, according to a pattern which can be imitated by no other known agency."

That the same process is going on in other parts of the ocean appears by observations made by Sir Leopold M'Clintock during the cruise of the Bulldog in 1860. He discovered that a calcareous ooze having the consistency of putty is spread out over extensive areas between the Faroe Islands and Iceland, and also between Iceland and Greenland. Of this mud about ninety-five per cent. is composed of Globigerinæ, which in some instances were brought up actually living to the surface, and busily engaged in secreting, by their vital powers, carbonate of lime from the waters of the sea.*

Professor Huxley goes yet one step further in following out the resemblance between the Chalk Rock that exists in the Crust of the Earth and the stratum of Chalk that is now growing up in the depths of the Atlantic. Not only are the Globigerinæ, of which the one is in great part composed, identical with the animalcules that make up about nine-tenths of the other, but even the minute granules that constitute the residue of each formation, correspond in a very remarkable manner. "In working over the soundings collected by Captain Dayman, I was surprised to find that many of what I have called the Granules of that mud were not, as one might have been tempted to think at first, the mere powder and waste of Globigerinæ, but they had a definite form and size. I termed these bodies Coccoliths, and doubted their organic nature. Doctor Wallich verified my observation, and added the interesting discovery that, not unfrequently, bodies similar to these Coccoliths were aggregated together into spheroids, which he termed Coccospheres. So far as we knew, these bodies, the nature of which is extremely puzzling and problematical, were peculiar to the Atlantic soundings.

"But a few years ago Mr. Sorby, in making a careful examination of the Chalk by means of thin sections and otherwise, observed, as Ehrenberg had done before him, that much of its granular basis possesses a definite form. Comparing these formed particles with those in the Atlantic soundings, he found the two to be identical; and thus

* Lyell, Elements of Geology, p. 318.

proved that the Chalk, like the soundings, contains these mysterious Coccoliths and Coccospheres. Here was a further and a most interesting confirmation, from internal evidence, of the essential identity of the Chalk with modern deep-sea mud."

We may, therefore, set it down as certain, first, that the formation of Chalk Rock is going on very extensively at the present day; and secondly, that the chief agency employed in its production is no other than the vital action of minute animalcules. This is no longer merely a plausible theory or an ingenious hypothesis: it is simply a matter of fact ascertained by direct observation. If then it is just and philosophical to ascribe like effects to like causes, the conclusion is plain that the White Chalk of Europe came into existence in some far distant age by just such a process as that which is now in operation on the bed of the Atlantic Ocean.

From the Chalk mud of the Atlantic we will now pass to the Coral Reefs that are growing up beneath the waters of the Pacific and the Indian Oceans. Every one has heard of Coral Reefs and Coral Islands; yet we fancy many persons have but vague and indefinite notions about them. We shall, therefore, in the first place, give a brief account of their general appearance, their extent, and their geographical distribution. Afterward we shall give some of the evidence which goes to show that these huge masses of rock owe their existence to the organic powers of minute living animalcules.

The Coral Reef is familiar to the navigator of tropical seas under a great variety of forms, and in many different stages of development. In one case it is a chain of hidden rocks rising not quite to the level of the sea; in another it appears just above the waters, but is washed over by each returning tide; while in another it rises up beyond the reach of the waves, is clothed with luxuriant vegetation, and inhabited by various species of animals, even by man himself. Again there is great diversity of outline among these rocks, whether they are sunk beneath the surface of the waters or lifted above them. But all may be reduced to four classes, of which we propose to give a short description.

First is the Atoll, or lagoon island. It is a circular strip of limestone rock enclosing a shallow lake within, and surrounded by a deep and often unfathomable ocean without. The scene presented by some of these circular reefs is described by travellers as equally striking for its singularity and its beauty. "A strip of land a few hundred yards wide is covered by lofty cocoa-nut trees, above which is the blue vault of heaven. This band of verdure is bounded by a beach of glittering white sand, the outer margin of which is encircled with a ring of snow-white breakers, beyond which are the dark heaving waters of the ocean. The inner beach encloses the still clear water of the lagoon, resting in its greater part on white sand, and, when illuminated by a vertical sun, of a most vivid green."

These lagoon islands are often found in groups stretching, with little interruption, for many hundred miles across the ocean. The Maldives, for example, which lie a little distance to the southwest of Hindostan, form a continuous chain, running due north and south, four hundred and seventy miles in length and fifty miles in breadth. Each successive link in this chain does not consist, as might be supposed, of a single circular reef, but it is rather a ring of small coral islets, sometimes more than a hundred in number, each of which is itself a perfect Atoll or lagoon island such as we have just described. Of these miniature islets many are from three to five miles in diameter; while the larger rings of which they form a part are from thirty to fifty. The Laccadive islands, a little more to the north, exhibit a similar arrangement, and indeed would seem tc be a continuation of the same group. In the Pacific are found some chains of coral islands yet more extensive; as for instance the Dangerous Archipelago, which is upward of eleven hundred miles in length, and from three to four hundred in breadth; but the islands within these spaces are thinly scattered, and insignificant in size.

Sometimes the annular strip of coral rock encloses within itself a lofty island, which rises up from the centre of the lagoon. In this case it is called an Encircling Reef; the lagoon being simply a broad channel surrounding the island in the centre, and encompassed itself by the coral rock. An example occurs in the island of Vanikoro, celebrated for the shipwreck of La Peyrouse, where the Encircling Reef runs at a distance of two or three miles from the shore, the channel between it and the land having a general depth of between two and three hundred feet. The well-known mountainous island of Tahiti in the South Pacific Ocean is also encompassed by an Encircling Reef, from which it is separated by a broad belt of tranquil water.

A third class of Coral Reefs consists of those which run parallel to the shores of continents or great islands, from which they are cut off by a broad channel, to which the sea has free access through certain open passages in the rock. They are called Barrier Reefs; and differ from the former only in this, that they do not surround the land, but run parallel to it at a distance of some miles. The Great Barrier Reef of Australia offers a noble example. It has been described as a huge, massive, submarine wall or terrace, fronting the northeastern coast of that continent, varying from ten to ninety miles in breadth, and extending, with some trifling interruptions, to a length of 1250 miles. Another reef of the same kind, 400 miles in length, faces the western coast of the long narrow island of New Caledonia.

When a chain of Coral rocks approaches close to the

shore, so as to leave no intervening channel of deep water, they are called Fringing Reefs ; and these constitute the fourth and last class of the Coral formation. They prevail everywhere in tropical regions, and appear as banks of Coral encrusting the rocky shores of islands and continents.

As regards the geographical distribution of Coral Reefs, the first circumstance that claims our notice, is that they are exclusively confined to the warmer regions of the globe. They exist in great profusion within the tropics, and are rarely to be found beyond the thirtieth parallels of latitude on each side of the Equator. The only remarkable exception is in the case of the Bermuda Islands in 32° north latitude; but here, it is to be observed, the ocean is warmed by the waters of the Gulf Stream. Another singular fact is the almost total absence of Coral Reefs from the Atlantic Ocean. In fact, the Bermudas, we believe, constitute here again the only exception. The Pacific, on the contrary, is wonderfully productive of coral; also the Indian Ocean, the Persian and Arabian Gulfs, and the Red Sea.

It may gratify, perhaps, the curiosity of some readers, if we add a word on the Red Coral which is now so favorite an ornament in the fashionable world. Though it never attains to the magnitude of those reefs and islands we have been describing, it partakes nevertheless of the same peculiar structure; and no doubt is entertained that, like them, it derives its existence from animal life, in the manner we shall presently explain. It is produced chiefly in the Mediterranean, in the Red Sea, and in the Persian Gulf; and is brought up from the great depths by means of a grappling apparatus attached to boats. The largest pieces have a shrub-like branching form, and are supposed to grow to the height of one foot in about eight years.*

* Lyell, Principles of Geology, vol. ii., chap. xlix.; Mantell, Wonders of Geology, Lecture VI.; Jukes, Manual of Geology, pp. 130–3.

So much for the existence of the Coral Formation. Next comes the question of its origin, with which, of course, we are chiefly concerned. It is now the received belief of all distinguished Naturalists, that these huge and wide-spread masses of limestone rock, against which the breakers of the ocean are ever thundering in vain, are the work of tiny marine animalcules, and chiefly of those seemingly insignificant creatures known by the name of Polyps or Zoophytes. The Zoophyte, they tell us, is a mason who himself produces the stones that he employs in his building. "He has neither plane, nor chisel, nor trowel; there is no sound of hammer in his city. He erects mighty and enduring edifices, yet has no mechanical power by which to raise his rocks to their summits. He can answer thee nothing—no tongue, no eyes, no hands, no brains has he—yet from the caves of old ocean has he raised that which fills you with admiration."* Surely if all this be true, these countless myriads of animalcules call aloud to us from the depths of the ocean in language that cannot be mistaken: "Know ye that the Lord He is God; it is He that hath made us, and not we ourselves."†

The Zoophyte belongs to the simplest form of the animal creation. Its body consists merely of a pouch or stomach, with tentacles arranged round the margin, which it can extend at pleasure to supply itself with food. In many species the individuals grow together on a common stem, from which new members are constantly shooting forth like buds from the branches of a tree. Hence the origin of the name Zoophyte, which literally means a plant-like animal. The common stem on which they grow is sometimes composed of a horny substance, but more generally it is pure carbonate of lime, which they secrete by the powers of

* Sacred Philosophy of the Seasons, by the Rev. Henry Duncan, D.D.; Summer, p. 168.

† Ps. xcix. 3.

organic action from the waters of the sea. It forms, therefore, a kind of internal skeleton or framework, to which the soft, gelatinous parts of the animal adhere, pretty much as, in the case of other animals, the flesh adheres to the bones. Thus we have, as it were, a community of living creatures, growing together upon one common stony framework, called a Polypidom or Polyp edifice, which they themselves build by the very fact of living.

The peculiar structure of these wonderful little communities may perhaps be made more intelligible by the aid of a few illustrations. Figure 4 exhibits the branching skeleton and, at the extremities of the branches, the several Polyps by whose vital action the skeleton has been constructed. Some of the animalcules are shown in a state of activity, with their tiny arms spread out in search of food : others are withdrawn within their cells, and appear in

Fig. 4.—Campanularia Gelatinosa.

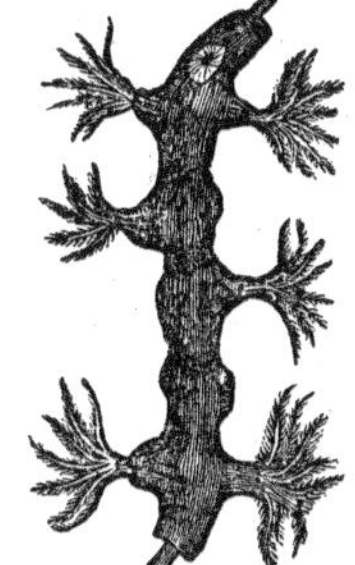

Fig. 5.—Gorgonia Patula.

a state of repose. This species of Zoophyte, which is highly magnified in the figure, flourishes abundantly on the shores of Ireland and England. It has received the name of Campanularia, from the bell-like form of its cells. Our next cut represents a Gorgonia from the

Mediterranean, which is also considerably magnified. The fleshy integument of this specimen is of a brilliant red colôr: the Polyps are arranged in rows on each side of the stem, and are shown in a state of expansion.

A mass of Coral animalcules, which are known by the name of Frustra Pilosa, is represented of the natural size in Figure 6. To the naked eye it seems like a piece of fine net-work, disposed around a fragment of sea-weed, which may be observed protruding in the upper part of our illustration. With the aid of an ordinary magnifier the

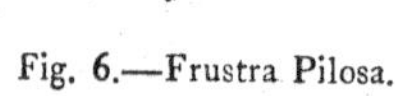

Fig. 6.—Frustra Pilosa. Fig. 7.—Madrepora Plantaginea.

net-like surface is seen to abound in minute pores arranged with much regularity. Each of these pores is the cell of a Zoophyte. And if a fragment of Frustra be examined with a powerful microscope, when immersed in sea-water, the curious little inhabitants themselves may be seen darting in and out of their cells, expanding and contracting their long feelers, and exhibiting altogether a wonderful activity. In the adjoining woodcut, Figure 7, is shown another interesting species of the arborescent Zoophyte. It belongs to the family of Madrepores, and abounds in almost all Coral Reefs. Alive under water it appears clothed in a gelatinous coating of rich and varied hues. But when removed from its native element this gelatinous coating, which is the living animal substance, quickly melts away; and, in some instances, runs off from the calcareous skeleton in a kind of watery slime.

A good idea of the celebrated red and pink Coral of commerce, so much admired for its brilliant color, and the high polish of which it is susceptible, may be gathered from our next illustration. As in the other species to which we have

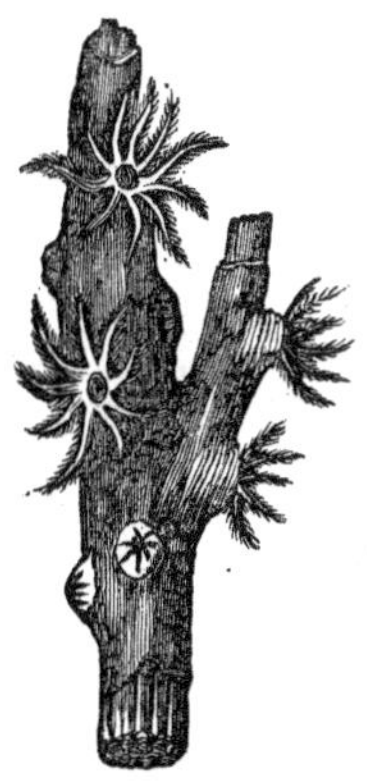

Fig. 8.—Corallium Rubrum.

referred, the calcareous skeleton is enveloped in a living gelatinous substance, from which the Zoophytes seem to shoot out like buds from the bark of a tree. Several of these animalcules are exhibited in our figure, in the active enjoyment of life; gathering in, with their expanded tentacles, the elements of their stony edifice from the surrounding waters. After death the fleshy integument is wasted away by the action of the sea; and the framework that remains behind, washed ashore by the waves, or hooked up by the coral fisherman, is wrought into brooches, bracelets, necklaces, and other ornaments of various kinds.

Not a few varieties of the Coral-producing Zoophytes are to be found in actual living reality on our own coasts, where the curious student may examine for himself their habits and general structure. But it is in the warmer regions of the Earth that they are developed in the greatest numbers, and decked in the brightest hues. Those who have seen them through the crystal waters of tropical seas, swarming in countless multitudes on the clear white sand below, speak with enthusiasm of their luxuriant profusion and of their striking beauty. Combining to a picturesque elegance of form a rich variety and pleasing harmony of colors, they present to the eye a scene which has been compared to a magnificent garden, laid out in diverse beds of rare and splendid flowers.

So far we have spoken only of the Polypidom, that is to say, the community of Polyps living together on a common stem of their own construction. Now this Polypidom is the first element of the Coral Reef. In some species of Zoophytes, the Red Coral for instance, the calcareous stem never attains a size greater than that of a diminutive shrub. But in others, and they are very numerous, especially in tropical seas, there seems to be no limit to the growth of the solid stony framework. As the existing generation of Zoophytes is dying out, new individuals are ever budding forth, which continue unceasingly to secrete carbonate of lime, as their predecessors had done before them, from the waters of the ocean; and thus the tree-like form spreads its branching arms on every side, growing upward and outward day by day. The soft gelatinous parts of those generations that have passed away are, in a short time, dissolved, and the stony skeleton alone remains behind. Ages roll on: the calcareous framework, ever increasing in size, becomes at length a formidable rock; and this rock is the Coral Reef.

Let it not be supposed we are here advancing a theory:

we are only stating a fact that has been established by close and repeated observations. All the phenomena exhibited in the development of the Polypidom, are exhibited no less plainly in every Coral Reef that has yet been examined. On the surface of the Reef are the living Zoophytes, clinging to the calcareous skeleton which is ever growing larger through the unconscious action of their vital functions; while immediately beneath may be seen the same stony skeleton, already divested of its fleshy integument, and beginning to assume the appearance of compact and massive rock. We can behold, therefore, the mason at work on the upper story of his building, and the structure already finished below. And so we have little less than ocular demonstration that the Coral Reef is the work of the Zoophyte.

It must not be supposed, however, that in every part of the Coral Reef, the form and outline of the stony skeleton are exactly preserved. Fragments of the rock are broken off by the force of the waves, and mixed up with the comminuted shells of oysters, mussels, and other crustaceous animals inhabiting the same waters. In this way a sort of calcareous gravel, sometimes a calcareous paste, is formed, which fills up the interstices, and connects the tree-like coral into a compact rock.

We have yet to explain how the Coral Reefs come, in many cases, to rise above the surface of the ocean, and to form dry land: for it has been found that the reef-building Zoophytes require to be continually immersed in salt water, and therefore, by their own efforts, they cannot raise their structure above the ordinary level of the sea. This question was for a long time involved in obscurity; but it has been cleared up by the actual observations of Naturalists in modern times. The following description, which is given to us by Chamisso, the companion of Kotzebue on his voyages, will convey a good idea of the process by which a sunken reef is often converted into a smiling, fruitful island. "When the reef is of such a height that it remains almost dry at low water, the corals leave off building. Above this line a continuous mass of solid stone is seen, composed of the shells of mollusks and echini, with their broken-off prickles and fragments of coral, united by calcareous sand, produced by the pulverization of shells. The heat of the sun often penetrates the mass of stone when it is dry, so that it splits in many places, and the force of the waves is thereby enabled to separate and lift blocks of coral, frequently six feet long and three or four in thickness, and throw them upon the reef, by which means the ridge becomes at length so high that it is covered only during some seasons of the year by spring tides. After this the calcareous sand lies undisturbed, and offers to the seeds of trees and plants cast upon it by the waves, a soil upon which they rapidly grow, to overshadow its dazzling white surface. Entire trunks of trees, which are carried by the rivers from other countries and islands, find here at length a resting place after their long wanderings: with these come some small animals, such as insects and lizards, as the first inhabitants. Even before the trees form a wood, the sea-birds nestle here; stray land-birds take refuge in the bushes; and, at a much later period, when the work has been long since completed, man appears and builds his hut on the fruitful soil." *

Another question that seems to call for some explanation is suggested by the well-known habits of the Zoophytes themselves. From the observations of Kotzebue and Darwin it appears that those species which are most effective in the construction of Reefs cannot flourish at a greater depth than twenty or thirty fathoms; whereas the coral rocks rise up in many cases from the bottom of an unfathomable

* Kotzebue's Voyages, 1815–18, vol. iii., pp. 331–33.

ocean. How, then, it may be asked, have the foundations of these wonderful structures been laid? This question opens a wide field for philosophical speculation; and we freely admit that no theory of Coral Reefs can be regarded as complete and satisfactory, which does not furnish a reasonable answer. But so far as the purpose of our argument is concerned, it is quite sufficient if a stratum of solid limestone, twenty fathoms thick, has been formed mainly through the agency of these minute animalcules. And this conclusion, so abundantly demonstrated by facts, is left quite untouched by the difficulty to which we now refer.

It will be interesting, however, to notice in passing the explanation of this phenomenon first suggested by Mr. Darwin, and now very generally accepted. He maintains that the whole Coral Reef—foundations and superstructure alike—is, in most cases, the result entirely of organic agency. The reef-building Zoophyte always begins his labors in water that is comparatively shallow. But as he is building upward, it often happens that the bed of the sea is sinking downward in pretty nearly the same proportion; and thus the reef is ever increasing in height from its original base, while the living mass of Zoophytes on its upper surface remains in about the same depth of water as when the building first began.

This theory is supported by a vast amount of curious and ingenious reasoning. In the first place, there is nothing more remarkable in the physical conformation of the Globe, than the immense predominance of water over land throughout those extensive tracts of ocean where Coral Reefs abound. Now this is just what we should naturally expect if the hypothesis of Mr. Darwin were admitted; for wherever the Crust of the Earth has been subsiding for many ages on a large scale, the domain of the sea must of necessity have been considerably enlarged, and that of the land contracted in proportion. Again, this hypothesis will be found to harmonize most perfectly with all the phenomena of Fringing Reefs, Barrier Reefs, Encircling Reefs, and Lagoon Islands. The Fringing Reef represents, as it were, the first stage of progress. The building operations have just commenced near the shore of some island or continent, and but little space intervenes between the land and the incrusting wall of coral. Then, as the Crust of the Earth gradually subsides, the water encroaches on the land, and forms a channel between it and the reef. Meanwhile the Zoophytes are at work, and the coral rock is growing upward as the foundation on which it rests is sinking downward : each year it is higher from the bed of the sea, and yet no nearer to the surface of the waters. And when at length the channel, which is ever growing wider and wider, has reached a certain limit, the Fringing Reef becomes a Barrier Reef, or if it encompasses an island, an Encircling Reef. Lastly, the Encircling Reef will finally become a Lagoon Island, when the highest peaks of the land it encloses have slowly disappeared beneath the surface of the waters.

In confirmation of this reasoning Mr. Darwin has pointed out numerous examples to illustrate each intermediate stage through which, according to his hypothesis, the Coral Reef must pass in the progress of its construction. He traces the gradual transition from the low bank of coral incrusting a rocky shore to the Encircling Reef that compasses round a lofty island, like Tahiti, with a broad channel between. Then he shows how this channel insensibly becomes wider and wider, encroaching more and more upon the land, until at length only a few high peaks remain above water. Finally he leads us on to the case of a perfect Atoll, within which no trace of land remains to be seen ; and the channel, now become a lagoon, is encompassed by a Reef of Coral Rock that rises steeply from an unfathomed ocean.

We do not mean to dwell upon this ingenious speculation, which would carry us too far from the object at which we are aiming. It seems to us, however, that the arguments in its favor are at least deserving of careful consideration; and we may add that they receive new strength from the facts we shall have occasion hereafter to bring forward, when we come to speak of the undulating movements to which the Crust of the Earth has been subject at many different times, and in many different localities, even within the historic period.

The formation and structure of existing Coral Reefs being once fairly established, Geologists have little difficulty in ascribing a similar origin to many of the limestone strata that are found in the Crust of the Earth. For though the internal texture has been considerably modified in the long course of ages, by chemical and other influences, nevertheless the stony skeletons of the reef-building Zoophytes can be distinctly recognized in great abundance. Indeed it is not an uncommon thing to meet with limestone rock exhibiting plainly to the eye all the appearance of Coral Reefs lifted up from the bed of the ocean. "The Oolite," says Doctor Mantell, "abounds in corals, and contains beds of limestone which are merely coral reefs that have undergone no change but that of elevation from the bottom of the deep, and the consolidation of their materials. The Coral-rag of Wilts presents in fact all the characters of modern reefs: the polypifera belong chiefly to the Astræidæ, the genera of which family principally contribute to the formations now going on in the Pacific. Shells, echinoderms, teeth, and bones of fishes, and other marine exuviæ, occupy the interstices between the corals, and the whole is consolidated by sand and gravel, held together in some instances by calcareous, in others by siliceous infiltrations. Those who have visited districts where the Coral-rag forms the immediate subsoil, and is exposed to view in the quarries or in natural sections, must have been struck with the resemblance of these rocks to modern coral banks."*

Even in many of our finest marbles the coral skeletons may be traced distinctly enough, and contribute not a little to that variegated color which is so much admired. Nay, it is recorded by Mr. Parkinson that he discovered in a piece of solid marble, the *animal membrane itself* by which the lime was originally abstracted from the sea. He immersed the marble in dilute muriatic acid; and he relates with delight how, as the calcareous earth dissolved, and the carbonic acid gas escaped, he observed the animal tissue begin distinctly to appear in the form of light, elastic membranes.†

* Wonders of Geology, p. 648.

† Organic Remains of a Former World, vol. ii., p. 16.

CHAPTER IX.

STRATIFIED ROCKS OF ORGANIC ORIGIN—ILLUSTRATIONS FROM VEGETABLE LIFE.

Origin of coal—Evident traces of plants and trees in coal-mines—Coal made up of the same elements as wood—Beds of coal found resting upon clay in which are preserved the roots of trees—Insensible transition from wood to coal—Forest-covered swamps—Accumulations of drift-wood in lakes and estuaries—Peat bogs—Beds of Lignite—Seams of pure coal with half-carbonized trees, some lying prostrate, some standing erect—Summary of the argument hitherto pursued—Objection to this argument from the Omnipotence of God—Answer to the objection.

S animals, by organic action, extract lime from the waters of the ocean they inhabit, which, being converted in the first instance into minute shells, or stony skeletons, afterward passes into a compact and solid rock, so in like manner do plants and trees extract carbon from the atmosphere in which they vegetate, and convert it into coal. No reasonable doubt can now be entertained that coal derives its existence, almost entirely, from the woody tissue of sunken swamps and forests. Though the nature of the process by which this transformation takes place, is yet but imperfectly understood, and is, indeed, at the present moment a subject of much discussion and controversy, nevertheless the *fact* that the change *has* taken place is fully accepted by all as an established truth, and is supported by an accumulation of evidence which it is not easy to resist.

The first circumstance to which we shall call attention, is the wonderful profusion of vegetable life that is always associated with coal. Every one who has descended at any time into a coal mine, or who has examined the specimens usually exhibited in a well-furnished museum, must have been struck by the countless forms of trees and plants, which still remain vividly impressed on this black and unsightly mineral. Dr. Buckland has described this phenomenon with much vigor and beauty in his celebrated Bridgewater Treatise: "The finest example I have ever witnessed is that of the coal mines of Bohemia just mentioned. The most elaborate imitations of living foliage upon the painted ceilings of Italian palaces, bear no comparison with the beauteous profusion of extinct vegetable forms with which the galleries of these instructive coal mines are overhung. The roof is covered as with a canopy of gorgeous tapestry, enriched with festoons of most graceful foliage, flung in wild irregular profusion over every portion of its surface. The effect is heightened by the contrast of the coal-black color of these vegetables with the light ground-work of the rock to which they are attached. The spectator feels himself transported, as if by enchantment, into the forests of another world; he beholds trees of forms and characters now unknown upon the surface of the earth, presented to his senses almost in the beauty and vigor of their primeval life; their scaly stems and bending branches, with their delicate apparatus of foliage, are all spread forth before him, little impaired by the lapse of countless ages, and bearing faithful records of extinct systems of vegetation, which began and terminated in times of which these relics are the infallible historians."

The next important fact that points to the vegetable origin of Coal is, that wood and Coal are both composed of the same ultimate elements—carbon, hydrogen, and

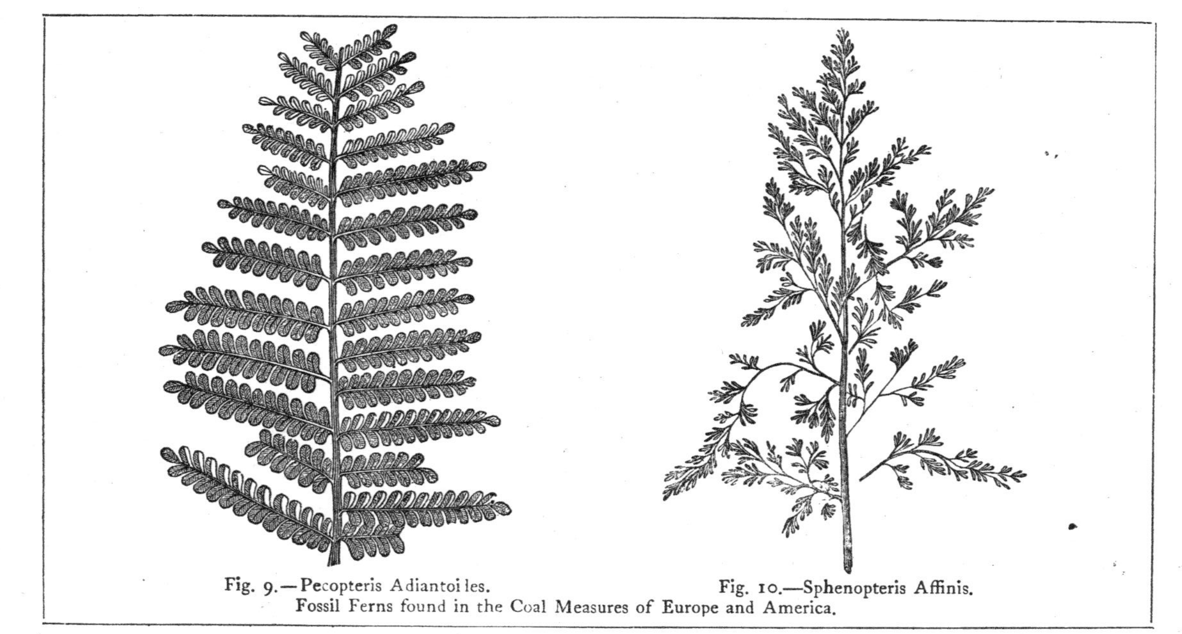

Fig. 9.—Pecopteris Adiantoi les. Fig. 10.—Sphenopteris Affinis.

Fossil Ferns found in the Coal Measures of Europe and America.

oxygen. This analogy is the more remarkable when we are told that no other rock except Coal exhibits anything approaching to this composition. It is true that the elements just enumerated do not exist in the same proportions in wood and in Coal. But the difference, when rightly understood, rather tends to confirm our theory that the one is derived from the other. There is more Carbon in Coal than in wood; while there is less oxygen and less hydrogen. To explain how this may have come to pass during the process of transition, we must call in the assistance of the chemist. It appears from the researches of Liebig that, when vegetable matter is buried in the earth, exposed to moisture, and partially or entirely excluded from the air, the process of decomposition sets in, and that under this process carbonic acid gas and carburetted hydrogen gas are slowly evolved. At the same time a portion of the oxygen when set free would naturally enter into a new combination with a portion of the hydrogen, and form water. The result of these several changes would necessarily be, that the accumulation of vegetable matter buried in the earth would part, in course of time, with no small share of its carbon, its hydrogen, and its oxygen, but not with all in the same proportions: for the new combinations would use up more of the oxygen than of the hydrogen, and more of the hydrogen than of the carbon.* In other words, if the process should have gone on for a sufficient lapse of ages, these elements would no longer exist together in the proportions which are necessary to constitute

* Carbonic acid gas contains two equivalents of oxygen to one of carbon, the chemical expression for the compound being CO_2; carburetted hydrogen, which is the gas we employ in illuminating our streets and houses, contains four equivalents of hydrogen to two of carbon, and is chemically expressed by the symbols C_2H_4; water is composed of one equivalent of oxygen, and one of hydrogen, the symbolic form being HO.

wood, but would rather exist in the proportions which are found to constitute coal.*

This explanation is confirmed by a fact with which our readers are no doubt familiar. According to the explanation, carbonic acid and carburetted hydrogen are evolved during the process by which coal is produced from wood. We should therefore expect to find these gases closely associated with Coal. If they are *not* so associated, their absence is a serious objection against our theory; but if they *are* so associated, their presence is a strong evidence in its favor. Now on this point, as every one knows, practical miners bear testimony that the fact corresponds exactly with our theory. They tell us that reservoirs of Choke-damp, which is carbonic acid, and of Fire-damp, which is carburetted hydrogen, are found very commonly pent up in the crevices and cavities of coal beds, and are the cause, when tapped, of many of the accidents which take place. They even assure us that some beds of coal are so saturated with gas that, when cut into, it may be heard oozing from every pore of the rock, and the coal is called *singing coal* by the colliers.†

To sum up, then, what we have said on this point: it appears, first, that the same constituent elements are found in wood and Coal; secondly, though they do not exist in the same proportions in the two substances, the difference is fully accounted for by the changes which we should naturally expect to take place when large accumulations of vegetable matter are buried in the earth; thirdly, in the hypothesis of these changes, carbonic acid and carburetted hydrogen would certainly be developed; and in point of fact, these gases are found intimately associated with Coal all over the world.

* See Jukes, Manual of Geology, pp. 138–141; Lyell, Elements of Geology, p. 500.

† Jukes, Manual of Geology, p. 140.

There is another remarkable fact which fits in most admirably with our theory. Coal is found at the present day in the Crust of the Earth, disposed in thin seams or beds, and each bed is almost uniformly found to rest upon a stratum of fine clay, sometimes several feet in thickness. This is just what our theory would lead us to expect. If coal is produced from plants and trees, these plants and trees must have grown upon some suitable soil ; and, therefore, in this hypothesis we should expect, ordinarily speaking at least, to find a bed of clay beneath every bed of coal. But this is not all. When we examine more closely the stratum on which the coal reposes, we find the roots and stems of trees mingled with the clay in the greatest profusion. In the Welsh coal field, in a depth of twelve thousand feet, there are from fifty to a hundred beds of coal, each lying on a stratum of clay abounding in these remains.*

We now come to an argument of apractical kind which appeals to common sense and common experience. Let us suppose that a person wholly unacquainted with the art of manufacturing paper, were to enter a paper-mill when the workmen are away, and the process of manufacture for a time suspended. At first sight he would probably find it difficult to persuade himself, that the piles of clean white paper, which attract his notice at one end of the building, are produced from the heaps of filthy rags which he sees accumulated at the other. But if he be a sagacious observer, he will soon find evidence to convince him that this is really the case. For he will perceive, upon close examination, that the self-same material is exhibited in every intermediate state of progress from one extreme to the other. First, there is the great chest with its numerous compartments, in which the rags are seen carefully sorted, accord-

* See Mantell, Wonders of Geology, pp. 680–2; also 760; Lyell, Elements of Geology, 464, 465.

ing to their various degrees of quality and texture. Next comes the fullin-gmill, where they are washed and bleached. Then the revolving cylinder, furnished on the exterior surface with sharp blades or cutters; and the vat in which it moves is filled with the rags, which now assume the form of a thin liquid pulp. Advancing still further he will see this pulp evenly spread out upon a wire-gauze frame, and now at last it is beginning to exhibit some likeness to the form and substance of paper. Further on it is seen pressed and dried; and last of all cut into sheets and laid aside in lofty piles.

Now it seems to us that we are placed in somewhat of the same position, as regards the manufacture of Coal. We cannot observe the process actually going on; for though, in this process, the work is never suspended, the workmen never at rest, yet extending as it does over a space of many centuries, it is too slow to be sensible; and besides it is conducted in great part beneath the surface of the Earth. Nevertheless, we can trace the progress of change through each intermediate stage of the transition, from one extreme to the other,—from the primeval swamps and forests through the numerous varieties of the Peat and Lignite to the richest beds of pure Coal.

First, then, we have the great forest-covered swamps, like those which now occupy the valley and delta of the Mississippi. They are composed in many cases of pure vegetable matter without any intermixture of earthy sediment. A dense growth of reeds, and shrubs, and herbage of every kind, covers the whole surface of the land, mixed up with the decaying leaves and prostrate trunks of forest-trees. Sir Charles Lyell mentions a very remarkable fact observed in the swamps of Louisiana. During an unusually hot season, when any part of a swamp is dried up, if the surface be set on fire, a pit is burned into the ground many feet deep, in fact, as far down as the fire can descend without meeting water; and it is then found that scarcely any residuum or earthy matter is left.*

Vegetable strata of this kind are produced, not only upon dry land by the growth and decay of forests, but also beneath the waters of lakes and estuaries, by the accumulation of Drift-timber borne along in the current of swollen rivers. The Mackenzie River, which drains a great part of Northwestern America, affords many admirable illustrations. Flowing as it does from south to north, it is subject to annual inundations when the snows begin to melt in the higher parts of its course, while the channel lower down, situated in colder latitudes, is still blocked up with ice. At this season then it overflows its banks, and sweeping through vast forests, carries away thousands of uprooted trees in its impetuous torrent.

"As the trees," says Dr. Richardson, "retain their roots, which are often loaded with earth and stones, they readily sink, especially when water-soaked; and accumulating in the eddies, form shoals, which ultimately augment into islands. A thicket of small willows covers the new-formed island as soon as it appears above water, and their fibrous roots serve to bind the whole firmly together. Sections of these islands are annually made by the river; and it is interesting to study the diversities of appearances they present according to their different ages. The trunks of the trees gradually decay until they are converted into a blackish-brown substance resembling peat, but still retaining more or less of the fibrous structure of the wood; and layers of this often alternate with layers of clay and sand, the whole being penetrated, to a depth of four or five yards or more, by the long fibrous roots of the willows. A deposition of this kind, with the aid of a little infiltration of

* Elements of Geology, p. 488.

bituminous matter, would produce an excellent imitation of Coal, with vegetable impressions of the willow roots.

"It was in the rivers only that we could observe sections of these deposits; but the same operation goes on, on a much more magnificent scale, in the lakes. A shoal of many miles in extent is formed on the south side of Athabasca Lake by the Drift-timber and vegetable débris brought down by the Elk River; and the Slave Lake itself must in process of time be filled up by the matters daily conveyed into it from Slave River. Vast quantities of Drift-timber are buried under the sand at the mouth of the river, and enormous piles of it are accumulated on the shores of every part of the lake."

Not unfrequently it happens that these strata of vegetable matter, with the roots and trunks of trees, their branches, fruits, and leaves, more or less perfectly preserved, are covered over by subsequent deposits. Such accumulations, we are assured by Doctor Mantell, have been found deep in the soil on the coast of England, in places that are still subject to periodical inundations. "The trees are chiefly of the oak, hazel, fir, birch, yew, willow, and ash; in short, almost every kind that is indigenous to this island occasionally occurs. The trunks and branches are dyed throughout of a deep ebony color by iron; and the wood is firm and heavy, and occasionally fit for domestic use; in Yorkshire and elsewhere, timber of this kind is sometimes employed in the construction of houses."* Here, then, is the first stage of the conversion of wood into Coal,—a stratum more or less compacted together of vegetable matter, spread out sometimes over the surface of the dry land, sometimes on the floor of lakes and estuaries, and often buried beneath an accumulation of subsequent deposits.

The next stage in the process of transformation may be represented by those Peat Bogs which constitute one of the

* Mantell, Wonders of Geology, p. 67.

most remarkable physical characteristics of Ireland, covering as they do an area equal to one-tenth of the whole island. In these the vegetable matter is more closely condensed, but the structure of the plants from which the Peat is derived is still preserved, and may be distinctly recognized by the naked eye. Nay, we have still the prostrate trunks of trees lying around on every side as they fell to the ground in their ancient forests. The researches recently pursued upon this subject have brought to light a fact which is very much to our present purpose; for it seems to prove our thesis by direct evidence. "In Limerick, in the district of Maine, one of the States of North America, there are Peat Bogs of considerable extent, in which a substance exactly similar to *cannel coal* is found at the depth of three or four feet from the surface amidst the remains of rotten logs of wood and *beaver sticks*: the peat is twenty feet thick, and rests upon white sand. This coal was discovered on digging a ditch to drain a portion of the bog, for the purpose of obtaining peat for manure. The substance is a true bituminous coal, containing more bitumen than is found in any other variety. Polished sections of the compact masses exhibit the peculiar structure of coniferous trees, and prove that the coal was derived from a species allied to the American Fir."* A similar phenomenon was observed by Doctor Dieffenbach in the Chathain Islands. In the same bed of peat he was able distinctly to trace a gradual transition from pure vegetable matter to a mineral substantially identical with common coal.†

But though Peat may thus, as it should seem, pass directly into pure Coal, there are many cases in which it first assumes a more imperfect form, known under the name of Lignite. This substance is described as of a brownish color, "soft and mellow in consistence when freshly quarried, but becoming brittle by exposure, the fracture

* Mantell, Wonders of Geology, p. 66. † Id. Ib.

following the direction of the fibre of the wood."* It clearly occupies an intermediate position between Peat and Coal. Like the former, it still exhibits the stems and woody fibre of the plants from which it is derived, very little altered in their structure; while on the other hand it is already beginning to acquire some of the consistency and density of Coal; to which also it approaches much more closely in its chemical composition. It should be remembered, moreover, that Lignite does not designate a substance of a fixed, invariable character. On the contrary, under the one general name are comprised a definite number of varieties, leading from one extreme to the other by a series of almost insensible gradations; the extreme variety on one side being scarcely distinguishable from Peat, while the extreme variety on the other is practically identical with ordinary Coal. It can hardly be doubted, therefore, that Coal must have the same origin as Lignite, while it is at least equally certain that Lignite has been derived from Peat; and we have already seen what overwhelming evidence may be adduced to show that the origin of Peat is to be sought for in the sunken swamps and forests of a long past age.

Lastly, when we come to examine the texture of Coal itself, we find much to confirm the conclusion at which we have thus arrived. In beds of pure Coal the remains of many species of plants have been detected, and sometimes in such abundance as to constitute visibly the bulk of the Coal. Even large trees are sometimes found standing erect in the Coal fields, with their bark actually converted into this mineral. The annexed Figure represents a portion of the stem, together with the roots of a tall forest tree, Sigillaria, discovered not long ago in a Coal mine at Saint Helens, near Liverpool. The stem, which was nine feet high, was found erect in the seam of Coal, while the roots,

* Chemical Technology, Ronalds and Richardson, vol. i., p. 32.

ten in number, stretched away into the vegetable soil beneath.

Not less than thirty such trees, some of them four or five feet in diameter, and all incrusted with Coal, were laid bare a short time since, in a Colliery near Newcastle, within an area of fifty yards square. "In 1830," writes Sir Charles Lyell, "a slanting trunk was exposed in Cragleith quarry,

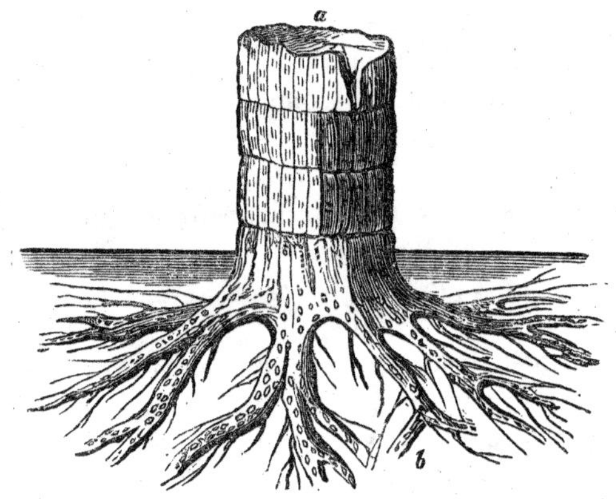

Fig. 11.—Stem and roots of a Forest Tree, Sigillaria. From a Coal-mine, near Liverpool.

a, The trunk traversing a bed of Coal.

b, The roots spreading out in the underclay.

near Edinburgh, the total length of which exceeded sixty feet. Its diameter at the top was about seven inches, and near the base, it measured five feet in its greater, and two feet in its lesser, width. The bark was converted into a thin coating of the purest and finest Coal." Again, "in South Staffordshire, a seam of Coal was laid bare in the year 1844, in what is called an open work at Parkfield Colliery, near Wolverhampton. In the space of about a quarter of an acre, the stumps of no less than seventy-three trees, with their roots attached, appeared, some of them more than eight feet in circumference. The trunks, broken off close to the root, were lying prostrate in every direction, often crossing each other. One of them measured fifteen, another thirty feet in length, and others less. They were invariably flattened to the thickness of one or two inches, and converted into Coal. Their roots formed part of a stratum of Coal ten inches thick, which rested on a layer of clay two inches thick, below which was a second forest resting on a two-foot seam of Coal. Five feet below this again was a third forest, with large stumps of Lepidodendra, Calamites, and other trees."*

We have now brought to a close a very important line of argument in the Science of Geology. We have pointed out that, in the strata which compose the Crust of the Earth, there are rocks of various kinds, distinguished from one another as well by the nature of the materials which compose them, as by the manner in which these materials are arranged together; and we have shown that rocks presenting the same general appearances, and composed of exactly the same materials, are being produced in the present age upon the Surface of the Earth, through the agency of natural causes. Moreover, we have closely examined, in certain cases, the nature of the process by which the formation of these rocks is accomplished at the present day; and we have seen how difficult it is, when the facts of the case are once clearly before us, to resist the conclusion that the rocks which we now find buried in the Earth, were produced in some former age, by the same causes which are still at work. We shall next proceed to inquire how far

* See Lyell, Elements of Geology, 477-81; Jukes, Manual of Geology, 138, 149-53; The English Cyclopædia, Natural History Department, Article, Coal; Mantell, Fossils of the British Museum, Chapter i., Part I.

this conclusion is confirmed by the independent evidence of Fossil Remains.

But before entering on a new line of argument, it is fit we should take notice of an objection which has sometimes been urged against the reasoning we have hitherto pursued, and which has done much to create and to keep alive a prejudice unfavorable to the Science of Geology. Religious writers have not unfrequently insinuated, and sometimes have plainly asserted, that, in ascribing the present structure of the Earth's Crust to the operation of natural causes, Geologists would seem to make no account of God's Omnipotence. A moment's reflection will convince the reader that this charge is utterly unphilosophical. Is it not plain that the more fully we appreciate and acknowledge the wonderful works of Nature, the more deeply must we become impressed with the power and wisdom of Him who is the Author and Ruler of Nature? To say that secondary causes exist, and to point out the monuments that bear witness to their operation in long passed ages, is not to deny, but rather to affirm the existence of a Great First Cause, upon whom they all depend for their existence, their preservation, and their guidance.

We are everywhere reminded by abundant evidence, that it has pleased the Great Creator to employ the agency of His creatures in the fashioning and the adorning of this material universe. He does not create at once, as He well might do, the great oak of the forest; but He allows the seed to sink into the earth, where it is watered by the gentle dews of Heaven, and fructified by the genial warmth of the sun; soon it puts forth a tender germ; the germ, in time, imbibing the elements of its support from the air and the earth, becomes a sappling, and the sappling a tree, which spreads its huge branches on every side, and serves for many purposes of ornament and of use. Or let us take the case of the honeycomb, that most curious and ingenious work, at once the palace and the storehouse of a vast and busy community. It is not produced in a moment by a simple act of creation. God has not made it Himself, but He has taught the bee to make it. In like manner He has provided for the little birds, not by building their nests, but by infusing into their nature that mysterious instinct which prompts them to build, and guides them in their work.

Geologists, therefore, when they undertake to explain the existence of Stratified Rocks, not by the immediate action of the Creator, but by the intervention of natural causes, are not on that account to be accused of impiety. They do not disparage, but rather magnify His glory, when they expatiate upon the endless variety of agents which, according to their theory, He has employed in the structure of the material world. If the honeycomb, as a work of contrivance and design, excites the wonder and admiration of the philosopher, what must we think of the contrivance and design exhibited by Him who has made, not the honeycomb only, but the bee that builds the honeycomb? And so, too, we get novel and unexpected views of God's Omnipotence, when, through the science of Geology, we come to understand the vast and harmonious series of secondary causes by which he has brought the Crust of the Earth into its present form and shape. The impress of His hand is stamped upon His works; and all that is wonderful and attractive in Nature is but the token of His power and the shadow of His beauty. And so our national poet has sung:

> "Thou art, O GOD, the life and light
> Of all this wondrous world we see;
> Its glow by day, its smile by night,
> Are but reflections caught from Thee.
> Where'er we turn, Thy glories shine,
> And all things fair and bright are Thine."

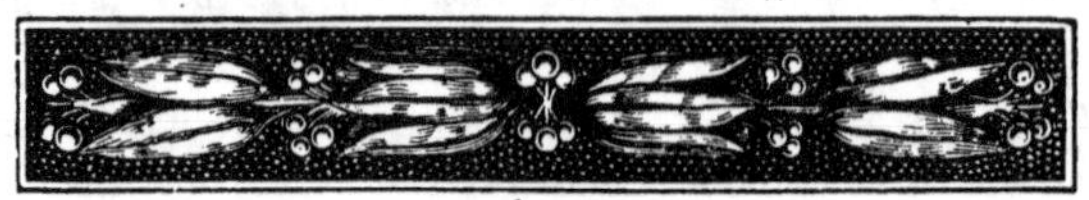

CHAPTER X.

FOSSIL REMAINS—THE MUSEUM.

Recapitulation—Scope of our argument—Theory of stratified rocks the framework of geological science—The theory brings geology into contact with revelation—the line of reasoning hitherto pursued confirmed by the testimony of fossil remains —Meaning of the word fossil—Inexhaustible abundance of fossils—Various states of preservation—Petrifaction—Experiments of Professor Göppert—Organic rocks afford some insight into the fossii world—The reality and significance of fossil remains must be tearned from observation—The British Museum—Colossal skeletons—Bones and shells of animals—Fossil plants and trees.

READER, you are beginning to suspect us. 'How long do we propose to detain people?' For anything that appears we may be designing to write on to the twentieth century. 'And *whither* are we going?' Toward what object? which is as urgent a quære as, *how far?* Perhaps we may be leading you into treason. You feel symptoms of doubt and restiveness; and like Hamlet with his father's ghost, you will follow us no further unless we explain what it is that we are in quest of."

These words of Thomas De Quincey to his readers, in the middle of one of his discursive essays, which, interesting as they certainly are in all their parts, yet sometimes beget a feeling of weariness from the uncomfortable apprehension that they will not come to an end, are, perhaps, scarcely less appropriate in our own case. It may be that our readers have been left too long in the uneasy state of suspense and hope deferred. They came to our pages to look for a practical solution of the question, Is Geology at variance with the Bible? And what avails it, they may ask, to discourse to them of the Gulf Stream, and Rivers, and Glaciers, and Alluvial Plains, and Coral Rocks, and Coal Mines? With painful steps they have been toiling after us through tedious disquisitions, straining their eyes to see the end, but the end is not yet in sight. Well, then, if they will rest for a few minutes by the way, we will pause, too, and tell them what we are about, and try to bring out more clearly the object at which we are aiming.

Our design from the beginning was to consider the points of contact between Geology and Revelation; to examine the relations that exist between these two departments of knowledge,—one resting upon reason and observation, the other given to us from Heaven; and to inquire how far it may be possible to adopt the conclusions of the former, while we adhere, at the same time, with unswerving fidelity, to the unchangeable truths of the latter. With this end in view, we proceeded at once to sketch out the more prominent features of Geological theory; not the particular theory of one writer, or of one school, but that more general theory which is adopted by all writers, and prevails in every school. This theory, we were all well aware, is in many points widely at variance with the common notions of sensible and even well-informed men who have not devoted much attention to the study of Physical Science. And it occurred to us that, possibly, many of our readers might be disposed to cut the controversy short by rejecting, in a summary way, the whole system of Geology, and treating it as an empty shadow or an idle dream. This, we were convinced, would be a mistaken and mischievous course. Geology is not a house of cards that it may be blown down by a breath. It is a hypothesis, a theory, if you will ; but no one can in fairness deny that behind this theory there are facts,—unexpected, startling, significant facts ; that these facts, when considered in their relation to one another, when illustrated by the present phenomena of Nature, and skilfully grouped together, as they have been by able men, disclose certain general truths, and suggest certain arguments, which do seem to point in the direction of those conclusions at which Geologists have arrived.

It follows that he who would investigate fairly the claims of Geology, must first learn to appreciate the significance of these facts, and to estimate the value of these arguments. And this is precisely what we have been trying to do. We are not writing a treatise on Geology. Certainly not : it would be presumptuous in us, with our scanty knowledge, to attempt it. Besides, Geology has it own professors, and its lecture-halls, and its manuals. Neither do we mean to assume the character of the advocates or champions of Geology. It does not ask our services ; in its cause are enrolled no small proportion of the most illustrious names which for the last fifty years have adorned the annals of Physical Science. Nor do we want even to enforce upon our readers that more general theory of Geology which we are endeavoring to explain and illustrate. Our purpose is merely to collect from various sources, and to string together, the evidence that may be adduced in its favor ; that so, when we come hereafter to consider this theory in its relation with the History of the Bible, we may not incur the risk of discomfiture by denying that which has been proved by facts, but rather approach the subject with such knowledge as may help us to discover the real harmony that we know to exist between the truths inscribed on the works of God, and those which are recorded in His Written Word.

In the accomplishment of this task we have devoted ourselves chiefly to the study of the Aqueous or Stratified Rocks. According to Geologists, these rocks, such as we find them now, were not the immediate work of creation, but were slowly produced in the long lapse of ages, and laid out one above another, by a vast and complex machinery of secondary causes. The elements of which they are composed were gathered together from many and various sources ; from the ocean, from the air, from other pre-existing rocks ; and, for aught we know, may have had a long and eventful history before they came to assume their present structure and arrangement. Thus, for example, the Conglomerates, and Sandstones, with which we are so familiar, are made up of broken fragments derived from earlier rocks, and then transported to distant sites by the mountain torrents, or the stately rivers of vast continents, or the silent currents of the sea ; the Limestone with which we build our houses is the work of living animals that once swarmed in countless myriads beneath the waters of the ocean ; and the Coal which supplies the motive power to our manufactories, our railways, our ships of war and commerce, is but the modern representative of ancient swamps and forests, which, having been buried in the earth, and there, by the action of chemical laws, endowed with new properties, were laid by for the future use of man in the great storehouse of Nature.

This mode of accounting for the origin and formation of Stratified Rocks constitutes in a manner the framework that supports and binds together the whole system of Geology. If it be once fairly established, Geology is entitled to take high rank as a Physical Science. If on the contrary it should prove to be without foundation, then Geology is no longer a science, but a dream. Moreover, it is this theory of stratification which, from the first, has brought Geology into contact with Revelation. For Geologists have been led to infer the extreme Antiquity of the Earth, from the immense thickness of the Stratified Rocks on the one hand, and, on the other, the very slow and gradual process by which each stratum in the series has been, in its turn, spread out and consolidated. Those likewise who claim for the Human Race a greater Antiquity than the Bible allows, seek for their proofs in the supposed origin and antiquity of those superficial deposits, in which the remains of Man or of his works are sometimes found entombed.

It is not to be wondered at, therefore, that the theory of Stratified Rocks should engage the largest share of our attention when we undertake to discuss the relation in which Geology stands to Revealed Religion. For the present we say nothing about the conclusions that flow from this theory, or the errors to which it has led when hastily or ignorantly applied : we are only investigating the evidence by which it is supported. In our former chapters we have drawn out at some length the line of reasoning which is derived from the character of the Aqueous Rocks themselves when considered in the light of Nature's present operations. We have shown that Stratified Rocks of many different kinds, just such as those which compose the Crust of the Earth, have been produced by natural causes within historic times ; and we have explained some of the more simple and intelligible parts of that complex machinery, which, even now, is busily at work gathering, sorting, distributing, piling up together, and consolidating the materials of new strata all over the world. These considerations, as we took occasion to point out, beget a strong presumption in favor of Geological theory. Here we have Nature at work, actually bringing into existence a stratum of rock before our eyes. And there, in the Crust of the Earth, we find another stratum of precisely the same kind already finished. What can be more reasonable than to ascribe the one to the action of the same causes which we see at work upon the other? And thus, by extending the area of our observations from one class of Aqueous Rocks to another, the idea gradually grows upon us that these rocks have been spread out, stratum upon stratum, during many successive ages, by the agency of secondary causes similar to those which are still in operation ; and that each stratum, in its turn, as it first came into existence, was for a time the uppermost of the series.

In support of this conclusion we are now about to bring forward a new and independent argument founded on the testimony of Fossil Remains. An eminent writer has summed up in a few words the value and importance of Fossil Remains in reference to Geological theory. "At present," he says, "shells, fishes, and other animals are buried in the mud or silt of lakes and estuaries; rivers also carry down the carcases of land animals, the trunks of trees, and other vegetable drift; and earthquakes submerge plains and islands, with all their vegetable and animal inhabitants. These remains become enveloped in the layers of mud and sand and gravel formed by the waters, and in process of time are petrified, that is, are converted into stony matter like the shells and bones found in the oldest strata. Now, as at present, so in all former time must the remains of plants and animals have been similarly preserved ; and, as one tribe of plant is peculiar to the dry plain, another to the swampy morass ; as one family belongs to a temperate, another to a tropical region, so, from the character of the embedded plants, we are enabled to arrive at some knowledge of the conditions under which they flourished. In the same manner with animals : each tribe has its locality assigned it by peculiarities of food, climate, and the like ; each family has its own peculiar structure for running, flying, swimming, plant-eating, or flesh-eating, as the case may be ; and by comparing Fossil Remains with existing races, we are enabled to determine many of the past conditions of the world with considerable certainty."*

* Page, Advanced Text-Book of Geology, n. 7, pp. 20, 21.

On this branch of our subject we do not mean to offer much in the way of argument strictly so called. We shall content ourselves with a simple statement of facts, and leave them to produce their own impression. It will be necessary at the outset to explain some technical matters, that what we have to say hereafter may be the better understood : and if in this we are somewhat dry and tiresome, we will try to make amends by the curious and interesting story of Nature's long buried works, which we hope in the sequel to unfold.

When the word *Fossil* was first introduced into the English language, it was employed to designate, as the etymology suggests, whatever is *dug out of the earth.** But it is now generally used in a much more restricted sense, being applied only to the remains of plants and animals embedded in the Crust of the Earth and there preserved by natural causes. When we speak of remains, we must be understood to include even those seemingly transient impressions, such as foot-prints in the sand, which having been made permanent by accidental circumstances, and thus engraved, as it were, on the archives of Nature, now bear witness to the former existence of organic life.

Now in every part of the world where the Stratified Rocks have been laid open to view, remains of this kind are found scattered on all sides in the most profuse abundance. In Europe, in America, in Australia, in the frozen wastes of Siberia, in the countless islands scattered over the waters of the Pacific, there is scarcely a single formation, from the lowest in the series to the highest, that, when it is fairly explored, does not yield up vast stores of shells, together with bones and teeth, nay, sometimes whole skeletons of animals ; also fragments of wood, impressions of leaves, and other organic substances.

* From the Latin *Fossilis, dug up.*

These Fossil Remains do not always occur in the same state of preservation. Sometimes we have the bone, or plant, or shell, in its natural condition; still retaining not only its own peculiar form and structure, but likewise the very same organic substance of which it was originally composed. Examples innumerable may be seen in the

Fig. 12.—Fossil Irish Deer (County Fermanagh). In the Museum of Trinity College, Dublin. From Haughton's Manual of Geology

British Museum, or, indeed, in almost any Geological collection: the fine skeletons of ancient Irish Deer, which are exhibited in the Museum of Trinity College, Dublin, and of which all the bones are in excellent preservation, must be familiar to many of our readers.

It happens, however, more frequently that the organic substance itself has disappeared, but has left an impression on the rock, that now bears witness to its former presence. Thus, for instance, when a shell has been dissolved and carried away by water percolating the rock, it has very often left after it, on the hard stone, a mould of its outer surface and a cast of its inner surface, with a cavity between corresponding to the thickness of the shell. In such cases we have the form, the size, and the superficial markings of the organic body, but we have no part of its original substance, and no traces of its internal structure. This form of fossilization, as Sir Charles Lyell has well put it, "may be easily understood if we examine the mud recently thrown out from a pond or canal in which there are shells. If the mud be argillaceous, it acquires consistency in drying, and on breaking open a portion of it, we find that each shell has left impressions of its external form. If we then remove the shell itself, we find within a solid nucleus of clay, having the form of the interior of the shell."* In many cases the space first occupied by the shell is not left empty when the shell has been removed, but is filled up with some mineral substance, such as lime or flint. The mineral thus introduced becomes the exact counterpart of the organic body which has disappeared; and has been justly compared to a bronze statue, which exhibits the exterior form and lineaments, but not the internal organization nor the substance of the object it represents.

There is a third form more wonderful still, in which Fossil Remains are not uncommonly found. The original body has passed away as in the former case, and yet not only does its *outward shape* remain, but even its *internal*

* Elements of Geology, p. 38.

texture is perfectly preserved in the solid stone which has taken its place. This kind of change is exhibited most remarkably in the vegetable kingdom. Fossil trees of great size have been discovered of which *the whole substance has been changed from wood to stone*: yet with such exquisite skill has the change been effected that the minute cells and fibres, and the rings of annual growth, may still be clearly traced; nay, even those delicate spiral vessels which, from their extreme minuteness, can be discerned only by the aid of the microscope. Thus the tree remains complete in all its parts; but it is no longer a tree of wood; it is, so to speak, a tree of stone.

The mystery of this extraordinary transformation has not yet been fully cleared up by scientific men; but the general principle, at least, is sufficiently understood. It is thus briefly explained by Sir Charles Lyell: "If an organic substance is exposed in the open air to the action of the sun and rain, it will in time putrefy, or be dissolved into its component elements, consisting usually of oxygen, hydrogen, nitrogen, and carbon. These will readily be absorbed by the atmosphere or be washed away by rain, so that all vestiges of the dead animal or plant disappear. But if the same substances be submerged in water, they decompose more gradually; and if buried in the earth, still more slowly, as in the familiar example of wooden piles or other buried timber. Now, if as fast as each particle is set free by putrefaction in a fluid or gaseous state, a particle equally minute of carbonate of lime, flint, or other mineral is at hand and ready to be precipitated, we may imagine this inorganic matter to take the place just before left unoccupied by the organic molecule. In this manner a cast of the interior of certain vessels may first be taken, and afterward the more solid walls of the same may decay and suffer a like transmutation."* This exposition, so simple

* Elements of Geology, p. 40.

and luminous in itself, may, perhaps, be rendered still more intelligible to the general reader by an ingenious illustration of Mr. Jukes. "It is," he says, "as if a house were gradually rebuilt, brick by brick, or stone by stone, a brick or a stone of a different kind having been substituted for each of the former ones, the shape and size of the house, the forms and arrangements of its rooms, passages, and closets, and even the number and shape of the bricks and stones, remaining unaltered."*

This singular kind of petrifaction, by which not only the external form, but even the organic tissue itself, is converted into stone, has been illustrated, in a very interesting way, by Professor Göppert of Breslau. With a view to imitate as nearly as he could the process of Nature, "he steeped a variety of animal and vegetable substances in waters, some holding siliceous, others calcareous, others metallic matter in solution. He found that in the period of a few weeks, or even days, the organic bodies thus immersed were mineralized to a certain extent. Thus, for example, thin vertical slices of deal, taken from the Scotch fir, were immersed in a moderately strong solution of sulphate of iron. When they had been thoroughly soaked in the liquid for several days, they were dried and exposed to a red heat until the vegetable matter was burnt up and nothing remained but an oxide of iron, which was found to have taken the form of the deal so exactly that casts even of the dotted vessels peculiar to this family of plants were distinctly visible under the microscope."†

If we have succeeded in making ourselves understood, the reader will now have a pretty accurate notion of what

* Manual of Geology, p. 375.

† Lyell, Elements of Geology, pp. 40–41. The reader will find a singularly clear and simple exposition of this subject in Doctor Haughton's Manual of Geology, Lecture III.; an exposition which it was not our good fortune to have read until our own brief summary was already in type.

is meant, in modern Geology, by Fossil Remains. They are the remains or impressions of plants and animals, buried in the earth by natural causes, and preserved to our time in any one of the three forms we have just described. Either the body itself remains, still retaining its own natural substance, together with its external form and its internal structure. Or secondly, the organic substance and the organic structure have both disappeared, but the outward form and the superficial markings have been left impressed on the solid rock. Or thirdly, the substance of the body has been converted into stone, but with such a delicate art, that it is in all respects, outwardly and inwardly, still the same body, with a new substance. We should observe, however, that these three different forms of fossilization, which we have successively described, are not always clearly distinct in actual fossil specimens, but are often curiously blended together according as the original organic substance has been more or less completely displaced, or the process of petrifaction has been more or less perfectly accomplished.

It will probably have occurred to the intelligent reader that we have already had some insight into the Fossil world, when investigating the origin of Organic Rocks. We have seen, for instance, that Coal is the representative to our age of swamps and forests which once covered the earth with vegetation; that Mountain Limestone is in great part formed from the skeletons of reef-building corals; that the White Chalk of Europe is almost entirely derived from the remains of marine shells. But it should be observed that these and such like rocks, while they afford us much valuable information about the ancient organic condition of our planet, are not, strictly speaking, Fossil Remains. For, not only does the substance of the organic bodies they represent exhibit an altered character, but the internal structure has been in great part effaced, and even the outward forms and superficial markings have disappeared. They contain, it is true, great multitudes of Fossils. In the Coal, for example, are found, as we have seen, trunks of trees, together with the impressions of plants and leaves: in the Chalk and Mountain Limestone, fragments of shells and corals are often discovered in a state of perfect preservation. But the bulk of these formations is made up not so much of Fossil Remains, as of that into which Fossil Remains have been converted. Coal, for instance, is something more than Fossil wood; Chalk, and Limestone, and Marble, are something more than Fossil shells and corals.

Fossil Remains properly so called present a very much more lively picture of the ancient inhabitants of our Globe. But it is a picture that can but faintly be conveyed to the mind by the way of mere verbal description. He who would appreciate aright the reality and the significance of Fossil Remains must gather his impressions from actual observation. Let him go, for instance, to the British Museum, and walk slowly through the long suite of noble galleries which are there exclusively devoted to this branch of science. He will feel as if transported into another world, the reality of which he could scarcely have believed if he had not seen it with his own eyes. Before him, and behind him, and on each side of him, as he moves along, are spread out in long array forms of beasts, and birds, and fish, and amphibious animals, such as he has never seen before, nor dreamt of in his wildest dreams. Yet much as he may wonder at these strange figures, he never for a moment doubts that they were once indued with life, and moved over the surface of the earth, or disported in the waters of the deep. Nay more, though the forms are new to him, he will be at no loss, however inexperienced in Natural History, to find many analogies between the creation in the midst of which he stands, and the creation with which he has been hitherto familiar. There are quadrupeds, and bipeds, and reptiles. Some of the animals were manifestly designed to walk on dry land, some to swim in the sea, and some to fly in the air. Some are armed with claws like the lion or the tiger, others have the paddles of a turtle, and others again have the fins of a fish. Here is an enormous beast that might almost pass for an elephant, though an experienced eye will not fail to detect an important difference; and there is an amphibious monster that suggests the idea of a crocodile; and again a little further on is an unsightly creature which unites the general characteristics of the diminutive sloth with the colossal proportions of the largest rhinoceros.

If left to mere conjecture, the visitor would perhaps suppose that these uncouth monsters had been brought together by some adventurous traveller from the remote regions of the world. But no: he will find on inquiry that the vast majority belong to species which for centuries have not been known to flourish on the Earth; and that many of the strangest forms before him have been dug up almost from beneath the very soil on which he stands,—from the quarries of Surrey, of Sussex, and of Kent, and from the deep cuttings on the many lines of railway that diverge from the great metropolis of London. The life they represent so vididly is, indeed, widely different from that which flourishes around us; but it is the life not so much of a far distant country as of a far distant age.

It must not be supposed, however, that such skeletons as those which first arrest the eye in the galleries of the British Museum—so colossal in their proportions and so complete in all their details—fairly exhibit the general character of Fossil Remains. Perfect skeletons of gigantic animals are rarely to be found. They are the exception and not the general rule,—the magnificent reward of long and toilsome exploration, or, it may be, the chance discovery that brings wealth to the humble home of some rustic laborer. Very different are the common every day discoveries of the working Geologist. Disjointed bones and skulls, scattered teeth, fragments of shells, the eggs of birds, the impressions of leaves,—these are the ordinary relics that Nature has stored up for our instruction in the various strata of the Earth's Crust: and these likewise constitute by far the greater part of the treasures which are gathered together in our Geological Museums.

We will suppose, then, that the visitor has gratified his sense of wonder in gazing at the larger and more striking forms, few in number, that rise up prominently before him, and seem to stare at him in return from their hollow sockets: he must next turn his attention to the cases that stand against the walls, and to the cabinets that stretch along the galleries in distant perspective. Let him survey that multitude of bones of every shape and size, and those countless legions of shells, and then try to realize to his mind what a profusion and variety of animal life are here represented. And yet he must remember that this is but a single collection. There are thousands of others, public and private, scattered over England, France, Germany, Italy, and beyond the Atlantic, on the continent of America, and even in Australia; all of which have been furnished from a few isolated spots,—scarcely more than specks on the surface of the Globe,—where the interior of the Earth's Crust has chanced to be laid open to the explorations of the Geologist.

Lastly, before he leaves this splendid gallery, let him take a passing glance at the Organic Remains of the vegetable world. There is no mistaking the forms here presented to his view. He will recognize at once the massive and lofty trunks of forest trees with their spreading branches; the tender foliage of the lesser plants; and, in particular, the graceful fern, which cannot fail to attract his eye by its unrivalled luxuriance. But if the forms are familiar, how strange is the substance, of this ancient vegetation! The forest tree has been turned into sandstone; many of the plants are of the hardest flint; and the rich green of the fern has given place to the jet black color of coal. Let him take a magnifying glass and scrutinize the internal structure of these mineralized remains ; for the more closely they are examined the more wonderful do they appear.

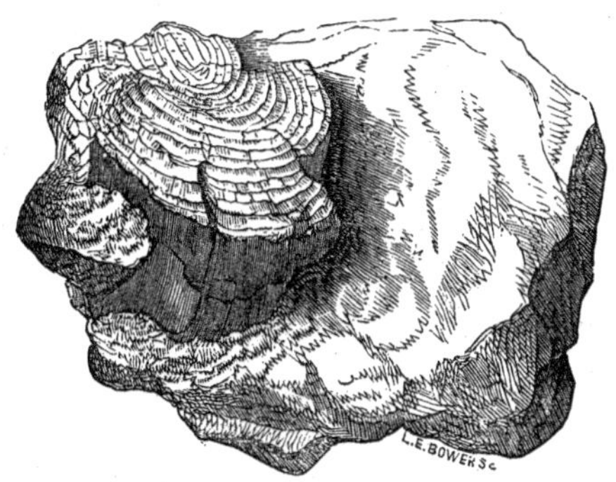

Fig. 13.—Fossil Wood, from the Carboniferous Limestone of Mayo, showing the rings of Annual Growth.

He can observe without difficulty their minute cells and fibres, the exact counterpart of those which may be seen in the plants that are now growing upon the earth ; he may detect the little seed-vessels on the under surface of the coaly fern ; nay, if he gets a polished transverse section of the sandstone tree, he may count the rings that mark its annual growth, and tell the age it attained in its primeval forest.

CHAPTER XI.

FOSSIL REMAINS—THE EXPLORATION.

From the museum to the quarry—Fossil fish in the limestone rocks of Monte Bolca—In the quarries of Aix—In the chalk of Sussex—The ichthyosaurus or fish-like lizard—Gigantic dimensions of this ancient monster—Its predatory habits—The plesiosaurus—The megatherium or great wild beast—History of its discovery—The mylodon—Profusion of fossil shells—Petrified trees erect in the limestone rock of Portland—Fossil plants of the coal measures—The sigillaria—The fern—The calamite—The lepidodendron—Coal mine of Treuil—Fossil remains afford undeniable evidence of former animal and vegetable life—Their existence cannot be accounted for by the plastic power of nature—Nor can it reasonably be ascribed to a special act of creation.

ROM the galleries of the Museum we must now descend into the subterranean recesses of the mine and the quarry. For it is not enough to be familiar with the appearance of Fossil Remains, as they are laid out for show by human hands: we must see them also as they lie embedded in the successive strata of the Earth's Crust, which are the shelves of Nature's cabinet. We shall begin with the celebrated quarries of Monte Bolca, in Northern Italy, not far from Verona. Here, in the hard limestone rock, fifty miles from the nearest sea, entire skeletons of many different species of fish are found

embedded in profuse abundance, and in a wonderful state of preservation. They lie parallel to the layers of the

Fig. 14.—Platax Papilio.
From the limestone of Monte Bolca.

rock; and, though flattened by pressure, still retain their scales, bones, fins, nay, even their muscular tissue, undisturbed and unharmed. Their color is a deep brown, which forms a remarkable contrast with the creamy hue of the limestone in which they are enveloped. The quarries

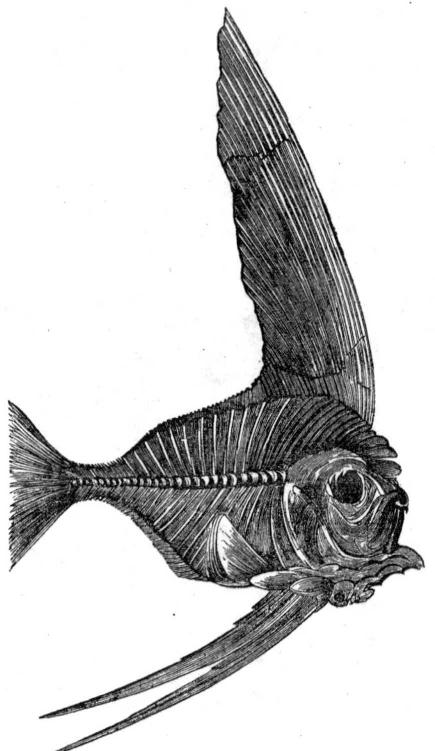

Fig. 15.—Semiophorus Velicans.
From the limestone of Monte Bolca.

have been worked only by students of Natural History for the sake of Organic remains, and are, therefore, of very limited extent; yet so abundant are these fossil treasures that upward of a hundred different species have been discovered, and thousands of specimens have been dispersed over the cabinets of Europe. So closely are they sometimes packed together that many individuals are contained in a single block.

From these facts Geologists have been led to conclude :— that the strata in question were deposited on the bed of an ancient sea in which these fishes swam; that the waters of the sea were suddenly rendered noxious, probably by the eruption of volcanic matter; that the fishes in consequence perished in large numbers, and were then almost immediately embedded in the calcareous deposits of which the strata are composed. These views receive no small confirmation from a very remarkable phenomenon to which we may be allowed, in passing, to call attention. In the year 1831 a volcanic island was suddenly thrown up in the Mediterranean between Sicily and the African coast; and the waters of the sea were at the same time observed to be charged with a red mud over a very wide area, while hundreds of dead fish were seen floating on the surface. Is it not pretty plain that when the mud subsided many of the fish were enveloped in the deposit, and thus preserved to future times? If so, then, we should have an exact modern parallel to the fossil fishes of Monte Bolca. But for the present it is our purpose rather to describe facts than to develop theories.*

Near the town of Aix, the ancient captial of Provence, in the south of France, is a group of strata, consisting chiefly of Conglomerate, Marl, Gypsum, and Limestone, which has earned for itself no small fame in the annals of Geology. Besides many curious relics of an extinct vegetation, these strata yield also an abundance of Fossil Insects, which emerge from the rocky bed in which they have slept for ages, with a surprising freshness and a life-like reality. But the quarrries of Aix, like those of Monte Bolca, are chiefly

* Buckland, Bridgewater Treatise, vol. i., p. 123; Mantell, Wonders of Geology, p. 269; Lyell, Elements of Geology, p. 687.

famous for their Fossil Fish. And in this case, too, as in the former, it would seem as if vast multitudes had suddenly perished together from some mysterious cause, and were then as suddenly entombed. They exhibit no mark of mechanical violence: and yet they are found, not unfrequently, crowded together as closely as they can fit, in every variety of position, on the same slab of limestone. A good example of such a block is represented in our woodcut.

Fig. 16.—Fossil Fish from Aix

The White Chalk Rock of Sussex has been rendered classical to the students of Geology by the skilful and laborious researches of the late Doctor Mantell. Previous to his time the Fish of the Chalk were known only by their teeth and bones, which abounded in every quarry. But he succeeded in bringing to light many whole skeletons, and disengaging them without injury from their chalky envelopment. In many cases these Fossil Fish appear to have suffered little from compression: the body still retains its rounded form; and even the most delicate scales and fins are as little disturbed or distorted as if the original had been surrounded by soft Plaster of Paris while floating in the water. For many years Doctor Mantell devoted himself, with indefatigable zeal, to the gathering of these interesting remains; and his magnificent collection now adorns the Galleries of the British Museum. In the annexed illustration is figured a specimen belonging to one of the most abundant species. It is closely allied to the common perch; and is popularly called Johnny Dory by the quarrymen of Sussex, but is entitled Beryx Lewesiensis by the learned.*

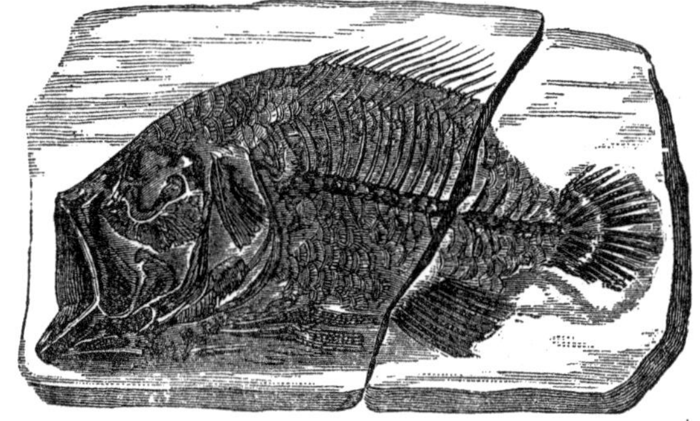

Fig. 17.—Beryx Lewesiensis, from the Chalk, near Lewes.

From Fossil Fish we now turn to Fossil Reptiles. Many of our readers have, perhaps, heard or read something about an important group of rocks known by the name of the Lias. This formation is well developed in England, and has received much attention from Geologists. It stretches in a belt of varying width from Whitby on the coast of Yorkshire to Lyme Regis on the coast of Dorsetshire; passing in its course through the counties of Leicester, Warwick, Gloucester, and Somerset. It is composed chiefly of Limestone, Marl, and Clay; and is celebrated for

* Mantell, Wonders of Geology, Lecture IV., Fossils of the British Museum, chapter V.; see, also, Medals of Creation, and Fossils of the South Downs, by the same Author.

8*

the number and size of its great Fossil Reptiles. Of these the most remarkable is the Ichthyosaurus or Fish-like Lizard.

This monster of the ancient seas combined, as its name denotes, the essential characters of a reptile with the form and habits of a fish. No such creature has been known to exist within historic times; nevertheless, all the various parts of its complicated structure have their analogies, more or less perfect, in the present creation. It had the head of a Lizard, the beak of a Porpoise, the teeth of a Crocodile, the back bone of a Fish, and the paddles of a Whale. In length it sometimes exceeded thirty feet; it had a short thick neck, an enormous stomach, a long and powerful tail. This last appendage, together with four great paddles or fins, constituted the chief organs of motion. But of all its parts the head was perhaps the most wonderful and characteristic. In the larger species the jaws were six feet long, and were armed with two rows of conical sharp-pointed teeth,—a hundred below, a hundred and ten above. The cavities in which the eyes were set measured often fourteen inches across, and the eyeballs themselves must have been larger than a man's head.

Now what we want particularly to impress upon our readers is, that the remains of this singular aquatic reptile abound throughout the whole extent of the Lias Formation in England. Far down below the surface of the earth they are found embedded in the marls, and clays, and limestones of Dorsetshire, and Gloucester, and Warwick, and Leicester, and Yorkshire. Sometimes whole skeletons are found entire, with scarcely a single bone removed from the place it occupied during life; but more frequently the scattered fragments are found lying about in a state of confused disorder; skulls, and jaw-bones, and teeth, and paddles, and the joints of the vertebral column and of the tail. The neighborhood of Lyme Regis is a perfect

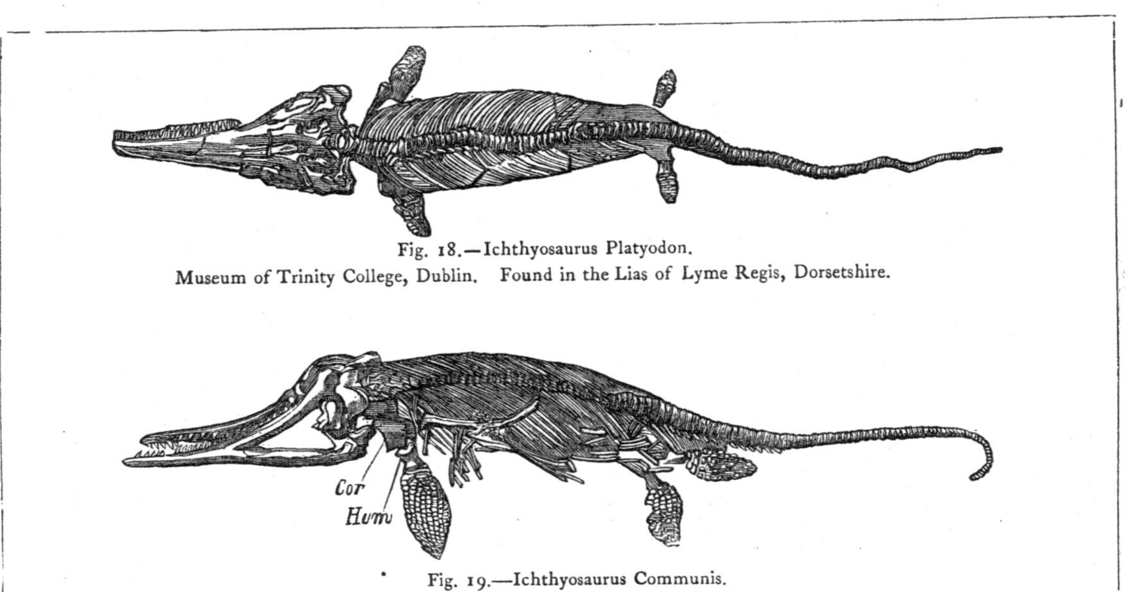

Fig. 18.—Ichthyosaurus Platyodon.
Museum of Trinity College, Dublin. Found in the Lias of Lyme Regis, Dorsetshire.

Fig. 19.—Ichthyosaurus Communis.
Museum of Trinity College, Dublin. Found in the Lias of Lyme Regis, Dorsetshire.

cabinet of these curious treasures. In some of the specimens there exhumed, a singular circumstance has been observed, which is deserving of special notice. We should naturally have expected, from the prodigious power of this animal, from the expansion of his jaws and the immense size of his stomach, that he preyed upon the other fish and reptiles that had the misfortune to inhabit the waters in which he lived. And so indeed it was. For here enclosed within his vast ribs, in the place that once was his stomach, are still preserved the remains of his half-digested food; and amidst the débris we can distinguish the bones and scales of his victims. Nay, in some of the more colossal specimens of this ancient monster, we can distinctly recognize the remains of his own smaller brethren; which, though less frequent than the bones of fishes, are still sufficiently numerous to prove that, when he wanted to appease his hunger, he did not even spare the less powerful members of his own species.*

It is with facts like these, which are revealed by the Crust of the Earth all over the world, that Geologists are called upon to deal. When they meet with skeletons and bones such as we have been describing, buried deep in the hard rock, hundreds of feet beneath the green grass, and the waving corn, they cannot help but ask the question: Where did these creatures come from? When did they live? And by what revolutions were they embedded here, and lifted up from beneath the waters of the deep?

In the same formation are found the remains of another ancient reptile, called the Plesiosaurus, that is to say, nearly allied to the Lizard. Of this extraordinary monster Cuvier observed that its structure was the most singular and anomalous that, up to his time, had been discovered

* Owen's Palæontology, pp. 200–9; Buckland, Bridgewater Treastise, vol. i., pp. 168–186; Mantell, Wonders of Geology, pp. 576–581; Lyell, Elements of Geology, pp. 420-425; Jukes, Manual of Geology, pp. 598–599.

amid the ruins of the ancient world. It is chiefly distinguished from the Ichthyosaurus, to which it has no small affinity, by the enormous length of its neck, which, in some species, resembles the body of a serpent. Dr. Buckland tells us that in the Plesiosaurus Dolichodeirus the neck is longer than the trunk ; the one being five times, the other only four times, as long as the head. Our illustration, for which we are indebted to the kindness of Doctor Haughton, represents a fine specimen of Plesiosaurus Cramptonii, which was found in the Lias Beds of Kettleness, near Whitby, in Yorkshire, and which is now a prominent object in the Museum of the Royal Dublin Society.

The habits and character of the Plesiosaurus have been thus sketched out by Mr. Conybeare :—"That it was aquatic is evident, from the form of its paddles ; that it was marine is almost equally so, from the remains with which it is universally associated ; that it may have occasionally visited the shore, the resemblance of its extremities to those of the turtle may lead us to conjecture. Its motion, however, must have been very awkward on land ; its long neck must have impeded its progress through the water ; presenting a striking contrast to the organization which so admirably fits the Ichthyosaurus to cut through the waves. May it not therefore be concluded (since, in addition to these circumstances, its respiration must have required frequent access of air), that it swam upon or near the surface ; arching back its long neck like the swan, and occasionally darting it down at the fish which happened to float within its reach. It may perhaps have lurked in shoal water along the coast concealed among the sea-weed, and raising its nostrils to a level with the surface from a considerable depth, may have found a secure retreat from the assaults of dangerous enemies ; while the length and flexibility of its neck may have compensated for the want of strength in its jaws, and its incapacity for swift motion through the water, by the sud-

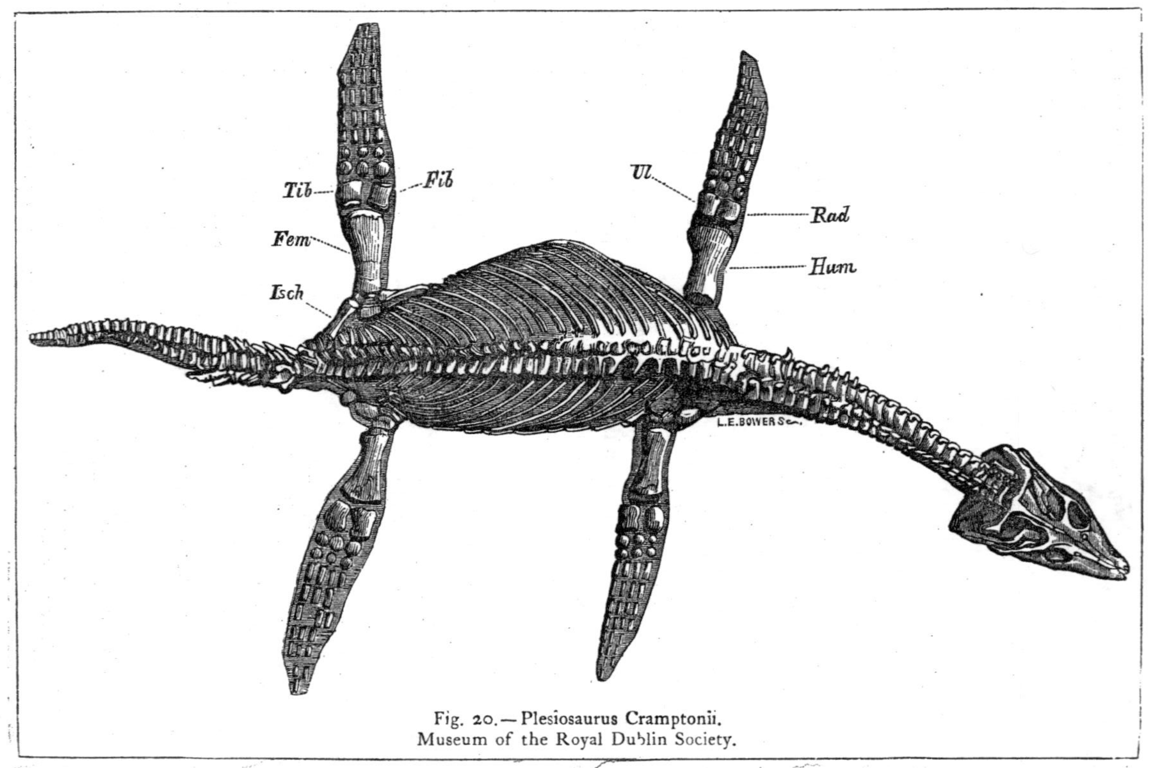

Fig. 20.—Plesiosaurus Cramptonii.
Museum of the Royal Dublin Society.

denness and agility of the attack which they enabled it to make on every animal fitted for its prey, which came within its reach."*

The Pampas of South America are not less famous in Geology for the remains of Gigantic quadrupeds, than the Lias of England for its colossal marine reptiles. These vast undulating plains, which present to the eye for nine hundred miles a waving sea of grass, consist chiefly of stratified beds of gravel and reddish mud; and it is in these beds that the remains of many unshapely but powerful terrestrial animals have been found embedded. So abundant are they, that it is said a line drawn in any direction through the country would cut through some skeleton or bones. Indeed, Mr. Darwin is of opinion that the whole area of the Pampas is one wide sepulchre of these extinct animals. It will be enough for our purpose to describe one in particular, which, from its prodigious bulk, has received the appropriate name of Megatherium, or the Great Wild Beast.

The Megatherium, like the Ichthyosaurus and the Plesiosaurus, had many affinities with the existing creation. In its head and shoulders it resembled the sloth which still browses on the green foliage of the trees in the dense forests of South America; while in its legs and feet it combined the characteristics of the Ant-Eater and the Armadillo. But it was eminently distinguished from these and all the other modern representatives of the family to which it belonged by its colossal proportions. It was often twelve feet long and eight feet high; its fore-feet were a yard in length and twelve inches in breadth, terminating in gigantic claws; its haunches were five feet wide, and its thigh bone was three times as big as that of the largest elephant. "His entire frame," as Dr. Buckland has admirably observed and carefully demonstrated, "was an apparatus of colossal mechan-

* Buckland's Bridgewater Treatise, vol. i., pp. 202–14; Owen's Palæontology, 223–232.

ism, adapted exactly to the work it had to do; strong and ponderous, in proportion as this work was heavy, and calculated to be the vehicle of life and enjoyment to a gigantic race of quadrupeds, which, though they have ceased to be counted among the living inhabitants of our planet, have, in their fossil bones, left behind them imperishable monuments of the consummate skill with which they were constructed,—each limb, and fragment of a limb, forming co-ordinate parts of a well adjusted and perfect whole; and through all their deviations from the form and proportions of the limbs of other quadrupeds, affording fresh proofs of the infinitely varied and inexhaustible contrivances of Creative Wisdom."

This Leviathan of the Pampas, as it has been justly called, became first known in Europe toward the close of the last century. In the year 1789 a skeleton was dug up, almost entire, about three miles southwest of Buenos Ayres, and was presented by the Marquis of Loreto to the Royal Museum at Madrid, where it still remains. Since that time other specimens, besides numerous fragments, have been discovered, chiefly through the zeal and energy of Sir Woodbine Parish; by the aid of which the form, structure, and consequently the habits of this clumsy and ponderous animal have been fully ascertained. The complete skeleton which forms so prominent an object of attraction in the British Museum, and which is represented in the woodcut on the adjoining page, is only a model; but it has been constructed with great care from the original bones, some of which are to be found in the wall-cases of the same room, and others in the Hunterian Museum of the Royal College of Surgeons."*

* Buckland, Bridgewater Treatise, vol. i., pp. 139–164; Owen's Palæontology, pp. 390–2; Mantell, Wonders of Geology, pp. 166–9; Fossils of the British Museum, pp. 465–480; The English Cyclopædia, Natural History Division, Article, Megatheridæ.

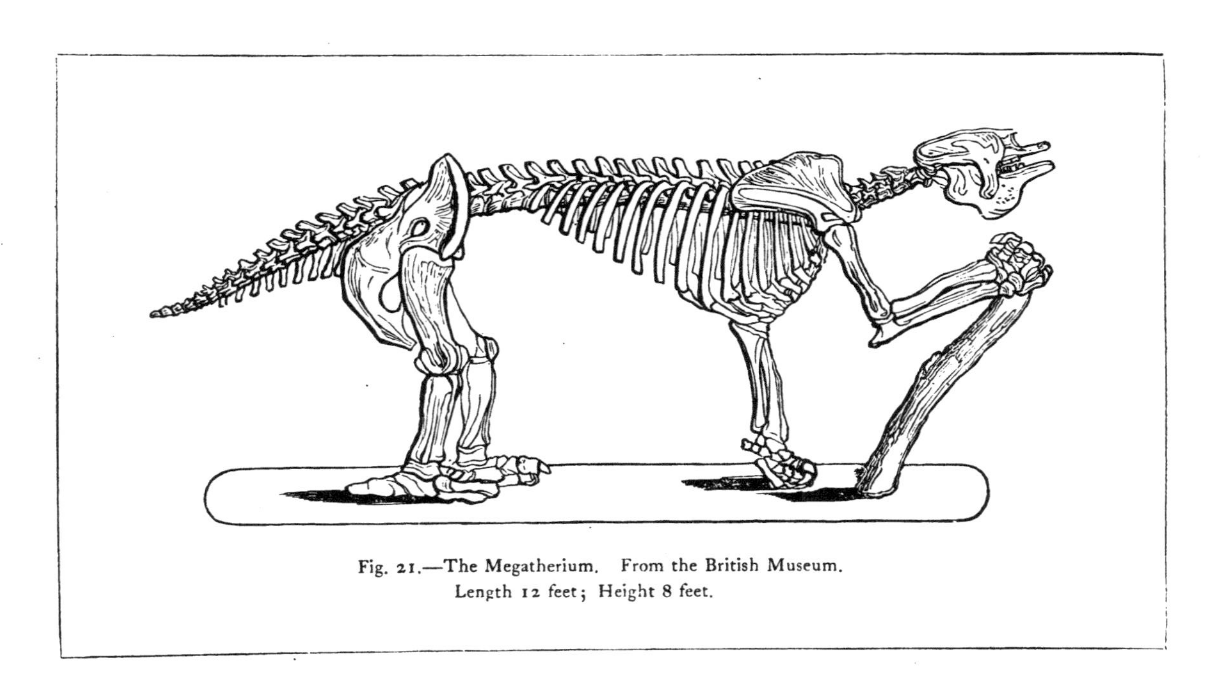

Fig. 21.—The Megatherium. From the British Museum.
Length 12 feet; Height 8 feet.

Closely allied to the Megatherium, but somewhat less colossal in its dimensions, is the Mylodon. Its remains are found associated with those of the Megatherium and other great animals of the same family, in the superficial gravels of South America. A splendid specimen, which

Fig. 22.—Mylodon Robustus, from Buenos Ayres.

measures eleven feet from the fore part of the skull to the end of the tail, was dug up, in the year 1841, a few miles north of Buenos Ayres. It is well figured in the adjoining woodcut, which we reproduce, by kind permission of the Author, from Dr. Haughton's admirable Manual of Geology.

Passing from the petrified fish, and the reptiles, and the

quadrupeds, that thus come forth, as it were, from their graves to bring us tidings of an extinct creation, we must next turn our attention for a moment to Fossil Shells. These relics of the ancient world, which are scattered with profuse abundance through all the strata of the Earth's Crust, may seem, indeed, of little value to the careless observer; but to the practised eye of science they are full of instruction. They have been aptly called the Medals of Creation; for, stamped upon their surface they bear the impress of the age to which they belong; and they constitute the largest, we may say, perhaps, the most valuable part of those unwritten records from which the Geologist seeks to gather the ancient history of our Globe.

As regards the prodigious abundance of Fossil Shells preserved in the Crust of the Earth, it is unnecessary for us here to speak. We have already seen that the great mass of many limestone formations is composed almost exclusively of such remains, broken up into minute fragments, and more or less altered by chemical agency; and besides, there are quarries within the reach of all, where they may collect at pleasure these interesting relics of the olden time. But there are one or two facts of peculiar significance connected with Fossil Shells, which it may be useful briefly to set down. In the first place, we would remind our readers that there is a marked and well-known difference between the shells of those animals that can live only in the sea, of those that inhabit rivers, and of those, finally, that frequent the brackish waters of estuaries. Now it has been made clear beyond all reasonable doubt, by the explorations of Geologists, that sea-shells abound in great numbers far away from the present line of coast, in the heart of vast continents. And they are found, not merely on the surface, but buried deep in the Crust of the Earth, and overlaid, in many cases, by numerous strata of solid rock, thousands of feet in thickness. It is also to be observed that they occur at all heights above the level of the ocean; having been discovered at an elevation of eight thousand feet in the Pyrenees, ten thousand in the Alps, thirteen thousand in the Andes, and above eighteen thousand in the Himalaya.* Such are the phenomena which are constantly forcing themselves on the attention of the Geologist, and which involve a number of problems that he cannot help attempting to investigate and explain. He is instinctively impelled to ask himself, how can the shells of marine animals have come to exist so far away from the sea? how have they been buried in the Crust of the Earth? how have they been lifted up to the highest pinnacles of lofty mountains?

Our subterranean exploration would be incomplete if it did not illustrate the Vegetable as well as the Animal Life of the ancient world. Let the reader then descend in fancy into the celebrated quarries of Portland on the south coast of England, and he will see the fossilized remains of a long past vegetation exhibited in a very striking manner. In one of these quarries a vertical section, extending from the surface downward to the depth of about thirty feet, presents the following succession of strata arranged in horizontal layers:—first, a light covering of vegetable soil, beneath which are thin beds of cream-colored limestone, forming a stratum of solid rock ten feet thick; then a bed of dark-brown loam, mixed with rounded fragments of stone, and varying in thickness from twelve to eighteen inches. This is known to the quarrymen by the name of Dirt-bed, and seems, in former ages, to have supported a luxuriant vegetation; for all around are scattered the petrified fragments of an ancient forest. The prostrate stems and shattered branches of great trees are met at every step; but what is most striking and peculiar is, that, in many cases, the petrified stumps are still standing erect, with their roots fixed

* Lyell, Elements of Geology, p. 4.

in the thin stratum of loam, and their trunks stretching upward into the hard limestone rock. Immediately below the Dirt-bed is another thick stratum of limestone, and below this again is a stratum of the famous Portland stone,

Fig. 23.—Section of a Quarry in the Island of Portland. Total thickness about thirty feet.

so highly prized for building purposes. As the quarries of Portland are worked chiefly for the sake of this building stone, little attention is paid to the Dirt-bed and its contents, which are commonly thrown aside by the quarrymen as rubbish.

The scene of this petrified forest is thus described by Doctor Mantell :—" On one of my visits to the island the surface of a large area of the Dirt-bed was cleared preparatory to its removal, and the appearance presented was most striking. The floor of the quarry was literally strewn with fossil wood, and before me was a petrified forest, the trees and plants, like the inhabitants of the city in Arabian story, being converted into stone, yet still remaining in the places which they occupied when alive! Some of the trunks were surrounded by a conical mound of calcareous earth, which had, evidently, when in the state of mud, accumulated round the roots. The upright trunks were generally a few feet apart, and but three or four feet high; their summits were broken and splintered, as if they had been snapped or wrenched off by a hurricane at a short distance from the ground. Some were two feet in diameter, and the united fragments of one of the prostrate trunks indicated a total length of from thirty to forty feet; in many specimens portions of the branches remained attached to the stem."*

The Coal Measures of Europe and America offer to the student of Geology a boundless field for the investigation of Fossil Plants and Trees. We have already had occasion to notice the Sigillaria. This ancient tree, remarkable for its beautiful sculptured stem, has no exact representative in the vegetable kingdom of the present day. But it abounds everywhere in the Coal Measures; and there seems little doubt that several great seams of Coal are composed almost entirely of its carbonized remains. Indeed the ancient soil, which commonly constitutes the floor on which the bed of Coal reposes, is often as thickly crowded with the branching roots of the Sigillaria, as the soil of a dense forest with the roots of the trees by which it is covered. The stem itself, when converted into Coal, generally assumes the form of long narrow slabs; having been flattened by pressure during the process of mineralization. Sometimes however, it is found uncompressed and erect. In this case the interior of the trunk is usually observed to have been filled up with sand or clay: and thus the forest tree, still retaining its external shape and character, is transformed

* Wonders of Geology, p. 400.

into a cylindrical shell of carbonized bark without, and a solid cylinder of sandstone or shale within. An interesting example is exhibited in our illustration, Figure 11.

Every Coal mine, too, is adorned with the imprint of the graceful Fern, which constitutes one of the most attractive features in the Flora of the ancient world. Not unfre-

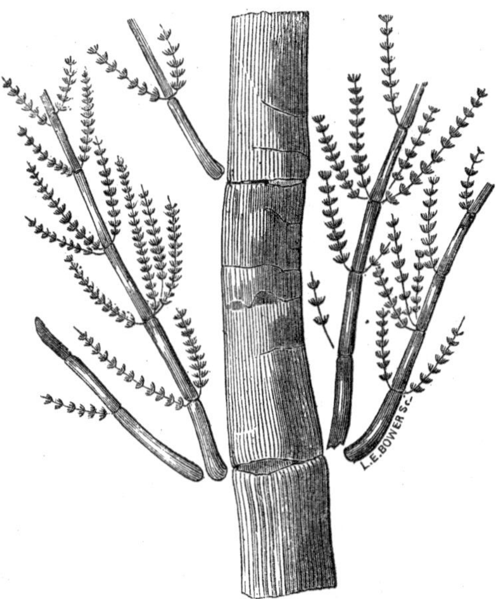

Fig. 24.—Calamites Nodosus
From the Coal Measures of Newcastle.

quently it assumes a tree-like character, as it often does even now in tropical countries; and then, indeed, it is an object of striking beauty, reaching to a height of forty or fifty feet, and expanding at the summit into an elegant canopy of foliage.

The Calamite is another plant in which the Coal abounds. Its true botanical character is not yet clearly ascertained; but it bears a general resemblance, except for its gigantic dimensions, to the common Horse-tail of our swamps and marshy grounds. It is a reed-like, jointed stem, sometimes thirty feet in length, hollow within, and curiously jointed without.

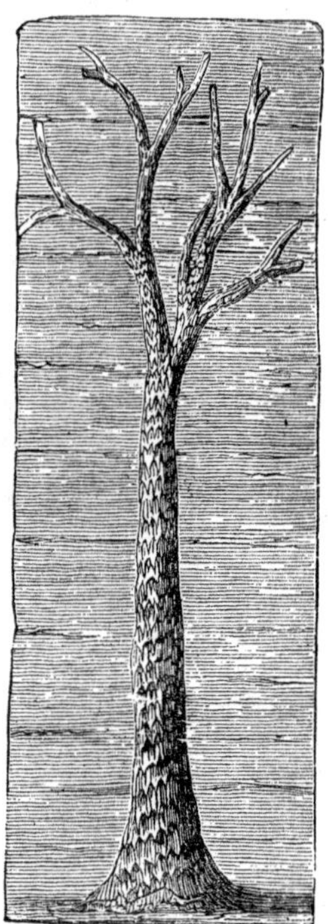

Fig. 25.—Lepidodendron Sternbergii; a Fossil Tree, 39 feet high. From a Coal Mine near Newcastle.

Scarcely less conspicuous than the Sigillaria, the Fern, and the Calamite, is the Lepidodendron or Scaly Tree, one of the most curious and interesting among the plants of the Coal-bearing period. Like the Sigillaria and the Calamite, it has been, and still is, a puzzle to the student of Botany. But it needs not the eye of science to see that it is unmistakably a stately forest tree, shut up in the Crust of the Earth, encased in a solid framework of indurated Shale, or Sandstone, or Coal, as the case may be, and overlaid with massive strata of rock hundreds of feet in thickness.

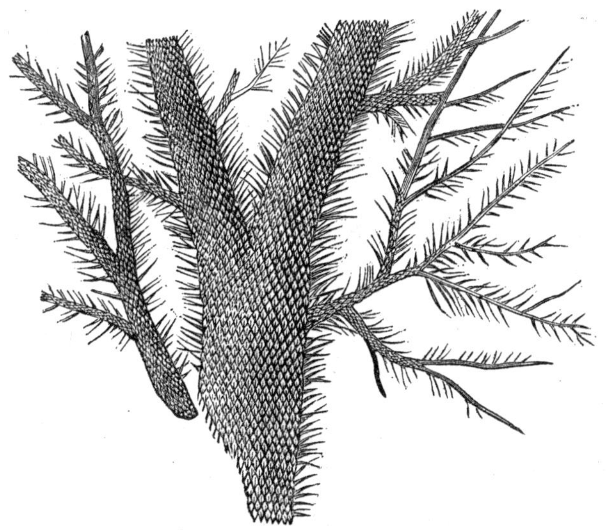

Fig. 26 Lepidodendron Elegans.
Portion of Stem and branches; Coal Mine, Newcastle.

Such a specimen as that represented in our woodcut was laid bare some years ago in Yarrow Colliery, near Newcastle.

In the same neighborhood was found a portion of the stem and branches of another variety, Lepidodendron Elegans, which will enable the reader to form a more complete idea of the appearance presented by this ancient tree as it stood in its primeval forest.

An unusually favorable illustration of our present subject may be seen at the colliery of Treuil, in France, not far from the city of Lyons. The beds of Coal are overlaid by a kind of slaty sandstone, ten feet thick; and this sandstone is traversed by the vertical stems of enormous petrified plants, chiefly Calamites. Here, then, to all appearance, we have an ancient forest enveloped in sandstone. We must suppose that the forest was submerged while the trees were still erect; that in this condition it received the sedimentary deposits carried down by the current of some great

Fig. 27.—Section of a Coal sandstone at Treuil, near Lyons. Showing the erect position of Fossil Trees. (Alex. Brongniart.)

river; and finally, that these deposits were, in the course of ages, compacted into sandstone by a process already explained. It would seem that after the sandstone had been partially, at least, consolidated, it was subjected to a sliding movement here and there, by which the continuity of the stems was broken; the upper part being pushed on one side, as shown in our Figure.

It is time we should bring to a close our survey, meagre and imperfect as it is, of Fossil Remains. Those who desire to pursue the inquiry for themselves will easily find an opportunity of doing so. There are few, we should suppose, who may not, occasionally, have access to one or other of those splendid Museums of Geology, which have been set up in all the great towns of Europe. And the still more extensive cabinets of Nature's Museum, spread out beneath our feet, are within the reach of all.

But even the scanty facts which have been set forth faithfully, we trust, though perhaps feebly, in these pages, are sufficient to satisfy all reasonable minds that the bones, the skeletons, the trunks and branches of trees, which have been exhumed from the Stratified Rocks are really the remains of Organic Life that once flourished on the earth, or in the waters of the ancient seas. Obvious, however, as this fact must appear to all who have fully realized the character and appearance of Fossil Remains, it has been often vigorously assailed and vehemenlty denounced. In the early days of Geology phenomena of this kind were ascribed, not uncommonly, to the "plastic power of Nature," or to the influence of the stars. Such notions, however, meet with little support among modern writers. They were nothing more than wild fancies, without any foundation either in the evidence of facts or in the analogy of Nature. The "plastic power of Nature" was a phrase that sounded well, perhaps, in the ears of unreflecting people; but no one ever undertook to show that Nature really possesses that "plastic power" which was so readily imputed to her. No one ever undertook to show that it is the way of Nature to make the stems, and branches, and leaves of trees, without the previous process of vegetation; or to make bones and skeletons which have never been invested with the ordinary appendages of flesh and blood. Yet surely this is a theory that requires proof; for all our experience of the laws of Nature points directly to the opposite conclusion. And as for the influence of the stars, we may be content to adopt the language of the celebrated painter Leonardo da Vinci :—"They tell us that these shells were formed in the hills by the influence of the stars; but I ask where in the hills are the stars now forming shells of distinct ages and species? and how can the stars explain the origin of gravel occurring at different heights and composed of pebbles rounded as if by the action of running water? or in what manner can such a cause account for the petrifaction in the same places of various leaves, sea-weeds, and marine crabs?"*

In modern times the form of objection has been somewhat changed. We are told by some writers that, when we seek to explain the existence of Fossil Remains by the action of natural laws, we seem to forget the Omnipotence of God. They urge upon us, with much solemnity, that He could have made bones, and shells, and skeletons, and petrified wood, though there had been no living animal to which these bones belonged, and no living tree that had been changed into stone. And if He made them, might He not disperse them up and down through His creation, on the lofty mountains, in the hidden valleys, and in the profound depths of the sea? and buried them in limestone rocks and in the soft clay? and arranged them in groups, or scattered them in wild confusion as He best pleased?

To this line of argument we must be content to reply, that we have no wish to limit the power of God. But we have learned from our daily experience that in the physical world He is pleased to employ the agency of secondary causes; and when we know that for many ages a certain effect has been uniformly produced by a certain cause, and not otherwise, then if we again see the effect, we infer the cause. When a traveller in the untrodden wilds of Western America, comes upon a forest of great trees, or a herd of unknown animals, surely he never thinks of supposing

* See Lyell, Principles of Geology, vol. i., p. 31, who refers to Da Vinci's MSS, now in the Library of the Institute of France.

that the wild beasts and the forest trees came directly from the hand of the Creator, in that state of maturity in which he beholds them. And why? for it might be argued that the power of God is unbounded, and he might have created them as they now are if He had so pleased. Is it not that the traveller is impelled, by an instinct of his nature, to interpret the works of God which he now sees for the first time, according to the analogy of those with which he has been long familiar? Now this is just the principle for which we are contending. According to all our experience of the works of God in the physical world, the living body comes first, and the skeleton afterward; the living tree comes first, and afterward the prostrate trunk and the splintered branches. Therefore when we meet with a skeleton, we conclude that it was once a living body; and when we find the petrified stems, and branches, and leaves of trees, we have no doubt that they are the remains of an ancient vegetation.

But, in truth, if any one, with all the facts of the case fully before his mind, were deliberately to adopt this theory, that Fossils, as we find them now, were created by God in the Crust of the Earth, we candidly confess we have no argument that we should think likely to shake his conviction; just as we should be utterly at a loss if he were to say that the Pyramids of Egypt, or the colossal sculptures of Nineveh, or the ruins of Baalbec, were created by God from the beginning. The evidence of human workmanship is certainly not more clear in the one case than is the evidence of animal and vegetable life in the other. We believe, however, that no such persons are to be found; that theories of this kind have their origin, not so much in false reasoning, as in imperfect knowledge of facts; and we have, therefore, judged it most expedient not to spend our time in a discussion of philosophical axioms, but to set forth the facts, and leave them to speak for themselves.

CHAPTER XII.

GEOLOGICAL CHRONOLOGY—PRINCIPLES OF THE SYSTEM EXPLAINED AND DEVELOPED.

Significance of fossil remains—Science of Palæontology—Classification of existing animal life—Fossil remains are found to fit in with this classification—Succession of organic life—Time in Geology not measured by years and centuries—Successive periods marked by successive forms of life—The Geologist aims at arranging these periods in chronological order—Position of the various groups of strata not sufficient for this purpose—It is accomplished chiefly through the aid of fossil remains—Mode of proceeding practically explained—Chronological table.

THE existence of Fossil Remains is, then, a fact. Go where you will through the civilized world, and every chief town has its Museum, into which they have been gathered by the zeal and industry of man; descend where you can into the Crust of the Earth,—the quarry, the mine, the railway cutting,—and there, notwithstanding the plunder which has been going on for two centuries or more, you will find that the inexhaustible cabinets of Nature are still teeming with these remains of ancient life.

When we are brought, for the first time, face to face with these countless relics of a former world, we are impressed with a sense of wonder and bewilderment. That the skeletons before us, though now dry and withered, were once animated with the breath of life; that the trees now lying shattered and prostrate, and shorn of their branches, once flourished on the earth, we cannot for a moment hesitate to believe. But beyond this one fact, all is darkness and mystery. These gaunt skeletons, these uncouth monsters, these petrified forests, are silent, lifeless, as the rocks within whose stony bosoms they have lain so long entombed. Had they speech and memory, they could tell us much, no doubt, of that ancient world in which they bore a part, of its continents, and seas, and rivers, and mountains; of the various tribes of animals and plants by which it was peopled; of their habits and domestic economy; how they lived, how they died, and how they were buried in those graves from which, after the lapse of we know not how many ages, they now come forth into the light of day. As it is, however, we can but gaze and wonder. We have nothing here but the relics of death and destruction: there is no feeling, no memory, no voice, in these dry bones; no living tenant in these hollow skulls, to recount to us the history of former times.

So thinks and reasons the ordinary observer. But far different is the language of the Geologist. These dry and withered bones, he tells us, *are* gifted with memory and speech; and, though the language they speak may seem at first unfamiliar and obscure, it is not, on that account, beyond our comprehension. Like the birds, reptiles, fish, and other symbols, inscribed on the obelisks of ancient Egypt, these bones and shells stored up in the Crust of the Earth, have a hidden meaning which it is the business of Science to search out and explain. They are Nature's hieroglyphics, which she has impressed upon her works to carry down to remote ages the memory of the revolutions through which our Globe has passed; and when we come to understand them aright, they do unfold to us the story of that ancient world to which they belonged.

The interpretation of Fossil Remains is, then, an important department of Geology. Of late years it has been admitted to the rank of a special science, under the name of Palæontology, which means, as the word denotes—παλαιῶν ὄντων λόγος—the science which is concerned about the organic remains of ancient life. The honor of having been the first to place this science on a solid basis, in fact we may say the honor of having brought it into existence, is justly accorded to the distinguished Cuvier, whose name shed a lustre upon France during the early years of the present century. It is therefore still in its infancy; but it has already rewarded the zeal of its students by many wonderful and unexpected revelations. We purpose in the first place to examine the principles on which it is founded, and then to take a rapid glance at the conclusions to which it has led.

At the outset it is worthy of notice that the very existence of Fossil Remains, buried deep in the Crust of the Earth, forcibly confirms the Geological theory of Stratified Rocks. These rocks, as the reader will remember, are said to have been slowly spread out, one above another, during the lapse of many ages, by the operation of natural causes; and we have seen how this doctrine is supported by arguments founded on an examination of the rocks themselves,—of the materials that compose them, and of the way in which these materials are piled together. Now let us observe how clearly the testimony of Fossil Remains seems to point in the same direction.

First, the bones and shells which we now find in such profusion, far down beneath the superficial covering of the Earth, must have belonged to animals which, when living, flourished on what was then the surface. Yet now they are buried in the bosom of the hard rock, and covered over with beds of solid limestone, and sandstone, and conglomerate, hundreds and thousands of feet in thickness. How can we explain this fact, unless we suppose that these animals, when they perished, were embedded in some soft materials, which afterward became consolidated, and above which, in the course of ages, more and more matter was deposited, until at length that lofty pile of strata was produced, beneath which the remains are now found buried?

Again, it is part of our theory that the formation of Stratified Rocks took place, for the most part, under water. The Organic Remains, therefore, which we should naturally expect to find preserved in the strata of the earth, would be those of aquatic animals; or, if the remains of land animals were to be looked for, it should be of those chiefly which live near the banks of rivers and estuaries, and which, after death, might have been carried down by the current and buried in the silt and mud with which almost all rivers are charged at certain seasons of the year. We know as a fact that such animals are buried at the present day in the Deltas of the Ganges and the Mississippi; and it would be reasonable to suppose that the same should have occurred in former ages. Now here again the evidence of Fossil Remains exactly fits in with our theory. For the vast bulk of them are manifestly the remains of animals that lived in water: and the terrestrial animals, comparatively few, whose bones are preserved in the Crust of the Earth, are such as frequent the banks of great rivers or the marshy swamps of estuaries.

Thus much we may learn even from a cursory glance at Fossil Remains. But these curious monuments of ancient times have a deeper meaning, which cannot be unfolded without a more minute and laborious investigation. Our readers are aware that all the animals at present existing on the face of the Earth have been scientifically grouped together, according to certain well-marked characteristics, into various Kingdoms, Classes, Genera, and Species. Thus, for example, the horse and the dog are two different Species, belonging to the same Class of Mammalia ; the eagle and the sparrow are two different Species of the same

Class called Birds. Then again the Class of Mammalia and the Class of Birds both belong to the one common Kingdom of Vertebrata ; because, though different in many other respects, they agree in this, that all the members of both Classes have a vertebral or spinal column, to which the other parts of the internal skeleton are attached.

Now when Cuvier began to examine closely the Organic Remains of former times, to which his attention was called by the bones dug up in the gypsum quarries of Montmartre, near Paris, about the close of the last century, he brought with him to the task a very large acquaintance with the various forms of life that, in the present age, prevail throughout the world. And he was greatly struck with the marked difference between those living animals with which he had been long familiar, and those with which he now became acquainted for the first time. The more he extended his researches, the more manifest did this difference appear ; until at last it became quite clear that the great bulk of the animals whose remains are preserved in the Crust of the Earth, have no representatives now living on its surface. Nevertheless, he observed that, though the Species no longer exists, it often happens that we have still other Species of the same Genus ; or if the Genus, too, be extinct, we have other Genera of the same Class. Here, then, is the first great truth at which Cuvier arrived, and which has been since confirmed by extensive observations :—that the animals which formerly dwelt on this Earth of ours, were, for the most part, widely different from those by which it is now inhabited : and yet there is a well-defined likeness between them ; that both have been created on a plan so strictly uniform, that the one and the other naturally find their place in the same system of classification.

As the science of Palæontology progressed, and new facts were day by day accumulated, another truth, not less important, was gradually but certainly developed. In the distribution of Fossil Remains through the various strata of the Earth, there is a certain order observed, a certain regular law of succession, which cannot have been the mere result of chance, and which it is the business of science to unravel and explain. The facts are these. If we follow a particular set of strata *in a horizontal direction*, we find that the same fossils continue to prevail over hundreds of square miles, nay, often over a space as large as Europe, though beyond certain limits this uniformity of Fossil Remains will gradually be observed to disappear. But when we penetrate *in a vertical direction* through the strata, the forms of animal and vegetable life that we meet with are constantly changing. After a few hundred yards at the most, we find ourselves in the midst of a group of fossils, altogether different from those which we have passed in the beds above: and so on, as we proceed downward, *each particular set of strata is found to have an assemblage of fossils peculiar to itself.**

There can be no reasonable doubt as to the truth of these facts. They have been established and confirmed by the positive testimony of a whole host of Geologists, whose researches have extended to all parts of the globe. And we have besides a kind of negative evidence on the subject which is scarcely less convincing than the positive. Nothing is more easy than to refute a universal proposition if it is false. If it is not a fact that each group of strata, as we proceed downward, exhibits a collection of Fossils peculiar to itself, the assertion may be at once disproved by pointing out two or three different groups with the same Fossils. There are thousands of practical Geologists at work all over the world, eager for fame; and any one of them would make his name illustrious if he could overturn a theory so

* See Lyell, Elements of Geology, pp. 94-96; Principles of Geology, p. 116; Jukes, Manual of Geology, pp. 410, 411.

generally received. Now, when a statement of facts can be easily disproved if untrue; and when, at the same time, there is a large number of men whose interest it would be to disprove the statement if possible; and when it is nevertheless *not* disproved; this circumstance, we contend, is a convincing argument that the alleged facts *are* true. And such precisely is the case before us. We therefore think it would be unreasonable not to accept the facts.

Let us next examine what is their significance. Each group of strata, be it remembered, represents to us the animal life that flourished on the Earth during the period in which that particular group was in progress of formation. It is, as it were, a cabinet in which are preserved for our instruction certain relics or memorials of that age in the world's history. Of course it is not a perfect collection; but only a collection of those remains that chanced to escape destruction, and by some natural embalming process to be saved from dissolution. When we learn, then, that there is a marked uniformity in the assemblage of Fossils that are spread over a large horizontal area, in any group of strata, we conclude that, when that group was in course of formation, there was a certain uniformity in the animal life that extended over the corresponding area of the globe; just as, at the present day, the same species of animals are found to flourish over a great part of Europe, or America. And if this uniformity of Fossil Remains does not extend horizontally to an indefinite distance, this is precisely what we should have expected from the analogy of the existing creation: for, when we examine the present distribution of animal life over the earth, we find a marked diversity to exist between countries that are removed from one another; as, for instance, between Europe and Australia.

In the next place, we are told that, as we proceed *downward* into the Crust of the Earth, each successive group of strata has an assemblage of Fossils clearly distinct in character from those of the group above and of the group below. The conclusion to which this fact points is obvious enough. If, in the former case, we inferred that the animal life of any one period, considered in itself, was the same over extensive areas, in this case we must infer that the animal life of each successive period was *peculiar to that particular age;* being altogether distinct in its character from the animal life of the period that went before and of the period that followed. It would appear, therefore, as Sir Charles Lyell puts it, "that from the remotest period there has been ever a coming in of new organic forms, and an extinction of those which pre-existed on the earth; some species having endured for a longer, others for a shorter time; while none have ever reappeared after once dying out." *

Now, from these principles, Geologists have been gradually led to build up a system of Geological Chronology; in other words, to determine the order of time in which the numerous groups of strata that make up the Crust of the Earth have been formed, and thus to fix the age of each group in reference to the rest. This Chronology is not reckoned by the common measures of time which are used in history, but rather by the successive periods during which each group of rocks was in its turn slowly deposited on the existing surface of the globe. For example, the Coal-measures that so abound in the North of England are very much older than the bluish clay of which London is built. But if we ask what is the difference between the age of the one and of the other, the answer is given not in days and years and centuries, but in the number of different Formations that intervened between the two. We are told that the Coal-measures belong to the Carboniferous Formation; that this Formation was fol-

* Elements of Geology, p. 95.

lowed by the Permian, and that again in succession by the Triassic, the Jurassic, and the Cretaceous; and that, upon this last was spread out the Eocene, to which the London clay belongs. Indeed, as regards the precise length of any given period, Geologists can offer nothing but the wildest conjectures. Some form their estimates in thousands of years; others in millions. And the wisest amongst them fairly confess they have no sufficient data to make an accurate computation. Nevertheless, they are all agreed in this, that the ages of which the memory is preserved in history, that is to say, the last six thousand years, are but a small part of one Geological period. Compared to the voluminous chronicles laid up in the Crust of the Earth, the records inscribed by human hands constitute but an insignificant fraction of the world's history. Our readers will be glad to learn something of the way in which this startling system of Geological Chronology is constructed and developed.

At first sight, perhaps, it might be imagined that the order of time in which the various strata were deposited, can be easily learned from the relative position in which they lie. Since each stratum, when first produced, was spread out on the existing surface of the globe, it is clear that the one which lies uppermost in the series must be the newest, then that which lies next below, and so on till we reach the lowest of the pile, which must be the oldest of all. Nothing could be more satisfactory than this reasoning, if each stratum was spread out over the whole Earth, and if, after having been once deposited, it was never afterward removed. We might then regard each stratum as a volume in the Natural History of the Globe, which, when it was finished, was laid down upon that which contained the chronicles of the preceding age; and thus the position of every stratum would be in itself a sufficient evidence of the age to which it belonged.

But such is not the case. Nowhere does the Crust of

the Earth exhibit a complete series of the Stratified Rocks laid out one above another. In any given section we can find but a few only of the long series of groups that are familiar to Geologists. And if we follow them on, in a horizontal direction, we shall invariably find that some of the strata will *thin out* and disappear, while new strata will gradually be developed between two groups that were before in immediate contact. Let it be observed, in passing, that this fact fits in most perfectly with the theory we have been all along defending. The Stratified Rocks were deposited under water; therefore, the strata of any given period were not *spread out over the whole Globe*, but at most over those parts only which, for the time, were submerged. With the next period came a change in the boundaries of land and water; and the formation of strata ceased in some localities and began in others: and so on from epoch to epoch. Thus the areas over which the process has been going on, have been, in every age, of limited extent, and have been ever shifting from place to place over the surface of the earth. Moreover, there is the opposite process of Denudation. Many of the strata deposited in the depths of the ocean must have been afterward swept away by the breakers, as they slowly emerged from the waters; or at a later time, reduced to their original elements, and carried back to the sea, by the action of rivers, rain, and frost. It should seem, therefore, as well from the *fact*, which is obvious to any one who will examine it, as from our *theory*, which harmonizes so completely with the fact, that the strata which we meet with in any given section of the Earth's Crust present to us but a very broken and imperfect series of monuments. They are, as it were, but odd volumes of a long series, and though they lie in juxtaposition, they may belong, nevertheless, to Geological epochs widely removed from each other.

Hence, in order to construct a complete system of Geological Chronology it is necessary to collect together these odd volumes, as they may be called, of the Great Geological Calendar, and to assign to each one its proper place in the series. This difficult and complicated task is accomplished chiefly by the aid of Fossil Remains. We have already shown that the Fossil Remains which are found embedded in each group of strata, represent the organic life of the period during which that group of strata was in progress of formation. Moreover, we have seen that each period was marked by the existence of an animal and vegetable creation peculiar to itself. If, therefore, we find that the Fossils of two different districts exhibit the same general character, we may conclude that the beds in which they are preserved were deposited about the same age, and consequently belong to the same Geological Period. Whereas, on the other hand, if, within certain limits, we discover two groups of strata, each of which has a collection of Fossils totally different from the other, it is a proof that these two groups were *not* deposited in the same age, and must, consequently, be referred to different Epochs of the Geological Calendar. Let us now see in what manner the practical Geologist proceeds to apply these general principles.

He takes first some one country, say England, and in that country he selects some one particular district to begin with. Here he examines a number of different sections, and makes himself familiar with all the strata of the neighborhood, and with the order in which they lie. Let us suppose that he finds three different groups spread out one above another, and let us call these groups A, B, and C; A being the lowest, B immediately above A, and C above B. The chronological order of these strata will be, therefore, A, B, C. He will study next the Fossil Remains which he finds embedded in each group. For convenience we may designate the Fossils of A by the letter a, those of

B by b, and those of C by c. Now, according to the principles above explained, these three collections of Fossils will be specifically distinct from one another, each collection being characteristic of one particular set of strata. Our Geologist next goes into a neighboring district, and there examines a number of sections as before. Let us suppose that he encounters again the groups A and B. He may, perhaps, have been able to trace the beds from one district to the other, by observations made upon his line of route: or it may be that the nature of the country has rendered such observations impossible; or the observations may have been so imperfect that from *them* he could arrive at no certain conclusion regarding the identity of the strata. But, at all events, if the new district yield an abundant supply of Fossils, he cannot long be at a loss. He will recognize the group A by the Fossils a, and the group B by the Fossils b. An important fact, however, soon attracts his attention. Group C has entirely disappeared, and is not to be found in this district; while between A and B there is a new group of rocks that he has not seen before, with a collection of Fossils different from a, b, and c. We will call this new group X, and its Fossils x. It is clear that the formation of X must have intervened between the formation of A and B; and the chronological order now stands A, X, B, C. In like manner another district may disclose a fourth group of strata, say Y, intervening between B and C. The chronological order will then stand A, X, B, Y, C. And thus the Geologist pursues his explorations until he has gone through the whole country, and arranged the principal groups of strata according to the order of time in which they were deposited.

In this way the whole of England has been minutely explored during the last half century. The task was first undertaken by William Smith, who is justly called the Father of English Geology. After multiplied researches, extending over a space of many years, during which he travelled the whole country on foot, this eminent man published in 1815 his Geological Map of England and Wales with part of Scotland ; a work which is described by Sir Charles Lyell as "a lasting monument of original talent and extraordinary perseverance." Hundreds followed in the same course, exploring every day new districts, and, by the new facts which they brought to light, supplying what was wanting in the work of Smith, correcting what was faulty, and confirming what was true ; until at length, in our day, it may be said that the Stratified Rocks of England are almost as well known and as completely mapped out as are its counties and its towns, its rivers, lakes, and mountains.

Meanwhile, Geologists were not idle in other parts of the world. Germany, France, Italy, even many districts of America and Australia, have been diligently explored according to the same principles as England. And by a comparison of the observations made, the Chronological order of strata over a considerable part of the Earth, but more particularly of Europe, has been now pretty fairly ascertained. This order we have attempted to set forth in an intelligible and sensible form by means of the table here annexed.

In the Woodcut are represented the strata hitherto examined by Geologists, laid out one above another, according to the order of time in which they are supposed to have been produced. The whole series is divided into a number of Formations, the names of which are given in the first column, together with an approximate estimate of their thickness, in feet. These Formations are distinguished from each other in the drawing by a difference of shading. Each of them, according to Geological theory, is believed to have come into existence by the accumulation of solid matter at the bottom of the sea ; and the Period of

TABLE OF STRATIFIED ROCKS,

CHRONOLOGICALLY ARRANGED.

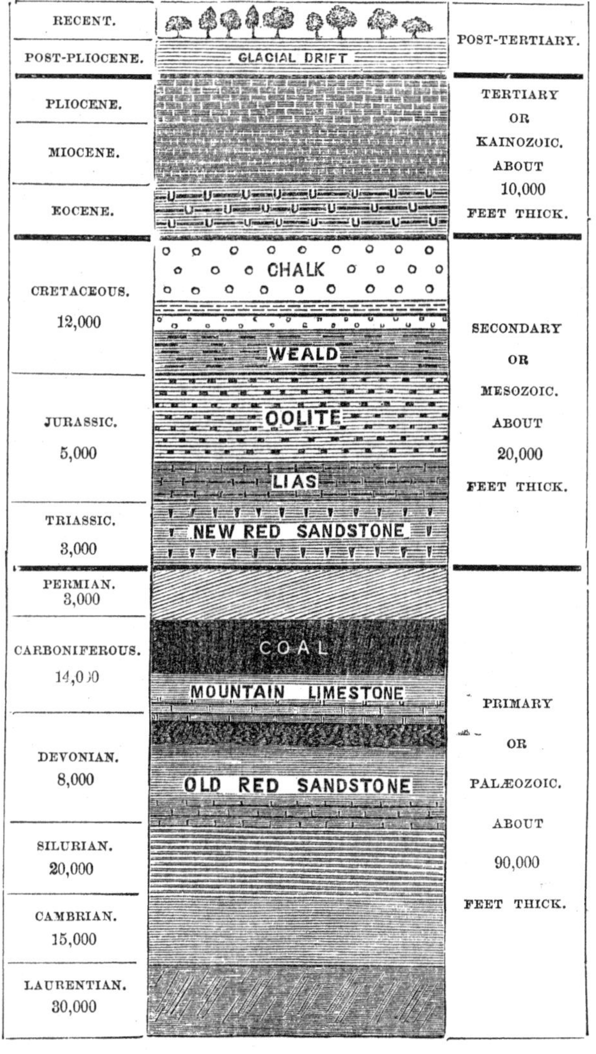

time occupied in its production is usually designated by the same name as the Formation itself. Thus we read of the Carboniferous Formation and the Carboniferous Period: by the former phrase is meant certain groups of strata contemporaneously deposited over various parts of the Earth's surface; and by the latter, the Period of time during which these groups of strata were spread out. In like manner, when we hear of the Carboniferous Fauna and Flora, we are to understand the animal and vegetable life that flourished during the Carboniferous Period. And again, when Geologists talk of the Cretaceous sea, and tell us that it rolled over a great part of what is now called Europe, they mean to speak of that sea on the bottom of which the Cretaceous rocks were deposited.

Most of the Formations comprise various groups of strata; and these groups are made up of different varieties of rocks, which are again divided into layers or beds of varying thickness. Even in these beds themselves we can often distinguish an indefinite number of laminæ or plates, scarcely thicker than a sheet of paper, which correspond to the periodical depositions of matter by which the rock was originally formed. These numerous subdivisions may be conveniently illustrated from the Carboniferous Formation. It is divided into two leading groups of strata; the Mountain Limestone below, the Coal Measures above. The upper group is the larger as well as the more important. It attains a maximum thickness in South Wales of 12,000 feet; and consists of numerous strata of Sandstone and Shale, with thin seams of Coal occasionally interposed. In one remarkable instance a hundred distinct layers of Coal, varying in thickness from six inches to ten feet, have been counted in one Coal-field, each resting on a bed of Shale, called in mining phraseology the Underclay. This Shale itself naturally divides into an indefinite number of thin plates, just like the stratum of mud accumulated by the annual inundations of the river Nile, and constituting the present soil of Egypt.

We have not attempted to represent in our Woodcut these various divisions and subdivisions of Stratified Rocks. But the names of some important and well-known groups we have had engraved, to impress more vividly on the mind the place to which they are to be referred in the Geological Calendar. Thus the reader may see at a glance the respective ages of the Coal and the Chalk ; of the Lias, in which are preserved the remains of extinct gigantic reptiles, and the Glacial Drift, in which the elephant, the rhinoceros, and the hippopotamus are found entombed ; of the Mountain Limestone, which is often nothing else than vast beds of Coral uplifted from beneath the waters of the ocean, and the Oolite, which includes the Portland quarries, where the petrified stems of ancient forest trees are found standing erect in the solid rock.

As the series of Stratified Rocks is divided by Geologists into a certain number or systems or Formations, so these are again grouped into still larger classes, called Primary, Secondary, and Tertiary; that is to say, first, second, and third, in the order of formation. These larger classes correspond to the Great Epochs or Ages of Geological time, each comprising within itself many distinct Periods. The Primary rocks are also called Palæozoic—παλαιόν, ancient, and ζῶον, an organic being—because they contain the oldest forms of organic life: in like manner the term Mesozoic—μεσον, middle, and ζῶον—is applied to the Secondary strata, inasmuch as they contain the middle or intermediate forms of organic life: and the name Kainozoic—καινόν, new, and ζῶον—is given to the Tertiary, which contain the newest forms of organic life.

The term Post-Tertiary has recently been adopted to designate those superficial deposits which are subsequent to the Tertiary Age. They are divided into two groups ;

the Recent, which corresponds with the period of history, and the Post-Pliocene which precedes it. Some writers seem to think that these deposits, being so very insignificant and so very modern when compared with the long series of Stratified Rocks, are not truly Geological. But this, we should say, is a mistaken view of the question. It seems to us that even the minute layer of mud that is deposited every day at the mouth of the Ganges or the Mississippi, is linked on to the long chain of events which have brought the Crust of the Earth into its present condition; and, therefore, truly belongs to the science of Geology, and is deserving of its proper place in Geological classification.

We may here observe that the names of the great Geological Epochs are descriptive names; that is to say, the obvious meaning of the words corresponds to the character of the strata they are used to represent. Primary, Secondary, Tertiary, mean First, Second, and Third, in the order of formation: Palæozoic, Mesozoic, and Kainozoic, signify that the strata so called are characterized by Ancient, Middle, and Modern, forms of organic life. But it is very often quite otherwise with the names of the several Formations: and this is a point of no small importance to the student of Geology. These names must be regarded simply *as names* employed to designate the strata formed in each successive period, and not exactly to describe their character. They generally had their origin in some accidental circumstance, or were derived from some particular locality; and afterward, being perpetuated, gradually came to receive a much more extended application than that which the words themselves would seem to suggest. Thus, for instance, the Cretaceous Formation is so called from the remarkable stratum of white chalk (creta) which was deposited during that period over a great part of Europe; but it would be a mistake to suppose that the whole Formation is made up of chalk. On the contrary, in different localities it is composed of very different materials; near Dresden, for example, it is a gray quartzose sandstone, and in many parts of the Alps it is hard compact limestone.* Again, the Devonian Formation derives its name from Devonshire, where the rocks of the Devonian period were first minutely examined; but we must not therefore infer that this Formation is peculiar to the county of Devon; it is to be found in many other parts of England, also in Ireland, and on the continent of Europe. So, too, another Formation has received the name of Carboniferous, which literally means Coal-bearing (carbo fero) because of the beds of Coal which are sometimes associated with its strata; yet this Formation is often found quite destitute of Coal over a very extensive area.

In looking over our Table of strata the reader must have noticed that the successive spaces in the Woodcut are not proportioned to the actual thickness of the successive Formations for which they stand. The Secondary and Tertiary Rocks taken together are scarcely one-third as thick, in reality, as the Primary; yet they occupy an equal space in the engraving: and, more remarkable still, the Cretaceous system is allowed double the space of the Laurentian, though less than half as thick. This circumstance calls for a passing word of explanation. In the early annals of a country there is generally a great scarcity of authentic records; and, from a simple dearth of facts, the history of a whole century is compressed, not unfrequently, into a few pages: whereas, in later times, when documentary evidence begins to accumulate, the historians will often spread out the events of two or three years over several chapters. Something of the same kind takes place in Geology. The Fossil Remains, from which, as from authentic documents, the Geologist chiefly derives his information regarding the history of the Earth's Crust, are scanty in the

* Lyell, Principles of Geology, vol. i., p. 115.

earlier Formations, and abundant in the more recent. And thus it happens that the older Geological Periods, notwithstanding the vast thickness of the rocks by which they are represented, do not occupy a very prominent position in the annals of Geology, and are compressed into a comparatively insignificant space in its Tables. Nevertheless, the immense depth of the earliest Stratified Rocks must be taken into account in any attempt to estimate the comparative duration of the several Geological Periods. We have, therefore, set down, under the name of each Formation, an approximate estimate of its actual thickness, taken chiefly from the works of Doctor Haughton and Sir Charles Lyell.

Before bringing this chapter to an end we would observe that the system of classification we have here endeavored to explain does not pretend to be final and complete. It is, on the contrary, little more than a temporary expedient to render intelligible the results at which Geologists have hitherto arrived ; and is liable to manifold modifications in proportion as their acquaintance with the records they have undertaken to interpret becomes more extensive and more minute. All that they now contend for is this : that the successive Formations represent successive Periods of time, which followed one another in the order here set forth, and during which the Earth was peopled with certain species of Plants and Animals, for the most part peculiar to their respective eras.*

* Lyell, Elements of Geology, p. 100.

CHAPTER XIII.

GEOLOGICAL CHRONOLOGY—REMARKS ON THE SUCCESSION OF ORGANIC LIFE.

Summary of the history of stratified rocks—Striking characteristics of certain formations—Human remains found only in superficial deposits—Gradual transition from the organic life of one period to that of the next—Evidence in favor of this opinion—Advance from lower to higher types of organic life as we ascend from the older to the more recent formations—Economic value of geological chronology—Illustration—Search for coal—The practical man at fault—The geologist comes to his aid, and saves him from useless expense.

ITH this sketch of Geological Chronology before us, we can now more fully realize to our minds the story we are told about the formation of the Earth's Crust. In the earliest age to which Geologists can trace back the history of the Aqueous Rocks—for they do not profess to trace it back to the beginning—this Globe of ours was, as it is now, partly covered with water, and partly dry land. The formation of stratified rocks went on in that age, as it is still going on, chiefly over those areas that were under water—not indeed throughout the entire extent of such areas, but over certain portions of them to which mineral matter happened to be carried by the action of natural causes. And the Earth was peopled then as now, though with animals and plants very different from those by which we are surrounded at the present day. Some of these happened to escape

destruction, and to be embedded in the deposits of that far distant age, and have thus been preserved even to our time. And these strata with their Fossils are the same that we now group together under the title of the Laurentian Formation: which being the oldest group of stratified rocks we can recognize in the depths of the Earth's Crust, occupies the lowest position in our table of Chronology. Ages rolled on; and the Crust of the Earth was moved from within by some giant force, the bed of the ocean was lifted up in one place, islands and continents were submerged in another, and so the outlines of land and water were changed. With this change the old forms of life passed away; a new creation came in; and the Laurentian period gave place to the Cambrian. But the order of nature was still the same as before. The deposition of stratified rocks still continued, though the areas of deposition were, in many cases, shifted from one locality to another. And the organic life that flourished in the Cambrian times left its memorials behind it buried in the Cambrian rocks. Then that age, too, came to an end, and gave place in its turn to the Silurian: and this was, again, followed by the Devonian. Thus one period succeeded to another in the order set forth in our table; and every part of the globe was, in the course of ages, more than once submerged, and covered with the deposits of more than one age, and enriched with the Organic Remains of more than one creation.

As we advance upward in the series of Formations we soon perceive that the Fossil Remains, which, in the earlier groups were scanty enough, become profusely abundant, until even the unpractised eye cannot fail to mark the peculiar character of each successive period;—the exuberant vegetation of the Carboniferous, with its luxuriant herbage and its tangled forests, its huge pines, its tall tree-ferns, and its stately araucarias; the enormous creeping monsters of the Jurassic, the ichthyosaurs, the megalosaurs, the iguanodons, which filled its seas, or crowded its plains, or haunted its rivers; and higher up in the scale, the colossal quadrupeds of the Miocene and the Pliocene, the mammoths, the mastodons, the megatheriums, which begin to approximate more closely to the organic types of our own age. But amidst these various forms of life, the eye looks in vain for any relic of human kind. No bone of man, no trace of human intelligence, is to be found in any bed of rock that belongs to the Primary, Secondary, or Tertiary Formations. It is only when we have passed all these, and come to the latest formation of the whole series, nay, it is only in the uppermost beds of this Formation, that we meet, for the first time, with human bones, and the works of human art.

Thus it appears pretty plain, even from the testimony of Geology, that man was the last work of the creation; and that, if the world is old, the human race is comparatively young. These broken and imperfect records, which have been so curiously preserved in the Crust of the Earth, carry us back to an antiquity which may not be measured by years and centuries, and then set before us, as in a palpable form, how the tender herbage appeared, and the fruit-tree yielding fruit according to its kind; and how the Earth was afterward peopled with great creeping things, and winged fowl, and the cattle, and the beasts of the field; and then, at length, they disclose to us how, last of all, man appeared, to whom all these things seem to tend, and who was to have dominion over the fish of the sea, and the fowl of the air, and every living thing that moveth upon the earth. We do not mean to dwell just now upon this view of the history of creation so clearly displayed in the records of Geology. But we shall return to it hereafter when we come in the sequel to consider how admirably the genuine truths of this science fit in with the inspired narrative of Moses.

It may here, very naturally, be asked, if the records of Geology give us any information as to the manner in which each period of animal and vegetable life was brought to an end? Did the old organic forms gradually die out, and the new gradually come in to take their places? or were the one suddenly extinguished and the others as suddenly produced? This question has been a subject of controversy among Geologists themselves; and therefore it is somewhat outside our scope, since we propose to exhibit only that more general outline of Geological theory which is accepted by all. Nevertheless, as it is a question that must needs occur to the mind of every reader, it seems to call for a few words of explanation as we pass along. In the early days of Geology, it was commonly held that each great period was brought to an end by a sudden and violent convulsion of Nature. The Crust of the Earth was burst open in many places all at once; the bottom of the ocean was upheaved with a tremendous shock; the waters, driven from their accustomed bed, rushed with furious impetuosity over islands and continents; and the whole existing creation perished in a universal deluge. Then succeeded an interval of chaotic confusion, and when at length the waters subsided, and dry land again appeared, a new age in the history of the Globe was ushered in, and the Earth was again peopled by a new creation.

But this old theory has gradually given way as the Stratified Rocks have been more and more fully examined, and at the present day it is almost universally abandoned. Geologists have observed that the same species of Fossil Remains which prevail in the upper beds of one Formation, are met with also in the lower beds of the next, though in less numbers and mixed up with new species; and that, as we ascend higher and higher into the later Formation, the old species gradually become more and more scarce, while the new gradually become more and more numerous;

until at length the characteristic forms of one age have disappeared altogether, and those of the succeeding age have attained their full development.

For this important fact, which was brought to light within the last half century, we are mainly indebted to the unwearied researches and great ability of Sir Charles Lyell. Speaking of the Formations of the Tertiary Epoch, to which, as is well known, he has principally devoted himself, this distinguished writer thus sums up the result of his long investigation:—"In passing from the older to the newer members of the Tertiary system we meet with many chasms, but none which separate entirely, by a broad line of demarkation, one state of the organic world from another. There are no signs of an abrupt termination of one fauna and flora, and the starting into life of new and wholly distinct forms. Although we are far from being able to demonstrate geologically an insensible transition from the Eocene to the Miocene, or even from the latter to the recent fauna, yet the more we enlarge and perfect our general survey, the more nearly do we approximate to such a continuous series, and the more gradually are we conducted from times when many of the genera and nearly all the species were extinct, to those in which scarcely a single species flourished which we do not know to exist at present."* Hence he concludes, and his conclusion is now the common doctrine of Geologists, that the extinction and creation of species has been "the result of a slow and gradual change in the organic world."†

It was long argued against this view, that we often meet, especially in the Primary and Secondary Formations, two groups of strata in immediate contact, in which there is a perfectly sudden transition from one set of Fossil Remains to another altogether different. Each group contains a countless variety of species, and yet there is not a single

* Principles of Geology, vol. i., p. 312. † Ib. 313.

species common to the two. Does it not appear that in such a case the organic life of one period was suddenly destroyed, and that of the next as suddenly introduced? Not so; there is one link wanting in the argument. It must be shown that these two strata which are now in *immediate contact* were originally deposited in *immediate succession*. But this it is impossible to prove: nay, it must needs be very often false. We have before observed that the areas of deposition were limited in every age, and were ever shifting from one locality to another. Therefore it must have been a frequent occurrence that, after one bed of rock was formed, the process of deposition ceased altogether in that locality, and did not begin again for many ages. Thus a long lapse of time often intervened between the deposition of two strata, which were laid out one immediately above the other. Furthermore, we have also seen that whole groups of strata may in any age be swept away by Denudation; and then the rocks which are next deposited in that locality, will be in immediate contact with strata indefinitely more ancient than themselves. From these considerations it is plain that two groups of strata which are now found in juxtaposition, may have been deposited in two Geological ages widely remote from each other. And consequently a sudden transition from the Organic Life of one group to the Organic Life of the other affords no proof of a sudden transition from the Organic Life of one Geological Period to the Organic Life of that which next succeeded. We may observe, however, that the recent researches, which have contributed so much to fill up the interstices of the Geological Calendar, have conduced in no small degree to fill up likewise some of the more remarkable gaps or chasms in the succession of Organic Life. It is, therefore, not unreasonable to suppose that, as our knowledge of the Earth's Crust becomes more and more minute, the sudden breaks in the continuity of the scale will be still further diminished and the successive stages of gradual transition will be made more clearly apparent.

This subject has been very happily illustrated by Sir Charles Lyell:—"To make still more clear the supposed working of this machinery [for the deposition of Stratified Rocks and the preservation of Organic Remains], I shall compare it to a somewhat analogous case that might be imagined to occur in the history of human affairs. Let the mortality of the population of a large country represent the successive extinction of species, and the birth of new individuals, the introduction of new species. While these fluctuations are gradually taking place everywhere, suppose commissioners to be appointed to visit each province of the country in succession, taking an exact account of the number, names, and individual peculiarities of all the inhabitants, and leaving in each district a register containing a record of this information. If, after the completion of one census, another is immediately made on the same plan, and then another, there will, at last, be a series of statistical documents in each province. When these belonging to any one province are arranged in chronological order, the contents of such as stand next to each other will differ according to the length of time between the taking of each census. If, for example, there are sixty provinces, and all the registers are made in a single year, and renewed annually, the number of births and deaths will be so small in proportion to the whole of the inhabitants, during the interval between the compiling of two consecutive documents, that the individuals described in such documents will be nearly identical; whereas, if the survey of each of the sixty provinces occupies all the commissioners for a whole year, so that they are unable to revisit the same place until the expiration of sixty years, there will then be an almost entire discordance between the persons enumerated in two consecutive registers in the same province.

"But I must remind the reader that the case above proposed has no pretentions to be regarded as an exact parallel to the Geological phenomena which I desire to illustrate; for the commissioners are supposed to visit the different provinces in rotation; whereas the commemorating processes by which organic remains become fossilized, although they are always shifting from one area to the other, are yet very irregular in their movements. They may abandon and revisit many spaces again and again, before they once approach another district; and besides this source of irregularity, it may often happen that, while the depositing process is suspended, Denudation may take place, which may be compared to the occasional destruction by fire or other causes of some of the statistical documents before mentioned. It is evident that where such accidents occur, the want of continuity in the series may become indefinitely great, and that the monuments which follow next in succession will by no means be equi-distant from each other in point of time.

"If this train of reasoning be admitted, the occasional distinctness of the fossil remains, in formations immediately in contact, would be a necessary consequence of the existing laws of sedimentary deposition and subterranean movement, accompanied by a constant mortality and renovation of species." *

There is another and a very striking fact in the succession of ancient organic life, which claims from us a moment's notice. As we proceed upward through the series of Stratified Rocks, from the oldest to the newest, we find a gradual advance in the types of animal organization therein preserved, from the humbler and more simple forms of structure to those of a higher and more perfect character. That form of organization is regarded among Zoologists as the more perfect in which there is "a greater number of

* Principles of Geology, vol. i., pp. 321, 322.

organs specially devoted to particular functions." Now all the forms of animal life with which we are acquainted, may be reduced to two great divisions, the Vertebrate and the Invertebrate,—the former having a *vertebral* or spinal column, the latter having none: and it is agreed in conformity with the notion set forth above, that the Vertebrate animals as a class exhibit a more perfect organization than the Invertebrate. Again, among the Vertebrate themselves there is a gradation; the Reptiles are ranked higher than the Fish, the Birds higher than the Reptiles, and the Mammalia higher again than the Birds.

All this we learn from Zoologists, who have pursued their investigations without any reference whatever to the science of Geology. It is, therefore, not a little remarkable that we should discover this very order and gradation of animal life in the successive groups of Stratified Rocks. All the Remains hitherto discovered in the earliest Geological Formations belong to Invertebrate animals, while the Vertebrate, which appear for the first time in the latter part of the Silurian Period, are, from that age on, more and more fully developed down to the present day, and now constitute, if not the most numerous, at least the most important part of the animal creation. Moreover, it is to be observed that the Vertebrate animals do not all make their appearance at once, but come in successively according to the same scale of organic perfection,—the Fish appearing first, then the Reptiles, then the Birds, and lastly the Mammalia. Even among the Mammalia a well-defined order of progressive succession has been observed, which finally culminates in the appearance of Man, the last created and the most perfect of animals.

This remarkable succession of animal life in the history of the Earth's Crust will be more readily understood by means of the annexed Table. The remains of Invertebrate animals have been traced as far back as the Lower Lauren-

TABLE OF GEOLOGICAL FORMATIONS,

SHOWING THE FIRST APPEARANCE ON THE EARTH OF THE VARIOUS FOR OF ANIMAL LIFE.

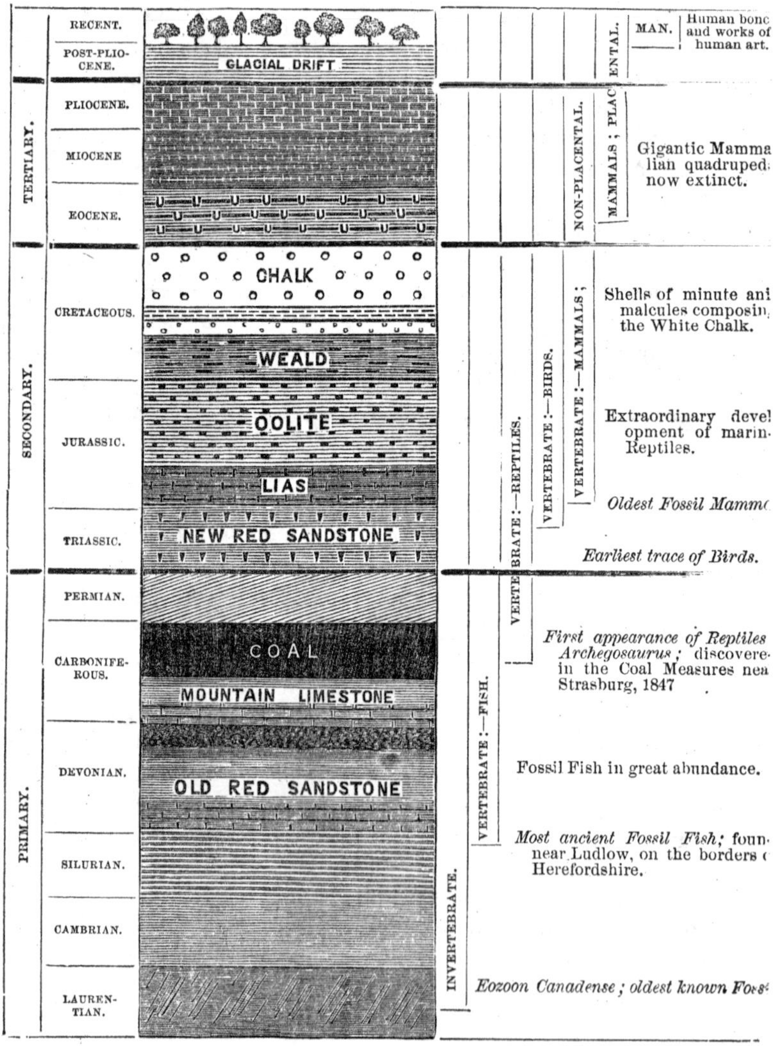

Era	Period	Formation	Animal life	Remarks
	RECENT.		MAN.	Human bonc and works of human art.
	POST-PLIO-CENE.	GLACIAL DRIFT	MAMMALS; PLAC ENTAL.	
TERTIARY.	PLIOCENE.		NON-PLACENTAL.	
	MIOCENE			Gigantic Mamma lian quadruped: now extinct.
	EOCENE.			
SECONDARY.	CRETACEOUS.	CHALK	VERTEBRATE:—MAMMALS;	Shells of minute ani malcules composin the White Chalk.
		WEALD	VERTEBRATE:—BIRDS.	
	JURASSIC.	OOLITE	VERTEBRATE:—REPTILES.	Extraordinary devel opment of marin Reptiles.
		LIAS		*Oldest Fossil Mamm*
	TRIASSIC.	NEW RED SANDSTONE		*Earliest trace of Birds.*
PRIMARY.	PERMIAN.			
	CARBONIFE-ROUS.	COAL		*First appearance of Reptiles Archegosaurus;* discovere in the Coal Measures nea Strasburg, 1847
		MOUNTAIN LIMESTONE	VERTEBRATE:—FISH.	
	DEVONIAN.	OLD RED SANDSTONE		Fossil Fish in great abundance.
	SILURIAN.			*Most ancient Fossil Fish;* foun near Ludlow, on the borders Herefordshire.
	CAMBRIAN.		INVERTEBRATE.	
	LAUREN-TIAN.			*Eozoon Canadense; oldest known Foss*

tian Rocks. The Vertebrate first become manifest in the Ludlow beds of the Upper Silurian; where they are represented by the bones of Fish, the lowest class belonging to the Province of Vertebrates. Next in order come the Reptiles: the oldest known Reptile having been found in the Coal Measures of Saarbrück between Strasburg and Treves. The skeletons of Birds are rare in the Stratified Rocks. It is supposed that their powers of flight have in all ages secured them, to great a extent, from being carried away by floods, like other land animals, and buried in the sedimentary deposits of rivers and estuaries. Nevertheless their presence in the ancient world is frequently attested by their footsteps, impressed originally on the sandy beach, and still preserved now that the soft sand has been converted into solid rock. Such traces have been discovered in great abundance on the New Red Sandstone of the Connecticut River in America; and afford the earliest evidence we possess in the records of Geology regarding the existence of the feathered tribe. This group of strata belongs to the lower Trias. In the higher beds of the same Formation we meet with the first relic of ancient Mammals. It was found near Stuttgardt, in 1847, and belongs to the more imperfect form of Mammalian life, the Non-Placental. Similar remains have been since discovered in the Upper Trias of Somersetshire. The Placental, or more perfect form of animal life in the same class, first appears in the Eocene Formation: and the bones of Man, the highest of the Placentals, are found for the first time in the upper deposits of the Post-Tertiary Age.

Let it be remembered that we are here but stating the facts which have been hitherto brought to light by the researches of Geologists. It may be, it is indeed most probable, that new discoveries will lead to numerous modifications in our Table. There is no reason to suppose that Geologists have yet exhumed the earliest remains of Vertebrates or Invertebrates preserved in the Crust of the Earth: that Fish may not hereafter be traced back beyond the Silurian, or Reptiles beyond the Carboniferous Period: that Birds may not be found among the Primary Rocks, and Placentals among the Secondary. But in a science which depends mainly upon observation, it is better to register the facts we have than to speculate idly about those we have not. And, having registered them, we cannot fail to be struck with the succession of animal life on the Earth, to which they seem to point. It is certainly deserving of notice that, as far as the Organic Remains hitherto discovered may be taken as a guide, Invertebrates and Vertebrates, Fish, Reptiles, Birds, and Mammals, Non-Placentals and Placentals, follow one another in the ascending series of Geological Formations exactly in the same order as they follow one another in the ascending scale of Zoological Classification.

And so Geologists go on ever searching out new phenomena, and grouping them together into classes, until from particular facts they lead us to general truths. Then starting with these general truths as the groundwork of their science, they proceed to sketch out the Natural History of our Globe from the remotest ages of the past down to the present time. They first study the stratified deposits of each succeeding age, and analyze the Fossil Remains embedded therein; afterward they make their inferences, and they compile their history. They describe the forms, the character, the habits, of the plants and animals that flourished of old in this world of ours; they tell us where the deep sea rolled its waves in each succeeding age, and where the dry land appeared; they point out the Deltas of its ancient rivers, they measure the breadth of its Estuaries, they trace the course of its Glaciers, they mark the outlines of its Mountain chains. But with these and such like speculations we are not here concerned. Many of them are open to controversy, and not a few are at this moment warmly disputed among Geologists themselves: besides, whether true or false, they do not in any way affect the relations between Geology and Revealed Religion. We shall be quite content, and it is all that our present scope demands, if we have made intelligible the general theory of Geological Chronology, and the kind of evidence on which it rests.

Before taking leave of this subject, however, we will venture to offer what seems to us an interesting illustration of the principles we have been explaining in the last two chapters;—one that will help to confirm the conclusions for which we have been contending, and that will also bring home to many minds the practical advantage to be derived from a thorough knowledge and just application of Geological science. Perhaps, too, it may help to revive the flagging attention of our readers; for the subject of our illustration is *Coal, and the way to find it.* In this age of manufactories and steam-engines,—when the atmosphere of great towns is heavy with smoke, and the quiet solitude of the country is so rudely disturbed by the shrieking of the railway-whistle and the snorting of the sooty locomotive,—this black, dirty mineral has acquired a value and importance, which may succeed in rousing even the practical money-making man to pay some heed to the lessons of science.

Coal might have been produced in any Geological Period; and in point of fact, beds of coal have been discovered in many different Formations. But in England, and in Western Europe generally, it has been found by long experience that the Coal-beds of the Carboniferous Formation are more abundant, and of better quality, than those of any other. Indeed the beds of Coal that occur in other Formations are so thin, and of such inferior quality, that they cannot be worked with profit. It is therefore of the highest importance in the search for Coal, before going to the enormous expense of sinking deep shafts, to discover whether or no the rocks in which the search is to be made belong to the Carboniferous Period. In this matter the more *practical man* is often seriously at fault. Coal-bearing strata generally consist pretty largely of dark-colored clay, black shales, and similar deposits. This is a fact which, as it strikes the eye, is perfectly familiar to all who are engaged in the working of Coal mines. Hence it happens, not unfrequently, that the practical man, when he meets with strata of this kind, is apt at once to infer that Coal is near at hand. The Geologist, on the contrary, knows well that such strata are not peculiar to the Carboniferous rocks, but are often found in other Formations in which there is no Coal at all, or at least no Coal that will repay the expense of working; and therefore he will pronounce it most rash to undertake costly works on the strength of these appearances. He has learned, however, that there are certain species of animals and plants which are found in the Carboniferous rocks and in them alone; he will search for these in the strata which it is proposed to explore, and by their presence or their absence he will know whether the strata in question belong to the Carboniferous Formation or not.

Again, it will often happen that, in the midst of an extensive region well known to abound in Coal, the rocks which appear at the surface in one particular locality, are not wholly devoid of Coal, but exhibit no resemblance either in mineral character or in Fossil Remains to the Coal-bearing strata. A question then arises of the highest practical importance. May it be that the Coal-bearing strata are spread out beneath this uppermost bed of rocks? and is it worth the expense to sink a shaft through the one in the hope of reaching the other? The practical miner has no very clear or certain principles to help him in the solution of this problem; and thus it has often happened that thousands upon thousands of pounds have been expended in sinking shafts to look for Coal, where, as it afterward proved, there was not the slightest chance of finding it. Now, though Geology cannot tell if we shall succeed in finding Coal beneath these rocks, it *can* tell if there is a *good chance* of succeeding. It can tell whether there is a reasonable hope, by penetrating into the Crust of the Earth at this particular spot, of reaching the Carboniferous Formation; and if we can reach the Carboniferous Formation in the midst of a Coal district, it is very likely we shall meet with beds of Coal.

His first object will be to ascertain what is the Formation to which the superficial rocks belong. If it be a Formation earlier in date than the Carboniferous,—the Silurian, for instance, or the Devonian,—he knows that it would be simply waste of money to look for Coal beneath them; because the Carboniferous rocks cannot possibly be found underneath the rocks of an earlier age. And so the Geologist can tell beforehand what the mere practical man would find out only when he had spent his money. If, on the other hand, the rocks which appear at the surface belong to a period later than the Carboniferous, the Geologist will not always conclude that it is expedient to sink a shaft in search of Coal. For though the Carboniferous rocks may, in this case, be underneath, they may be so far down in the Crust of the Earth that we should have no chance of ever reaching them. Suppose, for example, that the strata which appear at the surface belong to the Cretaceous Formation. He knows from his Chronological table that the Carboniferous age is separated from the Cretaceous by three intermediate Periods,—the Permian, the Triassic, the Jurassic. Therefore, when he finds the Cretaceous rocks at the surface in any locality, it is quite possible, though of course not certain, that before the Carboniferous Formation could be reached it would be necessary to bore through thousands of feet of Jurassic, Triassic, and Permian rocks. And even then there would be no certainty of meeting with the Coal-bearing strata. Perhaps they were never deposited over this area of the earth's surface; or, if deposited, perhaps they were subsequently swept away by Denudation. Hence our Geologist would reasonably conclude that, the probable expense of the search being so enormous, and the chance of success so remote, it would be much wiser not to make the attempt.

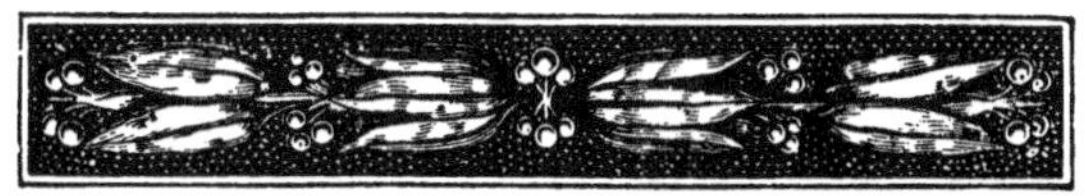

CHAPTER XIV.

SUBTERRANEAN HEAT—ITS EXISTENCE DEMONSTRATED BY FACTS.

Theory of stratified rocks supposes disturbances of the earth's crust—These disturbances ascribed by geologists to the action of subterranean heat—The existence of subterranean heat, and its power to move the crust of the earth, proved by direct evidence—Supposed igneous origin of our globe—Remarkable increase of temperature as we descend into the earth's crust—Hot springs—Artesian wells—Steam issuing from crevices in the earth—The geysers of Iceland—A glimpse at the subterranean fires—Mount Vesuvius in 1779 *—Vast extent of volcanic action—Existence of subterranean heat an established fact.*

N developing the modern theory of Geology, we have all along assumed that the Crust of the Earth has been subject to frequent disturbances from the earliest ages of the world. Again and again, in the course of our argument, we have talked of the bed of the sea being lifted up, and converted into dry land; and, on the other hand, of the dry land being submerged beneath the waters of the sea. We have not even hesitated to suppose that these two opposite movements of upheaval and submersion often took place by turns over the same area; nay, that there is scarcely a region on the surface of the Globe which has not been several times submerged, and several times again upheaved.

Yet all this has not been taken for granted without proof.

Our readers have seen what a long array of sober reasoning may be drawn out to show that the Stratified Rocks have been, for the most part, deposited *under water*:—first, from the nature and arrangement of the materials which compose them; secondly, from the character of the Organic Remains they contain. And since they are now *above water*, it is plain that either they have been lifted or the ocean has subsided. Furthermore, if we find, as we often do, two strata in immediate succession, the one underneath, exhibiting the trees of an ancient forest still standing erect with their roots attached, the other above, abounding in the remains of aquatic animals; we must conclude that when the ancient forest flourished this portion of the Earth's Crust was above the level of the sea; that afterward it was submerged, and a new deposit, in which the marine remains were embedded, was spread out above the earlier vegetation; and that, last of all it again emerged from the waters, and became once more dry land. Finally, when a vertical section of the Earth's Crust exhibits a continued series of such strata alternating with each other, it affords a proof that this particular area must have been several times under water, and several times again dry land, in the long course of ages.

These conclusions are now all but universally received among Geologists. The Crust of the Earth, we are assured, is not that unyielding and immovable mass which men commonly take it to be. On the contrary, it has been from the beginning ever restless and in motion, rising here and subsiding there, sometimes with a convulsive shock capable of upturning, twisting, distorting hard and stubborn rocks as if they were but flimsy layers of pliant clay; sometimes with a gentle, undulating movement, which, while it uplifts islands and continents, leaves the general aspect of the surface unchanged, the arrangement of the strata undisturbed, and even the most tender Fossils unharmed.

Disturbances of this kind have been going on in various parts of the world even within the period of history; and they may be distinctly traced to the action of subterranean Heat. In support of a theory so startling and unexpected, Geologists appeal to the direct evidence of facts: and we now propose to bring some of these facts under the notice of our readers.

At the outset, however, it is important to set forth clearly the doctrine we hope to illustrate and confirm. With the origin of the internal heat that prevails within the Crust of the Earth we have no concern. This is still an unsettled point among Geologists themselves. Some conjecture that our Globe, when first launched into space, was in a state of igneous fusion; that is to say, that all the solid matter of which it is composed was held in a molten condition by the action of intense heat; that, in course of time, as this heat passed off by radiation, the surface gradually cooled and grew hard; that an external shell of solid rock was thus formed, which has been ever growing thicker in proportion as the Earth has been growing cooler; and that the actual condition of our planet is the result of this process continued down to the present day,—a fiery mass of seething mineral within, and a comparatively thin crust of consolidated rock without. Others suppose that the internal heat of the Globe is developed by the agency of chemical changes constantly going on in the depths of the Earth; and others, again, look for a cause to the action of electricity and magnetism. But these and such like speculations are still under discussion, and not one of them can be regarded as anything more, at best, than a satisfactory hypothesis. Anyhow, it is not about the causes of internal heat that we are just now interested, but about the fact of its existence, and the nature of its effects. Is it true that an intense heat prevails very generally beneath the superficial covering of the Globe? and is that heat capable of producing those stupendous changes which are ascribed to it in our theory of Geology? These are the questions to which we mean to devote our chief attention.

It is a very significant fact, that *the deeper we penetrate into the Crust of the Earth, the hotter it is.* At first, no doubt, for a short distance, the reverse is the case. When we begin to descend we find it cooler below than above, because the further we depart from the surface the more we are removed from the influence of the Sun. But at a certain point—in our climate at about fifty feet below the surface—the influence of the Sun's heat ceases to be sensibly felt. When this limit is passed, the temperature begins to rise, and thenceforth the deeper we go the hotter the earth becomes.

This broad and general fact has been tested by experiments in every part of the world, and has been found true in all countries, in all climates, in all latitudes, whether in coal-pits, or mines, or deep subterranean caves. "In one and the same mine," says Sir John Herschel,* "each particular depth has its own particular degree of heat, which never varies: but the lower always the hotter; and that not by a trifling, but what may well be called an astonishingly rapid rate of increase,—about a degree of the thermometer additional warmth for every ninety feet of additional depth,† which is about 58° per mile!—so that, if we had a shaft sunk a mile deep, we should find in the rock a heat of 105°, which is much hotter than the hottest summer day ever experienced in England." Now if the temperature

* Familiar Lectures on Scientific Subjects: London, 1867; pp. 9, 10.

† It would be more strictly correct to say that the rate of increase varies considerably in different places, though the main fact is everywhere palpably apparent that the deeper we descend into the Earth the higher the temperature becomes. Sir Charles Lyell records a number of careful experiments made in England, France, Germany, and Italy, which seem to show that an increase of one degree Fahrenheit for every sixty-five feet of descent would represent pretty correctly the general average. See his Principles of Geology, vol. ii., pp. 205, 206.

continue to increase at this rate toward the centre of the Earth, it is quite certain that, at no very great distance from the surface, the heat would be sufficiently intense to reduce the hardest granite and the most refractory metals to a state of igneous fusion.

Again, every one is familiar with the existence of hot springs, which come up from unknown depths in the Earth's Crust, and which, appearing as they do in almost all parts of the world, testify in unmistakable language to the existence of internal heat. At Bath, for instance, in England, the water comes up from the bowels of the Earth, at a temperature of 117° Fahrenheit; and in the United States, on the Arkansas River, there is a spring at 180°—not much below the boiling point. This remarkable phenomenon, however, may be more closely investigated in the case of Artesian Wells, so called from the province of Artois, in France, where they first came into use. These wells are formed artificially, by boring down through the superficial strata of the Earth, sometimes to enormous depths, until water is reached. It has been found in every case that the water coming up from these great depths is always hot; and, furthermore, that the deeper the boring the hotter the water. A well of this kind was sunk in 1834 at Grenelle, in the suburbs of Paris, to a depth of more than 1800 English feet, and the water, which rushed up with surprising force, had a temperature of 82° Fahrenheit; whereas the mean temperature of the air in the cellars of the Paris Observatory is only 53°. The water has ever since continued to flow, and the temperature has never varied. At Salzwerth, in Germany, where the boring is still deeper, being 2,144 feet, the water which rises to the surface is 91° of our scale.

Then we have, in many countries, jets of steam which issue at a high temperature from crevices in the Earth, and which tell of the existence of heated water below, as plainly as the steam that escapes from the funnel of a locomotive or from the spout of a tea-kettle. Phenomena of this kind are very common in Italy, where they are sometimes exhibited at intervals along a line of country twenty miles in length. But in Iceland it is that they are displayed in the highest degree of splendor and power. On the southwest side of that island, within a circuit of two miles, there are nearly a hundred hot springs called Geysers, from some of which, at intervals, immense volumes of steam and boiling water are violently projected into the air. The Great Geyser is a natural tube, ten feet wide, descending into the Earth to a depth of seventy feet, and opening out above into a broad basin, from fifty to sixty feet in diameter. This basin, as well as the tube which connects it with the interior of the Earth, is lined with a beautifully smooth and hard plaster of siliceous cement, and is generally filled to the brim with water of a clear azure color, and a temperature little below boiling point. The ordinary condition of the spring is one of comparative repose, the water rising slowly in the tube and trickling over the edge of the stony basin. But every few hours an eruption takes place. Subterranean explosions are first heard, like the firing of distant cannon; then a violent ebullition follows, clouds of steam are given out, and jets of boiling water are cast up into the air. After a little the disturbance ceases, and all is quiet again. Once a day, or thereabouts, these phenomena are exhibited on a scale of extraordinary grandeur: the explosions which announce beforehand the approaching display are more numerous and violent than usual; then such volumes of steam rush forth as to obscure the atmosphere for half a mile around; and, finally, a vast column of water is projected to a height of from one to two hundred feet, and continues for a quarter of an hour to play like an artificial fountain. Geysers scarcely less grand and striking are to be seen in New Zealand, from which the water is thrown up at a temperature 214° Fahrenheit, or two degrees above boiling point.

Such are the evident symptoms of subterranean heat,—hot springs, jets of steam, fountains of boiling water,—which are manifested unceasingly at the surface of the Earth in every quarter of the Globe. But it is sometimes given us to behold, as it were, the subterranean fire itself, and to contemplate its power under a more striking and awful form. From time to time, in the fury of its rage, the fiery element bursts asunder the prison-house in which it is confined, and rushes forth into the light of day; then flames are seen to issue from the surface of the Earth, yawning chasms begin to appear on every side, the roaring of the furnaces is heard in the depths below, clouds of red-hot cinders are ejected high into the air, and streams of incandescent liquid rock are poured forth from every crevice, which, rolling far away through smiling fields and peaceful villages, carry destruction and desolation in their track. These are the ordinary phenomena of an active volcano during the period of eruption; and even while we write, most of them may be witnessed actually taking place for the hundredth time, on the historic ground of Mount Vesuvius. Our typical example, however, we shall take from the eruption of that mountain in the year 1779. It was not, indeed, especially remarkable for its violence or for the catastrophes by which it was attended; but it had the good fortune to be accurately recorded by an eye-witness, Sir William Hamilton, who, at that time, represented the English Government at the Court of Naples; and we are thus more minutely acquainted with all its various circumstances than with those of any other eruption of equal importance.

For two years before, the mountain had been in a state of excitement and disturbance. From time to time rumbling noises were heard underground, dense masses of smoke were emitted from the crater, liquid lava at a white heat bubbled up from crevices on the slopes of the mountain, and through these crevices a glimpse could be had here and there of the rocky caverns within, all "red-hot like a heated oven." But in the month of August, 1779, the eruption reached its climax. About nine o'clock in the evening of Sunday the eighth, according to the graphic description of Sir William Hamilton, "there was a loud report, which shook the houses at Portici and its neighborhood to such a degree as to alarm the inhabitants and drive them out into the streets. Many windows were broken, and, as I have since seen, walls cracked, from the concussion of the air from that explosion. In one instant, a fountain of liquid transparent fire began to rise, and, gradually increasing, arrived at so amazing a height, as to strike every one who beheld it with the most awful astonishment. I shall scarcely be credited when I assure you that, to the best of my judgment, the height of this stupendous column of fire could not be less than three times that of Vesuvius itself, which, you know, rises perpendicularly near 3,700 feet above the level of the sea. Puffs of smoke, as black as can possibly be imagined, succeeded one another hastily, and accompanied the red-hot, transparent, and liquid lava, interrupting its splendid brightness here and there by patches of the darkest hue. Within these puffs of smoke, at the very moment of their emission from the crater, I could perceive a bright but pale electrical light playing about in zigzag lines. The liquid lava, mixed with scoriae and stones, after having mounted, I verily believe, at least 10,000 feet, falling perpendicularly on Vesuvius, covered its whole cone, and part of that of Somma, and the valley between them. The falling matter being nearly as vivid and inflamed as that which was continually issuing fresh from the crater, formed with it a complete body of fire, which could not be less than two miles and a half in breadth, and of the extraordinary height above mentioned, casting a heat to the distance of at least six miles around it. The brushwood of the mountain of Somma was soon in a flame, which, being of a different tint from the deep red of the matter thrown out from the Volcano, and from the silvery blue of the electrical fire, still added to the contrast of this most extraordinary scene. After the column of fire continued in full force for nearly half an hour the eruption ceased at once, and Vesuvius remained sullen and silent." *

The existence, then, of intense heat within the Crust of the Earth may be regarded as an established fact whereever an active Volcano appears at the surface. Now let us consider for a moment, the very extensive scale on which these fiery engines of Nature are distributed over the face of the Globe. First, on the great continent of America. The whole chain of the Andes—that stupendous ridge of mountains which stretches along the western coast of South America, from Tierra del Fuego on the south to the isthmus of Panama on the north—is studded over with Volcanos, most of which have been seen in active eruption within the last 300 years. Passing the narrow isthmus of Panama, this line of Volcanos may still be traced through Guatemala to Mexico, and thence northward even as far as the mouth of the Columbia River. Here is a vast volcanic region extending fully 6,000 miles in length, and spreading out its fiery arms, we know not how far, to the right and to the left. At Quito, just on the Equator, a branch shoots off toward the northeast, and, passing through New Granada and Venezuela, stretches away across the West India Islands, taking in St. Vincent, Dominica, Guadaloupe, and many others; while, in the opposite direction, it is certain that the volcanic action extends westward, far away beneath the waters of the Pacific, though we have no definite means of ascertaining where its influence ceases to be felt.

* See Sir John Herschel, Familiar Lectures on Scientific Subjects, pp. 26, 27.

Another vast train of active Volcanos is that which skirts the eastern and southern coasts of Asia. Commencing on the shores of Northwestern America, it passes through the Aleutian Islands to Kamtschatka; then, in a sort of undulating curve, it winds its course by the Kurile Islands, the Japanese group, the Philippines, and the northeastern extremity of the Celebes, to the Moluccas. At this point it divides into two branches; one going in a southeasterly direction to New Guinea, the Solomon Islands, the Friendly Islands, and New Zealand; the other pursuing a northwesterly course through Java and Sumatra into the Bay of Bengal.

There is a third great line of volcanic fires which has been pretty well traced out by modern travellers, extending through China and Tartary to the Caucasus; thence over the countries bordering the Black Sea to the Grecian Archipelago; then on to Naples, Sicily, the Lipari Islands, the southern part of Spain and Portugal, and the Azores. Besides these there are numerous groups of Volcanos not apparently linked on to any regular volcanic chain, nor reduced as yet by scientific men to any general system; Mount Hecla, for instance, in Iceland, the Mountains of the Moon in Central Africa, Owhyhee in the Sandwich Islands, and many others rising up irregularly from the broad waters of the Pacific.

From this brief outline some idea may be formed of the magnificent scale on which volcanic agency is developed within the Crust of the Earth. It must be remembered, however, that any estimate based upon the enumeration we have given, would be, in all probability, far below the truth; for we have mentioned those Volcanos only which have attracted the notice of scientific men, or which have chanced to fall under the observation of travellers. Many others, doubtless, must exist in regions not yet explored, and in the profound depths of the seas and oceans, which cover nearly two-thirds of the area of our planet. Moreover, we have said nothing at all of *extinct* Volcanos—such as those of Auvergne in France, and of the Rocky Mountains in America—which have not been in active operation within historical times; but in which, nevertheless, the hardened streams of lava, the volcanic ashes, and the cone-shaped mountains terminating in hollow craters, tell the story of eruptions in bygone ages, not less clearly than the blackened walls and charred timbers of some stately building bear witness to the passing wayfarer of a long extinguished conflagation.

We contend, therefore, that the doctrine of intense subterranean heat is not a wild conjecture, but is based on a solid groundwork of facts. First, there is presumptive evidence. In every deep mine, in every deep sinking of whatever kind, the heat of the earth increases rapidly as we descend. Hot water comes from great depths, and never cold. Sometimes it is boiling: sometimes it has been converted into steam. All this is found to be the case universally, whenever an opportunity has occurred for making the trial; and it seems to afford a strong presumption that if one could go still deeper, the heat would be found yet more intense, and would at length be capable of reducing to a liquid state the solid materials of which the earth is composed. Next, there is the direct testimony of our senses. A channel is opened from the depths below, flames are seen, red-hot cinders are cast up, and molten rock is poured out over the surface of the Earth in a liquid stream of fire. This evidence, however, though direct and con clusive as far as it goes, is not universal. It proves that an intense white heat prevails within the Crust of the Earth, not everywhere, but at least in those numerous and extensive regions where active Volcanos exist. So stands the case, as it seems to us, for the doctrine of subterranean heat as far as regards the fact of its existance.

CHAPTER XV.

SUBTERRANEAN HEAT—ITS POWERS ILLUSTRATED BY VOLCANOS.

Effects of subterranean heat in the present age of the world—Vast accumulations of solid matter from the eruptions of volcanos—Buried cities of Pompeii and Herculaneum—Curious relics of Roman life—Monte Nuovo—Eruption of Jorullo in the province of Mexico—Sumbawa in the Indian Archipelago—Volcanos of Iceland—Mountain mass of Etna the product of volcanic eruptions—Volcanic islands—In the Atlantic—In the Mediterranean—Santorin in the Grecain Archipelago.

HAVING now sufficiently demonstrated the existence of intense subterranean heat, diffused, if not universally, at least very generally, beneath the superficial shell of the Earth, we shall next proceed to inquire if it is capable of effecting those physical changes which are ascribed to it in Geology;—of producing land where none before existed, of upheaving the solid Crust of the Earth, of driving the ocean from its bed, of dislocating and contorting solid masses of rock. The argument is still an appeal to facts. Such effects as these have been produced by the agency of internal heat, under actual observation, in the present age of the world; and it is not unreasonable to attribute to the same cause similar phenomena in ages gone by.

We will not run the risk of dissipating the force of this reasoning by attempting to expand it. It will be enough for us to state the facts: we shall leave it to our readers to estimate for themselves the value of the argument. There are three forms, more or less distinct, though closely associated, under which the subterranean fires have exerted their power in modern times to disturb and modify the Physical Geography of the Globe;—(1) the Volcano, (2) the Earthquake, (3) the gentle Undulation of the Earth's Crust. Of these we shall speak in order.

In the case of Volcanos, as we have already sufficiently conveyed, the hidden furnaces of the Earth find a vent for their surplus energies; and when this vent is once established, that is to say, when the active Volcano has begun to exist, it seems probable that there is little further upheaval, properly so called, of the surface. Nevertheless, Volcanos contribute largely to the formation of land by the vast accumulation of ashes, mud, and lava, which they vomit forth. The destruction of Herculaneum and Pompeii is a case in point. For eight days successively, in the year 79, the ashes and pumice stone cast up from the crater of Vesuvius, fell down in one unceasing shower upon these devoted cities; while at the same time floods of water, carrying along the fine dust and light cinders, swept down the sides of the mountain in resistless torrents of mud, entering the houses, penetrating into every nook and crevice, and filling even the very wine jars in the underground cellars.

At the present moment the layers of volcanic matter beneath which Pompeii has been slumbering for centuries, are from twelve to fourteen feet over the tops of the houses. Loftier still is the pile that overlies the buried Herculaneum. This city, situated nearer to the base of the Volcano, has been exposed to the effects of many successive eruptions; and accordingly, spread out over the mass of ashes and pumice by which it was first overwhelmed, in the time of Pliny, we now find alternate layers of lava and volcanic mud, together with fresh accumulations of ashes, to a height, in many places, of 112 feet, and nowhere less than 70. Nor was this ejected matter confined to these two populous towns. It was scattered far and wide over the country around, and has contributed in no small degree to that extraordinary richness and fertility for which the soil of Naples is so justly famed.

As regards the production of land where none before existed, here is one fact of singular significance. At the time of the eruption, in 79, Pompeii was a seaport town to which merchantmen were wont to resort, and a flight of steps, which still remains, led down to the water's edge: it is now more than a mile distant from the coast, and the tract of land which intervenes is composed entirely of volcanic tuff and ashes.

Gladly would we linger over the reminiscences of these luxurious and ill-fated cities. By the removal of the ashes, Pompeii is now laid open to view for at least one-third of its extent; and a strange sight it is, this ancient Roman city thus risen as it were from the grave,—risen, but yet lifeless,—with its silent streets, and its tenantless houses, and its empty Forum. Wherever we turn we have before us a curious and interesting picture, ghastly though it is, of the social, political, and domestic life of those ancient times, of the glory and the shame that hung around the last days of Pagan Rome;—in the theatres and the temples, in the shops and the private houses, in the graceful frescoes, in the elaborate mosaics, and, not least, in the idle scribblings on the walls, which, with a sort of whimsical reverence, have been spared by the destroying hand of Time. Then again, what a host of singular relics are there to be wondered at:—articles of domestic use and luxury, kitchen utensils and surgical instruments; female skeletons with the ornaments and vanities of the world, rings and bracelets and necklaces, still clinging to their charred remains; and strangest perhaps of all, eighty-four loaves of bread, which were put into the oven to bake 1800 years ago, and were taken out only yesterday, with the baker's brand upon them, and the stamp of the baker's elbow still freshly preserved in the centre of each. No subject could be more tempting to a writer, none more attractive to a reader. But our present purpose is to show the effects of Volcanos in elevating the level of the land; and so we must turn our back on the buried cities, and crossing the Bay of Naples, seek for a new illustration in the formation of Monte Nuovo, a lofty hill overlooking the ancient town of Pozzuoli.

About one o'clock at night, on Sunday, the twenty-ninth of September, 1538, flames were seen to issue from the ground close to the waters of the beautiful bay of Baiae. After a little, a sound like thunder was heard, the earth was rent asunder, and through the rent large stones, red-hot cinders, volcanic mud, and volumes of water, were furiously vomited forth, which covered the whole country around, reaching even as far as Naples, and disfiguring its palaces and public buildings. The next morning it was found that a new mountain had been formed by the accumulation of ejected matter around the central opening. This mountain remains to the present day, and is called the Monte Nuovo. In form it is a regular volcanic cone, four hundred and forty feet high, and a mile and a half in circumference at its base, with an open crater in the centre, which descends nearly to the level of the sea. An eye-witness who has left us a minute account of this eruption, relates that on the third day he went up with many people to the top of the new hill, and looking down into the crater, saw the stones that had fallen to the bottom, "boiling up just as a caldron of water boils on the fire." The same writer informs us—and it is very much to our present purpose to note the fact—that immediately before the eruption began, the relative position of land and sea was materially changed, the coast was sensibly upraised, the waters retired about two hundred paces, and multitudes of fish were raised high and dry upon the sand, a prey to the inhabitants of Pozzuoli.*

The Monte Nuovo is but a type of its class. If we travel westward 8,000 miles from Naples to the more stupendous Volcanos of the New World, we may witness the same phenomena on a still grander scale. In the province of Mexico, there is an elevated and extensive plain called Malpais, where for many generations the cotton plant, the indigo, and the sugar-cane, flourished luxuriantly in a soil richly endowed with natural gifts, and carefully cultivated by its industrious inhabitants. Everything was going on as usual in this smiling and prosperous region, and no one dreamed of danger, when suddenly, in the month of June, 1759, subterranean sounds were heard, attended with slight convulsions of the earth. These symptoms of internal commotion continued until the month of September, when they gradually died away, and tranquillity seemed to be restored. But it was only the delusive lull that precedes the fury of the storm. On the night of the twenty-eighth of September the rumbling sounds were heard again more violent than before. The inhabitants fled in consternation to a neighboring mountain, from the summit of which they looked back with wonder and dismay upon the utter annihilation of their homesteads and their farms. Flames broke out over an area half a square league in extent, the earth was burst open in many places, fragments of burning rock were thrown to prodigious heights in the air, torrents of boiling mud flowed over the plain, and thousands of little conical hills, called by the natives Hornitos or Ovens,

* See the elaborate work of Sir William Hamilton, entitled Campi Phlegraei, in which he gives a full account of the formation of Monte Nuovo, accompanied with colored plates. He has preserved two interesting narratives of the eruption written at the time by eye-witnesses. See also Lyell, Principles of Geology, vol. i., pp. 606–616.

rose up from the surface of the land. Finally a vast chasm was opened, and such quantities of ashes and fragmentary lava were ejected as to raise up six great mountain masses, which continued to increase during the five months that the eruption lasted. The least of these is 300 feet high, and the central one, now called Jorullo, which is still burning, is 1600 feet above the level of the plain. When Baron Humboldt visited this region just forty years after the eruption had ceased, the ground was still intensely hot, and "the Hornitos were pouring forth columns of steam twenty or thirty feet high, with a rumbling noise like that of a steam boiler."* Since that time, however, the face of the country has become once more smiling and prosperous; the slopes of the newly-formed hills are now clothed with vegetation, and the sugar-cane and the indigo again flourish luxuriantly in the fertile plains below.

On the opposite side of the Globe, 10,000 miles from Mexico, we have had, almost in our own time, an exhibition of volcanic phenomena not less wonderful than those we have been describing. The island of Sumbawa lies about two hundred miles to the east of Java in the Indian Archipelago; and it belongs to that remarkable chain of Volcanos which we have already described as stretching, with little interruption, along the coast of Asia from Russian America to the Bay of Bengal. In the year 1815, this island was the scene of a calamitous eruption, the effects of which were felt over the whole of the Molucca Islands and Java, as well as over a considerable portion of Celebes, Sumatra, and Borneo. Indeed, so extraordinary are the incidents of this eruption, that we might well hesitate to believe them if they had not been collected on the spot with more than ordinary diligence, and recorded with an almost scru-

* Sir John Herschel, Familiar Lectures on Scientific Subjects, p. 34; see also Lyell, Principles of Geology, chap. xxvii.; Mantell, Wonders of Geology, pp. 872–4.

pulous care. Sir Stamford Raffles, who was at the time governor of Java, then a British possession, required all the residents in the various districts under his authority to send in a statement of the circumstances which occurred within their own knowledge; and from the accounts he received in this way, combined with other evidence, chiefly obtained from eye-witnesses, he drew up the narrative to which we are mainly indebted for the following facts.

The explosions which accompanied this eruption were heard in Sumatra, at a distance of 970 geographical miles; and in the opposite direction at Ternate, a distance of 720 miles. In the neighborhood of the Volcano itself, immense tracts of land were covered with burning lava, towns and villages were overwhelmed, all kinds of vegetation completely destroyed, and of 12,000 inhabitants in the province of Tomboro, only twenty-six survived. The ashes, which were ejected in great quantities, were carried like a vast cloud through the air, by the southeast monsoon, for 300 miles in the direction of Java; and, still farther to the west, we are told that they formed a floating mass in the ocean two feet thick and several miles in extent, through which ships with difficulty forced their way. It is recorded, too, that they fell so thick on the island of Tombock, 100 miles away, as to cover all the land two feet deep, destroying every particle of vegetation, insomuch that 44,000 people perished of the famine that ensued. "I have seen it computed," writes Sir John Herschel, "that the quantity of ashes and lava vomited forth in this awful eruption would have formed three mountains the size of Mont Blanc, the highest of the Alps; and if spread over the surface of Germany, would have covered the whole of it two feet deep." Finally, it appears that this eruption was accompanied, like that of Monte Nuovo, by a permanent change in the level of the adjoining coast; in this case, however, it was a movement, not of upheaval, but of subsidence: the town of Tomboro sunk beneath the ocean, which is now eighteen feet deep where there was dry land before.*

Once more we will ask our readers to take a rapid flight over the map of the world, passing, this time, from the Indian Archipelago to the island of Iceland,—that "wonderful land of frost and fire." Besides the famous Volcano of Hecla, there are five others scarcely less formidable, all of which have been in active eruption within modern times. Of these the most celebrated is that of Skaptar Jokul. In the year 1783, this Volcano poured forth two streams of lava, which, when hardened, formed together one continuous layer of igneous rock, ninety miles in length, a hundred feet in height, and from seven to fifteen miles in breadth. The phenomena which accompanied the eruption are thus vividly described by Sir John Herschel :—"On the tenth of May innumerable fountains of fire were seen shooting up through the ice and snow which covered the mountain; and the principal river, called the Skapta, after rolling down a flood of foul and poisonous water, disappeared. Two days after, a torrent of lava poured down into the bed which the river had deserted. The river had run in a ravine 600 feet deep and 200 broad. This the lava entirely filled; and not only so, but it overflowed the surrounding country, and ran into a great lake, from which it instantly expelled the water in an explosion of steam. When the lake was fairly filled, the lava again overflowed and divided into two streams, one of which covered some ancient lava fields; the other re-entered the bed of the Skapta lower down, and presented the astounding sight of a cataract of liquid fire pouring over what was formerly the waterfall of Stapafoss. This was the greatest eruption on record in Europe. It lasted in its violence till the end of August, and closed with a violent earthquake; but for nearly the

* See Herschel, Familiar Lectures on Scientific Subjects, pp. 34–6. Lyell, Principles of Geology, vol. ii., pp. 104–6.

whole year a canopy of cinder-laden cloud hung over the island: the Faroe Islands, nay, even Shetland and the Orkneys, were deluged with ashes; and volcanic dust and a preternatural smoke which obscured the sun, covered all Europe as far as the Alps, over which it could not rise. The destruction of life in Iceland was frightful: 9,000 men, 11,000 cattle, 28,000 horses, and 190,000 sheep perished; mostly by suffocation. The lava ejected has been computed to amount in volume to more than twenty cubic miles."*

With these very significant facts before us, it is hard to resist the conclusion that the great mountain mass of Etna, 11,000 feet high and ninety miles in circumference, is formed entirely of volcanic matter ejected during successive eruptions. For the whole mountain is nothing else than a series of concentric conical layers of ashes and lava, such as have been poured out more than once upon its existing surface in modern times. Just, then, as Monte Nuovo was produced by an outburst of volcanic power in a single night, and the far larger mountain of Jorullo in the course of a few months, so may we believe that the more stupendous Etna is the work of the same power operating through a period of many centuries. And applying this conclusion to many other mountains throughout the world of exactly the same structure, we come to form no very mean estimate of the permanent changes wrought on the physical geography of our Globe by the operations of volcanic agency.

We must remember, too, that volcanic eruptions are not confined to the land; they often break out in the bed of the sea. In such cases the waters are observed in a state of violent commotion, jets of steam and sulphurous vapor are emitted, light scoriaceous matter appears floating on the surface, and not unfrequently the volcanic cone itself slowly rises from the depths below, and continues to

* Familiar Lectures on Scientific Subjects, pp. 31, 32.

grow from day to day, until at length it becomes an island of no inconsiderable magnitude. Sometimes when the violence of the eruption has subsided, the new island, consisting chiefly of ashes and pumice-stone, is gradually washed away by the action of the waves; but in the other cases, these lighter substances are compacted together by the injection of liquid lava, and being thus able to withstand the erosive power of the ocean, assume the importance of permanent volcanic islands. Many examples of the former kind are recorded within the last hundred years. In 1783 an island was thrown up in the North Atlantic Ocean, about thirty miles to the southwest of Iceland. It was claimed by the King of Denmark, and called by him Nyöe or New Island; but before a year had elapsed, this portion of his Majesty's dominion disappeared again beneath the waves, and the sea resumed its ancient domain. A cone-shaped island of the same kind, called Sabrina, three hundred feet high, with a crater in the centre, appeared amongst the Azores in 1811, but was quickly washed away again.

A more interesting example, because the circumstances are more minutely recorded, is the island which made its appearance in the Mediterranean, off the southwest coast of Sicily, in the year 1831. During its brief existence of three months, it received from contemporary writers seven different names; but the name of Graham Island seems to be the one by which it is most likely to be known to posterity. "About the tenth of July," writes Sir Charles Lyell, "John Corrao, the captain of a Sicilian vessel, reported that, as he passed near the place, he saw a column of water like a waterspout, sixty feet high, and eight hundred yards in circumference, rising from the sea, and soon afterward a dense steam in its place, which ascended to the height of 1800 feet. The same Corrao, on his return from Girgenti, on the eighteenth of July, found a small island, twelve feet high, with a crater in the centre, ejecting volcanic matter and immense columns of vapor; the sea around being covered with floating cinders and dead fish. The scoriae were of a chocolate color, and the water, which boiled in the circular basin, was of a dingy red. The eruption continued with great violence to the end of the same month, at which time the island was visited by several persons, and amongst others by Captain Swinburne, R. N., and M. Hoffman, the Prussian Geologist."* By the fourth of August the new island is said to have attained a height of 200 feet, and to have been three miles in circumference. Yet this was nothing more than the top of the volcanic cone; for, a few years before, Captain W. H. Smyth, in his survey, had found a depth of 600 feet at this very spot; and therefore the total height from the base of the mountain must have been 800 feet. From the beginning of August it began to melt away; and at the commencement of the following year, nothing remained of Graham Island but a dangerous shoal.

But even of the islands that occupy a prominent place on the map of the world, there is not wanting evidence to show that a large number derive their origin from the action of volcanic power. Among these may be mentioned many of the Molucca and Philippine groups, also several in the Grecian Archipelago, and not a few of the Azores and the Canaries,—in particular the lofty peak of Teneriffe, rising 12,000 feet above the level of the sea. In some cases, indeed, the actual process of their birth, and of their subsequent growth and development, has been minutely observed. A remarkable example occurs among the Aleutian Islands already referred to. In the year 1796 a column of smoke was seen to issue from the sea; then a small black point appeared at the surface of the water; then flames broke out, and other volcanic phenomena were ex-

* Principles of Geology, vol. ii., pp. 59, 60.

hibited; then the small black point grew into an island, and the island increased in size until it was at last several thousand feet high, and two or three miles in circumference. And such it remains to the present day.

The neighborhood of Santorin in the Grecian Archipelago has been noted from very remote times as the theatre of submarine eruptions. This island, which is itself to all appearance the crater of a vast volcano, has the form of a crescent, and, with the aid of two smaller islands

Fig. 28 – Bird's-eye view of Santorin during the volcanic eruption of February, 1866. (Lyell.)

a. Therasia.
b. The northern entrance, 1068 feet deep.
c. Thera.
d. Mount St. Elias, rising 1887 feet above the sea.
e. Aspronisi.
f. Little Kaimeni.
g. New Kaimeni.
h. Old Kaimeni.
i. Aphroessa.
k. George.

which stretch across between the horns of the crescent, encloses an almost circular bay. We learn from Pliny that in the year 186 before Christ, within this bay an island rose up which was called Hiera or the Sacred island. It was twice enlarged during the Christian era, once in 726, and again in 1427, and still exists under the name of Palaia Kaimeni, that is to say, the Old Burnt Island. In 1573 a second island made its appearance, and received the name of the Little Burnt Island, Mikra Kaimeni. In 1707 and 1709, a third island was thrown up, and was distinguished from the other two as Nea Kaimeni, the New Burnt Island. Lastly, in 1866 the hidden volcanic power again became active, and two new vents were formed, called respectively Aphroessa and George. "At the end of January," writes Sir Charles Lyell, "the sea had been observed in a state of ebullition off the southwest coast, and part of the Channel between New and Old Kaimeni, marked seventy fathoms in the Admiralty chart, had become, on February the eleventh, only twelve fathoms deep. According to M. Julius Schmidt, a gradual rising of the bottom went on until a small island made its appearance called afterward Aphroessa. It seems to have consisted of lava pressed upward and outward almost imperceptibly by steam, which was escaping at every pore through the hissing scoriaceous crust. 'It could be seen,' says Commander Lindesay Brine, R.N., 'through the fissures in the cone that the rocks within were red hot, but it was not till later that an eruption began.' On February the eleventh the village of Vulcano on the southeast coast, where there had been a partial sinking of the ground, was in great part overwhelmed by the materials cast out from a new vent which opened in that neighborhood, and to which the name of George was given, which finally, according to Schmidt, became about two hundred feet high.

"Commander Brine having ascended on February the twenty-eighth, 1866, to the top of the crater of Nea Kaimeni, about three hundred and fifty feet high, looked down upon the new vent then in full activity. The whole of the cone was swaying with an undulating motion to the right and left, and appeared sometimes to swell to nearly double its size and height, to throw out ridges like mountain spurs, till at last a broad chasm appeared across the top of the cone, accompanied by a tremendous roar of steam and the shooting up from the new crater, to the height of from fifty to a hundred feet, of tons of rock and ash mixed with smoke and steam. Some of these which fell on Mikra Kaimeni, at a distance of six hundred yards from the crater, measured thirty cubic feet. This effort over, the ridges slowly subsided, the cone lowered and closed in, and then, after a few minutes of comparative silence, the struggle would begin again with precisely similar sounds, action, and result. Threads of vapor escaping from the old crater of Nea Kaimeni proved that there was a subterranean connection between the new and the old vents. Aphroessa, of which the cone was at length raised to a height of more than sixty feet, was united in August with the main island. This was due in part at least to the upheaval of the bottom of the sea, which is now only seven fathoms deep in the channel dividing the New and Old Kaimenis, whereas in the Admiralty chart the soundings gave a hundred fathoms."*

* Principles of Geology, vol. ii. pp. 69, 70.

CHAPTER XVI.

SUBTERRANEAN HEAT—ITS POWERS ILLUSTRATED BY EARTHQUAKES.

Earthquakes and volcanos proceed from the same common cause—Recent earthquakes in New Zealand—Vast tracts of land permanently upraised—Earthquakes of Chili in the present century—Crust of the Earth elevated—Earthquake of Cutch in India, 1819—*Remarkable instance of subsidence and upheaval—Earthquake of Calabria,* 1783—*Earthquake of Lisbon,* 1755—*Great destruction of life and property—Earthquake of Peru, August,* 1868—*General scene of ruin and devastation—Great sea wave—A ship with all her crew carried a quarter of a mile inland—Frequency of earthquakes.*

HE chief effect of volcanic eruptions on the Geological structure of our Globe consists in the accumulation of cinders and molten rock, either upon the Surface of the Earth, or in the crevices and caverns that abound within its solid Crust. Sometimes, indeed, the operations of an active Volcano are accompanied by a movement of upheaval or of subsidence. Thus for instance, we have seen that a portion of the Italian coast was elevated when Monte Nuovo was thrown up, that the town of Tomboro was submerged on the occasion of the eruption of Sumbawa, and that the bottom of the sea was notably upheaved by the last outbreak of the volcanic fires of Santorin. Nevertheless it appears to be generally the case that when the Crust of the Earth is once burst open, and a means of

escape thus afforded to the fiery agent below,—in other words, when the active volcano is established,—the process of upheaval gives place to that of eruption. But when, as is often the case, no such safety-valve is offered to the surplus energies of the subterranean fires, then the giant power of heat, in its struggle to escape, shakes the foundation of the hills, and uplifts the superincumbent mass of solid rocks.

This theory which ascribes the phenomena of Earthquakes and Volcanos to the same common cause, acting under different circumstances, is now almost universally adopted by Geologists; and it may be briefly enforced by the following considerations. First, though Earthquakes have sometimes occurred far away from any known volcanic region, yet they are more frequent in the neighborhood of active or extinct Volcanos. Secondly, almost all volcanic eruptions are preceded by Earthquakes; and the Earthquakes generally cease, or, at least become less violent, when the subterranean fire breaks out in the form of a Volcano. And, Thirdly, it is plain that the condensed steam which is generated by internal heat, and the expansive power of the heat itself, must, of necessity, when pent up in the caverns of the Earth, tend to produce those very phenomena by which Earthquakes are distinguished.

Let it be observed, however, that while we explain the phenomena in question by the agency of subterranean heat, this doctrine is by no means necessary for the main purpose of our present argument. Whatever may be the cause from which the Earthquake shock proceeds, it is enough for us to show that the Crust of the Earth has been from time to time upraised, and dislocated, and rent asunder in modern times, just as it is supposed in Geological theory, to have been upraised, and dislocated, and rent asunder from time to time in by-gone ages. We will set down a few out of the many examples observed and recorded during the last hundred and twenty years.

When the English colonists settled in New Zealand about fifty years ago, they were told by the natives that they might expect a great Earthquake every seven years. This alarming prediction has not been literally fulfilled; but it is fully admitted that the total number of such disturbances within the last half century has not fallen short of what it should have been according to the above estimate. During the years 1826 and 1827 several shocks were felt in the neighborhood of Cook Strait, after which it was observed that the sea-shore had been uplifted on the north side of Dusky Bay. So transformed was the outline of the coast that its former features could no longer be recognized; and a small cove called the Jail, which had previously afforded a commodious harbor to vessels, engaged in seal fishing, was completely dried up.

But the most memorable convulsion took place on the night of January the twenty-third, 1855. A tract of land, about as large as Yorkshire, on the southwest coast of the North Island, was permanently upraised from one to nine feet. The harbor of Port Nicholson, together with the valley of the Hutt, was elevated four to five feet; and a sunken rock, regarded before as dangerous to navigators, has remained since the Earthquake three feet above the level of the water. The shock was felt by ships at sea a hundred and fifty miles from the coast; and it is estimated that the whole area affected was not less than three times the extent of the British Islands.

The whole coast of Chili has been subject to great disturbances and changes of level during the present century. In November, 1837, the town of Valdivia was destroyed by an Earthquake, and at the same moment, a whaling vessel, a short distance out at sea, was violently shaken, and lost her masts. The bottom of the sea was afterward found to have been raised in some places more than eight feet; and several rocks appeared high above the water which had previously been covered at all times by the sea. Two years before, in 1835, the town of Conception and several others were reduced to ruins by a like visitation. After the first great convulsion the Earth remained for many days in a state of commotion. More than three hundred lesser shocks were counted from the twentieth of February to the fourth of March. On this occasion, too, the bed of the sea was upheaved; and the whole island of Santa Maria, seven miles in length, was lifted up from eight to ten feet above its former level.

The Earthquake of 1822 was more violent, perhaps, and more striking in its effects, than either of those just mentioned. On the nineteenth of November in that year a sudden convulsive shock was simultaneously felt over a space 1200 miles in length. At Valparaiso, and on either side for a considerable distance, the coast was permanently upheaved. When Mrs. Graham, who was then living on the spot, and who has left us an account of the Earthquake, went down to the shore on the following day, she "found the ancient bed of the sea laid bare and dry, with beds of oysters, mussels, and other shells adhering to the rocks on which they grew, the fish being all dead, and exhaling most offensive effluvia." Some idea may be formed of the gigantic power here in operation, when it is remembered that to uplift the coast of Chili, it was necessary to move the mighty chain of the Andes, and, amongst the rest, the colossal mass of Aconcagua, 24,000 feet in height. How far this process of upheaval extended out to sea, beneath the bed of the ocean, has not been accurately ascertained: but certain it is that, for a considerable distance, the soundings were found to be shallower than before the Earthquake. It is roughly estimated that the Crust of the Earth was elevated over an extent of 100,000 square miles, or about half the area of France.

On the western coast of India, near the mouth of the

river Indus, is the well-known district of Cutch. In the month of June, 1819, this extensive territory, not less than half the size of Ireland, was violently shaken by an Earthquake, several hundred people were killed, and many towns and villages were laid in ruins. The shocks continued for some days, and ceased only when the outburst of a Volcano seemed to open a vent for the troubled spirit within. But what is particularly worthy of note is that when the Earthquake had passed away, a permanent change was found to have been effected in the level of the surrounding country. The town and fort of Sindree, situated on the eastern arm of the Indus, together with a tract of land 2,000 square miles in extent, were submerged beneath the waters. The principal buildings, however, still remained standing, with their upper parts above the surface ; and many of the inhabitants, who had taken refuge in one of the towers attached to the fort, were saved in boats when the Earthquake had ceased. On the other hand, within five miles and a half of this very spot, the level surface of the Earth was *upheaved*, so as to form a long elevated bank, fifty miles in length and sixteen in breadth, which has been called the Ullah Bund, or the Mound of God. Nine years after this event, Sir Alexander Burnes went out in a boat to the ruins of Sindree, and standing on the summit of the tower, which still rose two or three feet above the surface of the water, he could see nothing around him but a wide expanse of sea, save where a blue streak of land on the edge of the horizon marked the outline of the Ullah Bund. Here was a striking illustration, on a small scale, of those changes which Geologists suppose to have been going on since the world first began ; the dry land had been converted into the bed of the sea, and the level plain had been elevated into a mountain ridge.

Toward the close of the last century the province of Calabria, in Southern Italy, was the scene of an Earthquake which offers a very apposite illustration of our present argument. This celebrated convulsion is not, however, chiefly remarkable for its violence, or for its duration, or for the extent of the territory moved. In all these respects it has been surpassed by many Earthquakes, experienced in other countries, within the last hundred and fifty years. But the Calabrian Earthquake has an especial claim on our attention, mainly from this unusual circumstance, that the region of disturbance was visited, as Sir Charles Lyell tells us, "both during and after the convulsions, by men possessing sufficient leisure, zeal, and scientific information, to enable them to collect and describe with accuracy such physical facts as throw light on geological questions."

The shocks were first felt in February, 1783, and continued for nearly four years. Over a very considerable area of country all the common landmarks were removed, large tracts of land were forced bodily down the slopes of mountains; and vineyards, orchards, and cornfields were transported from one site to another; insomuch that disputes afterward arose as to who was the rightful owner of the property that had thus shifted its position. Two farms near Mileto, occupying an extent of country a mile long and half a mile broad, were actually removed for a mile down the valley; and "a thatched cottage, together with large olive and mulberry trees, most of which remained erect, was carried uninjured to this extraordinary distance." In other places the surface of the Earth heaved like the billows of a troubled sea; many houses were lifted up above the common level, while others subsided below it. Again and again the solid Crust of the Earth was rent asunder, and chasms, gorges, ravines, of various depths, were suddenly produced, in less time than it takes to tell it. Sometimes when the strain was removed, the yawning gulf as quickly closed again, and then houses, cattle, and men were swallowed up in the abyss, leaving not a trace behind. It has even been recorded—strange though it may seem—that when two shocks rapidly followed one another at the same spot, the people engulphed by the first, were again cast forth by the second, being literally disgorged alive from the jaws of death. About 40,000 persons perished in this dreadful visitation, the greater number being crushed to death beneath the ruins of the towns and villages, others swallowed up in the yawning fissures as they fled across the open country, and others again burned in the conflagrations which almost always followed the shocks of Earthquake.

Every one has heard of the famous Earthquake of Lisbon. It is chiefly memorable for the extreme suddenness of the shock, for the immense extent of the area affected, and for the amount of havoc and destruction done. On the morning of the fatal day—it was the first of November, 1755—the sun rose bright and cheerful over the devoted city, no symptom of impending danger was visible in the sky above or on the Earth below, and the gay-hearted people were pursuing their accustomed rounds of pleasure or business, when, suddenly, at twenty minutes before ten o'clock, a sound like thunder was heard underground, the Earth was violently shaken, and in another moment, the greater part of the city was lying in ruins. Within the brief space of six minutes, 60,000 people were crushed to death. The mountains in the vicinity of the town were cleft asunder. The waters of the sea first retired from the land, and then rolled back in a huge mountain-like wave fifty feet above the level of the highest tide. A new quay, built entirely of marble, had offered a temporary place of refuge to the terrified inhabitants as they fled from the tumbling ruins of the city. Three thousand people are said to have been collected upon it, when, all at once, it sunk beneath the waves, and not a fragment of the solid masonry, not a vestige of its living freight, was ever seen again. The bottom of the sea where the quay then stood is now a hundred fathoms deep.

From Lisbon as a centre the shock of this Earthquake radiated over an area not less than four times the extent of Europe. Like a great wave it rolled northward, at the rate of twenty miles a minute, upheaving the Earth as it moved along, to the coasts of the Baltic Sea and the German Ocean. The waters of Loch Lomond, in Scotland, were violently disturbed from beneath, and at Kinsale, in Ireland, the sea rushed impetuously into the harbor without a breath of wind, and mounting over the quay, flooded the market-place. Eastward the convulsion was felt as far as the Alps, and westward it extended to the West India Islands, and even to the great lakes of Canada. On the north coast of Africa the disturbance was as violent as in Spain and Portugal; and it is recorded that at a distance of eight leagues from Morocco, the earth opened and swallowed up a considerable town with its inhabitants, to the number of eight or ten thousand people.

Even on the high seas the shock was felt no less distinctly than on dry land. "Off St. Lucar," says Sir Charles Lyell, "the captain of the ship Nancy felt his vessel so violently shaken, that he thought she had struck the ground, but, on heaving the lead, found a great depth of water. Captain Clark, from Denia, in latitude 36° 24′ N., between nine and ten in the morning, had his ship shaken and strained as if she had struck upon a rock, so that the seams of the deck opened, and the compass was overturned in the binnacle. Another ship, forty leagues west of St. Vincent, experienced so violent a concussion, that the men were thrown a foot and a half perpendicularly up from the deck." It is worthy of note that this, the most destructive Earthquake recorded in history, was not attended with any volcanic eruption; which goes to confirm our theory that the active Volcano serves as a kind of safety-valve for the escape of the struggling powers confined within the Crust of the Earth.*

We must not bring our notice of Earthquakes to an end without at least some brief account of one which has startled the world even since we began to put together the materials of this Volume. On the Western Coast of South America there is a long, narrow strip of land, lying between the lofty crests of the Andes and the shores of the Pacific Ocean, which from the earliest times has been the familiar home of Earthquakes. Toward evening on the thirteenth of August, 1868, this fated region was the scene of a convulsion the most appalling and destructive that has been recorded within the present century. The disturbance was felt in its extreme violence for a distance of 1500 miles along the coast; from Ibarra one degree north of the Equator to Iquique more than twenty degrees south. In ten minutes from the first shock, 20,000 people perished, and a vast amount of property, roughly estimated at sixty millions sterling, was utterly destroyed. Many thriving towns—Iquique, Mexillones, Pisagua, Arica, Ylo, Chala, and others—were levelled to the ground. Even the very ruins were not spared. The sea rushed in when the Earthquake shock had ceased, and carried everything before it in one universal wreck: so that in some cases not a vestige remained behind to tell the dismayed survivors where their homesteads once had stood. It might be fancied perhaps that the cities seated aloft in the security of the Eternal Hills were beyond the reach of the convulsion that shook the plain below. But no: Arequipa, far up on

* For the account of these various Earthquakes we are mainly indebted to the indefatigable industry of Sir Charles Lyell, who has collected the facts with great care partly from the descriptions of eye-witnesses, and partly from authentic documents written upon the spot. See his Principles of Geology, vol. ii., chap. xxviii., xxix., xxx. See also Mr. Mallet's Earthquake Catalogue; and the first of Sir John Herschel's Lectures on Familiar Subjects.

the slopes of the western Cordillera, and Pasco, the highest city in the world, situated on a level with the snowy summit of the Jungfrau, were shattered into fragments with the same violence as the cities of the coast.

The various incidents recorded by the survivors are full of fearful interest. At Iquique, according to one account, about five o'clock in the evening of the thirteenth of August, a rumbling noise was heard, then the earth shook violently for some minutes, then the sea, with a great moan, retired from the shore, and rearing itself up into a tremendous wave, rushed back upon the land and swept away the town. "I saw," says one writer, "the whole surface of the sea rise as if a mountain side, actually standing up. Another shock, accompanied with a fearful roar, now took place. I called to my companions to run for their lives on to the Pampa. Too late! With a horrid crash the sea was on us, and at one sweep—one terrible sweep—dashed what was Iquique on to the Pampa. I lost my companions, and in an instant was fighting with the dark water. The mighty wave surged and roared and leaped. The cries of human beings and animals were dreadful. A mass of wreck covered me and kept me down, and I was fast drowning when the sea threw me on to a beam, but a nail piercing my coat, the timber rolled me again under, and I lost all sense. I suppose, as in all such cases, I must have struggled after sensation had left me, for when returning consciousness came I was grasping under one arm a large plank. Looking round, all was wreck and desolation. In a moment I was by a returning wave swept into the bay, and meeting a mass of broken timber, I was struck a fearful blow on the chin, and the broken end of the plank passed through my thigh. I knew no more until I found myself on the Pampa, and all dark around me. I was without trousers, coat, shoes, or hat. Trying to collect myself, I thought of another wave, and crawled away to the mountain side, scooped a hole in the ground, and got in; here, wet and shivering, I spent the night. My wound bled freely. In the morning I looked out and found Iquique gone, all but a few houses round the church."

A good deal of shipping was lying in the bay of Arica. When the waters first receded the vessels were all carried out to sea, chains, cables, and anchors snapping asunder like packthread. A moment afterward they were borne back irresistibly by the returning wave, and dashed to pieces on the coast. One more fortunate than the rest, the Wateree, a vessel of war belonging to the United States Government, was caught up on the crest of the wave, and with the loss of only one man, was landed high and dry among the sand-hills a quarter of a mile from the shore.

Before the Earthquake, Arequipa was a prosperous town of 30,000 inhabitants. It enjoyed a considerable trade, and, in importance as well as size, it was regarded as the third city of Peru, being inferior only to Lima and Cuzco. The houses were constructed with especial regard to security against the shock of Earthquakes. They were but one story high, built of solid stone, and massive to an extraordinary degree. But these precautions, though the fruit of long experience, were all of no avail. At Sunset on the fatal thirteenth of August the populous and thriving city of Arequipa was little better than a heap of ruins. "Not a church is left standing," writes an eye-witness, "not a house habitable. The shock commenced at twenty minutes past five in the afternoon, and lasted six or seven minutes. The houses being solidly built and of one story, resisted for one minute, which gave the people time to rush into the middle of the streets, so that the mortality, although considerable, is not so great as might have been expected. If the Earthquake had occurred at night, few indeed would have been left to tell the story. As it is, the prisoners in the public prison, and the sick in the hospital, have perished.

The Earthquake commenced with an undulating movement, and as the shock culminated, no one could keep his feet: the houses rocked as a ship in the trough of the sea, and came crumbling down. The shrieks of the women, the crash of falling masonry, the upheaving of the earth, and the clouds of blinding dust, made up a scene that cannot be described. We had nineteen minor shocks the same night, and the earth still continues in motion. Nothing has as yet been done toward disinterring the dead; but I do not think any are buried alive, as certain death must have been the fate of all those who were not able to get into the street. The earth has opened in all the plains around, and water has appeared in various places."*

These are a few typical examples of the more violent convulsions by which the Crust of the Earth has been disturbed within little more than a century; and they leave no doubt as to the kind of changes which may fairly be ascribed to similar agency in the past history of the Globe. Nor must it be supposed that, because our examples are few in number, the Earthquake is itself a rare and exceptional event. On the contrary, the state of partial disturbance and convulsion would seem to be the natural and ordinary condition of our planet. From the interesting Catalogue drawn up by Mr. Mallet, it appears that, in our own times, the number of Earthquakes actually observed and recorded is, on an average, not less than from two to three every week. Now this catalogue cannot represent more than one-third of the Globe: for the disturbances

* The following are the sources from which we have chiefly derived our information regarding the Peruvian Earthquake of 1868: (1) a series of letters written upon the scene of the catastrophe, and published in *The Times* of September 26, 1868; amongst them is one from the British Vice-consul, and one from the agent of the Pacific Steam Navigation Company, who were both at the time residents of Arica: (2) a letter of Mr. Clements Markham in *The Times* of September 15, 1868: (3) Captain Powell's Report to the Admiralty, dated September 14, 1868.

which take place in the profound depths of the ocean must for the most part escape observation, and many parts even of the inhabited Earth are still beyond the reach of scientific researches. It is, therefore, quite a reasonable speculation of Sir Charles Lyell, that "scarcely a day passes without one or more shocks being experienced in some part of the Globe."

Moreover, in Mr. Mallet's Catalogue no account is taken of those minor vibrations or tremblings of the Earth's Crust, which are not attended by any striking or noteworthy event. And yet such phenomena, when often repeated, may produce a very important change of level, and are far more frequent than most persons would be likely to suppose. In our quiet region of the Globe people are too apt to take for granted the general stability of the Earth: but in other countries the inhabitants, warned by long experience, are no less deeply impressed with a conviction of its instability. Sir John Herschel says that, in the volcanic regions of Central and Southern America, "the inhabitants no more think of counting Earthquake shocks, than we do of counting showers of rain:" nay, he adds that, "in some places along the coast a shower is a greater variety." And in Sicily, we are told they make provision against movements of the Earth's Crust, just as we make provision against lightning and storms; so much so that it is quite a common thing for architects to advertise their houses as Earthquake-proof.

CHAPTER XVII.

SUBTERRANEAN HEAT—ITS POWERS ILLUSTRATED BY UNDULATIONS OF THE EARTH'S CRUST.

Gentle movements of the Earth's Crust within historic times—Roman roads and temples submerged in the bay of Baiæ—Temple of Jupiter Serapis—Singular condition of its columns—Proof of subsidence and subsequent upheaval—Indications of a second subsidence now actually taking place—Gradual upheaval of the coast of Sweden—Summary of the evidence adduced to establish this fact—Subsidence of the Earth's Crust on the west coast of Greenland—Recapitulation.

SO far we have spoken of the disturbance of the Earth's Crust in modern times by sudden and violent convulsions. But there are many phenomena with which the Geologist is familiar, that cannot be fairly accounted for unless by supposing that the surface of the Earth was often elevated and depressed in ancient times, without any sudden shock, by a slow and almost insensible movement. And, accordingly, gentle undulations of this kind enter largely into that general theory of Geology which we have been attempting to draw out and illustrate. It may be asked, therefore, if we are able to support this part of our system by examples of similar phenomena occurring within the period of history. In reply, we shall endeavor to set forth, as briefly as we can, some of the evidence which has recently come to light on this subject, and which seems to us not less conclusive than it is interesting and unexpected.

In the bay of Baiæ, to the west of Naples, two ancient Roman roads may be distinctly traced, at the present day, for a considerable distance, permanently submerged beneath the waters. There are, also, in the same neighborhood, the ruins of the temple of Neptune and of the temple of the Nymphs, both likewise submerged. "The columns of the former edifice stand erect in five feet of water, the upper portions just rising to the surface;* the pedestals are supposed to be buried in the mud below. Again, on the opposite side of Naples, near Sorrento, "a road with fragments of Roman buildings, is covered to some depth by the sea;" † and in the island of Capri, at the opening of the bay of Naples, one of the palaces of Tiberius is also under water. Here, therefore, it is clear that the Crust of the Earth has subsided over a very considerable area; since what is now the bed of the sea, was in the days of the Romans dry land, traversed by roads, and dotted over with buildings. That the subsidence was slow and gradual may be inferred, partly from the absence of any record or tradition of a sudden convulsion producing such a change, and partly, too, from the unshaken and undisturbed condition of the monuments themselves.

But while this conclusion falls in most happily with our present argument, it would seem on further examination to bring with it a very serious difficulty. For, while those ancient monuments testify that the Crust of the Earth in this locality has *subsided*, the structure of the sea-coast, interpreted according to Geological principles, would indicate, on the contrary, that the Crust of the Earth has been *upheaved*. Close to the sea, at the present day, on the bay of Baiæ, there is a low, level tract of fertile land, and at a lit-

* Lyell, Principles of Geology, vol. ii., p. 176. † Id. ib.

tle distance inland, a lofty range of precipitous cliffs, eighty feet high, parallel to the line of the coast. This fertile tract, lying between the sea-beach and the perpendicular cliffs, is about twenty feet above the sea level, and is composed of regularly stratified deposits abounding in marine shells of recent species, together with works of human art, such as tiles, squares of mosaic pavement, fragments of bricks, and sculptured ornaments. Upon these facts a Geologist would pronounce without hesitation :—First, that at some period since the district around Naples was first inhabited by man, the waters of the sea washed the base of the perpendicular cliffs; secondly, that the strata in which we now find the recent marine shells, and the remains of man's workmanship, were formed during that period by the process of deposition at the bottom of the sea; and thirdly, that at some subsequent time, by an upheaval of the Earth's Crust, these strata were lifted up so as to form a pretty considerable area of dry land, fit for agriculture and the arts of life.

Does it not seem, therefore, that we have here a direct contradiction between the evidence of ancient Roman buildings and the inferences of modern Geology? Doubtless, they both agree in the main point about which we are concerned just now, that the Crust of the Earth has been moved in recent times on the shores of the bay of Naples; but according to the testimony of the Roman temples, now covered by water, this movement has been one of *subsidence*, while, according to the inferences of Geological theory, it has been one of *upheaval.* This apparent contradiction seems to call for some elucidation.

If we were left in this matter to mere conjecture, we might offer the following hypothesis as a fair and reasonable solution. We might suppose that since the days of the Roman Empire, there have been *two successive movements* of the Earth's Crust in the neighborhood of Naples; first, a movement of subsidence, by which the ancient temples and roads were submerged to a considerable depth beneath the sea; afterward, a movement of upheaval, by which the marine strata were lifted up. If this second movement were exactly equal to the first, it is plain that the ancient roads and buildings would have been just restored to their former level. But let us suppose that the amount of upheaval was something less than the amount of previous subsidence, and we should have these roads and buildings still submerged, as they are in point of fact, in a few feet of water. By such an hypothesis, therefore, the two classes of phenomena might be brought into perfect harmony.

But we are not obliged to take refuge in hypothesis: for it is now distinctly proved by a very curious kind of evidence, that the Crust of the Earth in and about the bay of Baiæ, has been successively depressed and upraised since the third century of the Christian era; nay more, that the subsidence in the first case was greater than the subsequent upheaval. Near Pozzuoli, on the level tract of land which, as we have said, intervenes between the sea and the lofty range of inland cliffs, are to be seen at the present day the ruins of a splendid Roman edifice, usually called the temple of Jupiter Serapis, though, according to some writers, it was not a temple at all, but a public establishment for baths. These ruins first attracted attention about the middle of the last century. Three magnificent marble columns were still standing erect, with their lower parts buried in the stratified deposits already described, and their upper portions, which projected above the surface of the land, partly concealed by bushes. When the soil was removed the original plan of the building could be distinctly traced. "It was of a quadrangular form, seventy feet in diameter, and the roof had been supported by forty-six noble columns, twenty-four of granite and the rest of marble." Many of the pillars have been shattered in the course of time, and lie strewn in fragments on the pavements. The three which are still standing erect, are upward of forty feet in height, each carved out of a solid block of marble; and, what is chiefly to our purpose, they exhibit, curiously inscribed on their surface, memorials of the physical changes in which they have borne a part.

The base of these lofty columns is, at present, slightly below the level of the sea. Their outer surface is smooth for about twelve feet above the pedestals; then, for the next nine feet the marble is everywhere bored by a well-known species of mussel, which it is certain can live only in the sea. Above this band of perforations the pillars again present a smooth surface, and continue smooth to the top. The first inference from these facts is, that the columns in question must have been at one time submerged to a height of twenty-one feet above the pedestals; otherwise they could not have been bored at that height by a species of animal that can only exist in sea-water. Since that time, therefore, the land at this spot must have been upraised twenty-one feet. Furthermore, the temple of Jupiter was certainly not built at the bottom of the sea, but upon dry land; therefore, after the temple had been built, the Crust of the Earth must have subsided at least twenty-one feet. Once more: as the floor of the temple is now somewhat below the level of the sea, and as it is not very likely it was at first so built, we may fairly infer that it is now lower than it originally stood; and consequently, that the total amount of upheaval has not been equal to the total amount of subsidence. Though we cannot fix the exact date at which the subsidence began, it was probably not earlier than the third century; for in the atrium of the temple is an inscription recording that it was adorned with precious marbles by the emperor Septimus Severus.

It cannot be supposed for a moment that these changes were effected by a rise and fall in the level of the sea rather than by a movement of the Earth's Crust. A permanent change in the level of the Mediterranean, in any given locality, would, of necessity, imply a change of level over its entire extent; and therefore, if the phenomena exhibited in the bay of Baiæ arose from such a cause, we should meet with phenomena of the same kind along the whole length of the Italian coast. Now, in point of fact, no such changes of level are elsewhere apparent; and consequently, they must be ascribed in the bay of Baiæ, not to an upward and downward movement of the sea, but to an upward and downward movement of the land.

We must not omit to state, before leaving the subject, that it is now ascertained, by a series of accurate observations, that the Crust of the Earth in this interesting locality is once again slowly and gradually subsiding. At the beginning of the century the platform of the temple stood at about the level of the sea; it is now more than a foot below it. Nay, this second subsidence appears to have begun even before the present century. "In the year 1813," writes a modern traveller, "I resided for four months in the Capuchin convent of Pozzuoli, which is situated between the road from Naples and the sea, at the entrance of the town of Pozzuoli. In the Capuchin convents the oldest friar is called 'il molto reverende,' and the one who then enjoyed the title in this convent was ninety-three years old. He informed me that, when he was a young man, the road from Naples passed on the *seaward side* of the convent; but that, from the gradual sinking of the soil, the road was obliged to be altered to its present course. While I was staying at the convent, the refectory as well as the entrance gate, were from six inches to a foot under water whenever strong westerly winds prevailed, so as to cause the waters of the Mediterranean to rise. Thirty years previously, my old informant stated, such an occurrence never took place. In fact, it is not probable that the builder of the convent would have placed the ground-floor so low as to expose to inundation as it now is."*

On the shores of the Baltic Sea we find another illustration of our theory upon a more extended scale. About a century and a half ago the Swedish naturalist, Celsius, expressed a belief that a remarkable change of level was taking place along the eastern coast of Scandinavia; and he ascribed the change to a subsidence of the waters of the Baltic Sea. This opinion was received at first with no small amount of incredulity; but the arguments of Celsius were plausible and attractive enough to excite a controversy, and the controversy once aroused was not easily set at rest. Accordingly, since his time the facts upon which he relied have been more strictly examined, difficulties have been started and investigated, many new facts, at first unknown or unnoticed, have been brought to light, and the whole question has been rigorously discussed by scientific men. It would be tedious to go through the history of the discussion, or to develop at any length the arguments which in the end have proved successful, involving as they do a multitude of minute observations and nice measurements, made at a great variety of different places with hard-sounding names. But the general result may be readily stated and as readily understood.

It appears that numerous sunken reefs, well known to navigators, have, within the last two centuries, become visible above water; that many ancient ports have become inland towns; that many small islands have become united to one another and to the mainland by grassy plains; that rocky points which in former times just peeped above the water, and afforded refuge only to a solitary sea-bird, are now grown into little islets; and that several of the old fish-

* Letter from C. Hullmandel, Esq.; see Mantell, Wonders of Geology, Appendix G., p. 470. For a full and elaborate disquisition on the Temple of Jupiter Serapis, see also Lyell, Principles of Geology, vol. ii., chap. xxv.

ing grounds are now deserted for their shallowness, nay, in some cases, altogether dried up. From these facts the inference is plain; either the solid Crust of the Earth has been uplifted, or the waters of the sea have subsided. Now it is certain there has been no subsidence of the sea; for such a subsidence, as we before observed, if it took place at all, should have been general; whereas there are many points on the shores of the Baltic, especially along the coasts of Denmark and Prussia, where it can be proved that no change of level has taken place for centuries. And therefore the phenomena above described we must attribute to an upheaval of the Earth's Crust.*

Such is the kind of reasoning with which this inquiry has been pursued; and it may now be set down as a received and established fact, that a slow and gradual process of upheaval is going on, at the present day, on the shores of the Baltic Sea, at the rate of from two to four feet in a century; and this is over an area of unknown breadth, and not less than 1000 miles in length. Evidence of a similar kind has lately been adduced to prove that the west coast of Greenland is just now gradually subsiding for a space of more than 600 miles from north to south. "Ancient buildings on low, rocky islands, and on the shore of the mainland, have been gradually submerged, and experience has taught the aboriginal Greenlander never to build his hut near the water's edge. In one case the Moravian settlers have been obliged more than once to move the poles upon which their large boats were set, and the old poles still remain beneath the water as silent witnesses of the change."†

It should seem, therefore, that the Crust of the Earth is not that fixed and immovable mass of unyielding rock which it is often supposed to be. Whatever the gigantic power is which lies shut up within it, and which seems, clearly

* Lyell, Principles of Geology, vol. ii., chap. xxxi. † Ibid.

enough, to be developed in some way or another—perhaps in many ways at once—from internal heat, that power exercises a mighty influence from age to age on the outward form of our planet. Like the wind, indeed, it bloweth where it listeth, and we cannot tell whence it cometh or whither it goeth; but we can hear the sound thereof, and witness its effects when it breaks out now in this quarter of the world, and now in that, bursting open the massive rocks, and furiously vomiting forth whole mountains of smouldering ashes and molten mineral; or again, when, failing to find a vent, it shakes the foundations of the hills, and shivers into fragments the most enduring works of man—castles, temples, palaces,—filling every heart with terror and dismay; or, in fine, when it gently upheaves the bottom of the ocean, or by withdrawing the strain, allows the Crust of the Earth to subside, with a movement so gradual and insensible as to escape the notice of the multitudes who are toiling in the busy cities on its Surface. That phenomena of this kind have been going on in all past ages, is now universally assumed in the speculations of Geology: that they are going on in the present age, we have here endeavored to prove by the evidence of facts. If we have succeeded according to our expectations, the reader will be prepared to admit that, on this point at least, it is not the Geologist who may fairly be charged with having recourse to the inventions of his fancy, but rather those who, assuming as a first principle that Geology is false, perseveringly shut their eyes to the physical changes that are going on around them.

PART II.

THE ANTIQUITY OF THE EARTH CONSIDERED IN RELATION TO THE HISTORY OF GENESIS.

CHAPTER XVIII.

STATEMENT OF THE QUESTION AND EXPOSITION OF THE AUTHOR'S VIEW.

The general principles of geological theory accepted by the author—These principles plainly import the extreme antiquity of the earth—Illustration from the coal, the chalk, and the boulder clay—This conclusion not at variance with the inspired history of creation—Chronology of the Bible—Genealogies of Genesis—Date of the creation not fixed by Moses—Progress of opinion on this point—Cardinal Wiseman, Father Perrone, Father Pianciani—Doctor Buckland—Doctor Chalmers, Doctor Pye Smith, Hugh Miller—Author's view explained—Charge of rashness and irreverence answered—Admonitions of Saint Augustine and Saint Thomas.

HE reader has now before him a general outline of Geological theory, together with some familiar illustrations of the evidence by which it is supported. We shall not attempt to enforce this evidence by any remarks of our own. Indeed it is of a kind that can derive but little aid from the arts of logic or rhetoric. It needs but to be fairly understood, and if it does not

altogether compel our assent, it begets at least a presumption so strong as to leave little room for doubt or hesitation.

Nobody, so far as we know, has ever hesitated to believe that the Round Towers of Ireland are the work of human hands. And yet if some incredulous skeptic were to raise the cry against this common opinion, were to argue that it is a mere hypothesis, and call for proof, we should be embarrassed how to answer him. We could only say that these monuments have all the characteristic marks of man's handiwork; and that buildings of this kind have never been known to come into existence except through the agency of Man. But should our vexatious skeptic contend that they were possibly produced by a freak of Nature; or that they were built in the beginning by the Creator of the World, who certainly might have made them had He been so minded, we should think him very unreasonable, and probably not feel much disposed to prolong the discussion. In like manner the theory of Geology which we are defending, cannot be established by a rigid demonstration: but we believe there is not one man of sense and judgment, who, being fully master of the evidence on which it rests, hesitates to accept that theory, at least in its more general outlines. No doubt many able and eminent men are to be found arrayed against Geology; but it would be easy to show from their writings that they have never thoroughly examined the facts about which they talk so flippantly, and which they often set aside so lightly.

For ourselves, therefore, we frankly avow that while we attach but little importance to the mere conjectures and speculations of Geological writers; while we look with doubt and suspicion on many plausible theories commonly enough adopted at the present day; and while we consider that the discoveries of modern times, wonderful though they are, have given rise to far more problems than they are yet able to solve; yet we do fully assent to those general principles which we have been attempting to develop and to illustrate in this Volume. Absolutely metaphysical certainty we have not; but we have a firm and rational conviction. We feel quite satisfied that the great Creator of the Universe did not bring suddenly into existence the withered remains and broken fragments of animals which had never lived; that He did not stamp upon the massive rocks, buried in the profound recesses of the earth, the impress of a luxuriant vegetation which had never flourished; that He did not, in short, create under millions of forms, the delusive appearances of things which had never been, and scatter them through this world of ours in wild profusion, well knowing that after many centuries they would come to light to bewilder human reason, and to lead it into error. This conclusion, of course, we are prepared to abandon if it should be found to clash with any certain truth or with any demonstrated fact. But, in the mean time, it seems to us as well grounded and as fairly established as the conclusions we are accustomed to accept without hesitation in the matter of other sciences, and in the common business of life.

It is argued, however, that Geological theory is, in fact, at variance with the very highest order of truth; with that truth which comes to us on the authority of God Himself. The Bible tells us that the world first came into existence about six or eight thousand years ago: Geology, on the contrary, tells us that six or eight thousand years are but as yesterday in the history of the revolutions through which our Globe has passed. This is the argument to which we are now about to address ourselves; and it well deserves our best attention, not only from its intrinsic importance, but also from the interesting nature of the discussion to which it has given rise.

In the first place, we fully admit that the extreme

Antiquity of the Earth is a necessary consequence of our theory. Setting out from the present stage of the world's existence, Geology carries us back from epoch to epoch, through a long succession of ages, each extending over many thousand years, until the mind is lost in the seeming infinity of the past. It may be asked, perhaps, in what way Geology can testify to the great length of each successive period in the history of the Globe. A familiar example will furnish the most convenient reply to such a question.

Let the reader call to mind what we have already explained about the origin and formation of Coal; and then let him examine the structure of the Carboniferous Rocks. In the great Coal-fields of Wales, for instance, he will find, in a depth of 12,000 feet, from fifty to a hundred distinct beds of coals, spread out one above another, with intervening strata of clay several feet thick. Now each one of these beds represents an ancient forest which must have grown up and flourished and decayed; or else an immense and varied mass of Drift-wood, transported from a distance by the action of moving water, and deposited near the mouth of some great river. In either case a considerable lapse of time would have been necessary for such an accumulation of vegetable matter as would furnish the elements even of a single seam of Coal. And, when that period came to an end, only one little stage in the long series had been accomplished: one stratum of a few feet had been laid down in that great Formation which was to reach at length a height of more than two miles. A new condition of things then ensued. This layer of vegetable matter, sunk below the waters, was gradually covered over with a thick deposit of clay, which, in course of time, was to emerge, and become dry land, and give birth to a second forest, destined in its turn to wither and decay. Or, at least, when the stratum of clay had been deposited, it was to be overlaid, in some way or another, with a second layer of vegetable matter sufficient for the production of a second bed of coal. And so this process must have gone on, doubtless with many and long interruptions, for a hundred times in succession.

Then it must be remembered that the Coal-bearing strata represent but one of many periods, and that not the longest in the Geological Calendar. Before the age of the Coal, England was for centuries at the bottom of the sea, while the Old Red Sandstone was slowly spread out over its existing surface. And after the age of the Coal, England was again submerged, and gigantic Ichthyosaurs with their companions of the deep, sported in the waters that rolled over her plains and covered the tops of her mountains; and, when they had run their course, left their remains buried in the clays of Oxfordshire and Warwickshire and Dorsetshire.

Furthermore, the beds in which these monstrous reptiles are entombed were overlaid by a stratum of calcareous ooze, now forming a solid mass of Chalk Rock, often a thousand feet in thickness. This Chalk, as we have seen, is nothing else than a vast accumulation of shells, so minute that millions of them would fit together on the blade of a small penknife, and hundreds of millions are carried about by every carpenter in his waistcoat pocket. How many generations of animalcules it took to pile up such an immense thickness of rock, by the action of their vital powers, and how many ages were consumed in the process it is beyond the reach of science to calculate, almost beyond the power of imagination to conceive. And yet the Chalk itself was followed by the various Formations of the Tertiary Age; while the last of these is separated by the Drift and Boulder Clay from the superficial deposits which correspond with the period of history, and which go by the name of Recent.

This topic has been illustrated in a lively and striking manner by Professor Huxley, in a Lecture delivered not long ago before the working-men of Norwich. "At Cromer," he says, "one of the most charming spots on the coast of Norfolk, you will see the Boulder Clay forming a vast mass, which lies upon the Chalk, and must consequently have come into existence after it. Huge boulders of chalk are, in fact, included in the clay, and have evidently been brought to the position they now occupy by the same agency as that which has planted blocks of syenite from Norway side by side with them.

"The Chalk, then, is certainly older than the Boulder Clay. If you ask how much, I will again take you no further than the same spot upon your own coasts for evidence. I have spoken of the Boulder Clay and Drift as resting upon the Chalk. That is not strictly true. Interposed between the Chalk and the Drift is a comparatively insignificant layer, containing vegetable matter. But that layer tells a wonderful history. It is full of stumps of trees standing as they grew. Fir-trees are there with their cones, and hazel-bushes with their nuts; there stand the stools of oak and yew trees, beeches and alders. Hence this stratum is appropriately called the Forest-bed.

"It is obvious that the Chalk must have been upheaved and converted into dry land before the timber trees could grow upon it. As the trunks of some of these trees are from two to three feet in diameter, it is no less clear that the dry land thus formed remained in the same condition for long ages. And not only do the remains of stately oaks and well-grown firs testify to the duration of this condition of things, but additional evidence to the same effect is afforded by the abundant remains of elephants, rhinoceroses, hippopotamuses, and other great wild beasts, which it has yielded to the zealous search of such men as the Reverend Mr. Gunn.

"When you look at such a collection as he has formed, and bethink you that these elephantine bones did veritably carry their owners about, and these great grinders crunch in the dark woods of which the Forest-bed is now the only trace, it is impossible not to feel that they are as good evidence of the lapse of time as the annual rings of the tree-stumps.

"Thus there is a writing upon the wall of cliffs at Cromer, and whoso runs may read it. It tells us with an authority which cannot be impeached, that the ancient bed of the Chalk sea was raised up and remained dry land until it was covered with forest, stocked with the great game whose spoils have rejoiced your Geologists. How long it remained in that condition cannot be said; but the 'whirligig of time brought its revenges' in those days as in these. That dry land, with the bones and teeth of generations of long-lived elephants hidden away among the gnarled roots and dry leaves of its ancient trees, sank gradually to the bottom of the icy sea, which covered it with huge masses of Drift and Boulder Clay. Sea-beasts, such as the walrus, now restricted to the extreme north, paddled about where birds had twittered among the topmost twigs of the fir-trees. How long this state of things endured we know not, but at length it came to an end. The upheaved glacial mud hardened into the soil of modern Norfolk. Forests grew once more, the wolf and the beaver replaced the reindeer and the elephant; and at length what we called the history of England, dawned.

"Thus evidence which cannot be rebutted, and which need not be strengthened, though, if time permitted, I might indefinitely increase its quantity, compels you to believe that the Earth from the time of the Chalk to the present day, has been the theatre of a series of changes as vast in their amount as they were slow in their progress. The area on which we stand has been first sea and then land for at least four alternations, and has remained in each of these conditions for a period of great length.

"Nor have these wonderful metamorphoses of the sea

into land, and of land into sea, been confined to one corner of England. During the Chalk Period not one of the present great physical features of the Globe was in existence. Our great mountain ranges, Pyrenees, Alps, Himalayas, Andes, have all been upheaved since the Chalk was deposited, and the Cretaceous sea flowed over the sites of Sinai and Ararat.

"All this is certain, because rocks of Cretaceous or still later date have shared in the elevatory movements which gave rise to these mountain chains, and may be found perched up, in some cases, many thousand feet high upon their flanks. And evidence of equal cogency demonstrates that, though in Norfolk the Forest-bed rests directly upon the Chalk, yet it does so, not because the period at which the forest grew immediately followed that at which the Chalk was formed, but because an immense lapse of time, represented elsewhere by thousands of feet of rock, is not indicated at Cromer.

"I must ask you to believe that there is no less conclusive proof that a still more prolonged succession of similar changes occurred before the Chalk was deposited. Nor have we any reason to think that the first term in the series of these changes is known. The oldest sea-beds preserved to us are sands and mud and pebbles, the wear and tear of rocks which were formed in still older oceans."*

It is needless to pursue this subject further, or to seek for other illustrations. We may reject Geology if we will: but if we put any faith even in its main principles, we must believe that the Crust of the Earth has passed through an indefinite series of revolutions, during which the Stratified Rocks were slowly built up by the action of natural causes. And it would be utterly ridiculous to suppose that the history of these revolutions can be compressed into the narrow compass of six thousand years.

* On a Piece of Chalk: A Lecture to Working Men.

Turning now to the other side of the question, we maintain that this extreme Antiquity of the Earth, which we have learned from Geology, is perfectly consistent with the historical narrative of the Bible. The Bible, indeed, does fix the Chronology of the Human Race at a comparatively recent period; but as for the Chronology of the World itself, the Bible simply tells us that, "In the beginning God created the Heavens and the Earth." For all that appears to the contrary, this Earth of ours may have been in existence for millions of years before man was introduced upon the scene; and during that time may have been peopled with those countless tribes of plants and animals which play so important a part in the records of Geology. This view, which is not only fully tolerated by the Church, but now largely supported by her Divines and Commentators, we hope to bring home clearly to our readers in the following pages; and thus to satisfy them that, as regards the Antiquity of the Earth, the discoveries of Geology can offer no prejudice to our religious belief.

At the outset it is of some importance to understand clearly the nature of that system of Chronology which is gathered from the Bible. Nowhere in the Sacred Text is the age of the human race explicitly set forth. But various data are found scattered here and there through the historical narrative, which afford us sufficient materials to compute the years that elapsed from the Creation of Adam to the Birth of Christ. Unfortunately, however, these data are in some respects obscure, and in some respects uncertain. And thus it has come to pass that many different systems of Chronology have come into vogue, even amongst those who profess to be guided entirely by the authority of the Bible.

The whole period may be conveniently divided into two parts;—from the Creation of Adam to the Call of Abraham; and from the call of Abraham to the Birth of Christ. As regards the latter interval, the difference of opinion between Chronologists is not very substantial; the length of the period may be roughly set down at about 2,000 years. But in the computation of the former interval a very wide difference prevails, arising from a diversity of reading in the earliest versions of the Pentateuch.

The materials for the computation are derived from two genealogical lists, one extending from Adam to Noah,* the other from Noah to Abraham.† In these lists we have not only the direct line of descent from father to son, extending through the whole period in question, but, moreover, we have the age of each individual member of the genealogy at the time when the next in succession was born. As, for example :—"Adam lived *a hundred and thirty years, and begot a son* to his own image and likeness, and called his name Seth. And the days of Adam, after he had begot Seth, were eight hundred years: and he begot sons and daughters. And all the time that Adam lived came to nine hundred and thirty years, and he died. Seth also lived *a hundred and five years, and begot Enos.* And Seth lived, after he begot Enos, eight hundred and seven years, and begot sons and daughters. And all the days of Seth were nine hundred and twelve years, and he died. And Enos lived *ninety years, and begot Cainan:*"‡ and so on. Now it is plain, according to this statement, that from the Creation of Adam to the birth of Seth was a hundred and thirty years; to the birth of Enos, a hundred and thirty, more a hundred and five years; to the birth of Cainan, a hundred and thirty, more a hundred and five, more ninety years. And in this way, following the genealogies of the Book of Genesis, we may easily compute the time from the Creation of Adam to the Birth of Abraham. Adding seventy-five years to this period, we reach the epoch known as the Call of Abraham; for we are told that "Abraham

* Genesis, v. 3–32. † Ib., xi. 10–26. ‡ Ib., v. 3–9.

was seventy and five years old when he went forth from Haran."*

Now every one knows that when a long catalogue of names and numbers is copied and recopied from age to age, errors are very likely to creep in and be perpetuated. And so it has been in the present case. The three earliest versions of the Pentateuch are the Hebrew, the Samaritan, and the Septuagint: and between these three versions there is a very great discrepancy with regard to the figures in question; so great, indeed, as to make up, on the whole, a difference of 1500 years, or more, in the age of the human race. In the table that appears on the following page, for which we are mainly indebted to the work of a modern writer,† this diversity of reading is set forth in a very simple and intelligible form.

It is plain that of these three different versions, one only can represent the true age of the human race when Abraham went forth, at the command of God, from his country and his kindred and his father's house, to go into the land of Canaan: and at this distance of time, it is impossible to determine with anything like certainty, which of the three has the greatest claim on our acceptance. The Church has not pronounced upon the subject; and the question is freely discussed among Biblical scholars. But the details of this controversy have little to do with our present argument. Enough it is for us to know that, from the Creation of Adam to the Birth of Christ, cannot have been more than six thousand years at the highest computation, nor much less than four thousand at the lowest. Adding 1869 years of the Christian Era, the present age of the Human Race according to the data of the Bible would seem to lie between six and eight thousand years.

* Genesis, xii. 4.

† The Genesis of the Earth and Man, Edited by Reginald Stuart Poole: London; Williams and Norgate; 1860.

Genealogies of Genesis.

List of Patriarchs.	Age of each when the next was born. According to		
	Septuagint.	Hebrew.	Samaritan.
Adam, ...	230	130	130
Seth, ...	205	105	105
Enos, ...	190	90	90
Cainan, ...	170	70	70
Malaleel, ...	165	65	65
Jared, ...	162	162	62
Henoch, ...	165	65	65
Mathusala, ...	167	187	67
Lamech, ...	188	182	53
Noe, ...	500	500	500
Sem, ...	100	100	100
From the creation of Adam to the birth of Arphaxad, two years after the Flood,*	2242	1656	1307
Arphaxad, ...	135	35	135
Cainan,†	130	—	—
Sale, ...	130	30	130
Heber, ...	134	34	134
Phaleg, ...	130	30	130
Reu, ...	132	32	132
Sarug, ...	130	30	130
Nachor, ...	79	29	79
Thare, ...	70	70	70
Abraham called by God, .	75	75	75
From the Flood to the Call of Abraham, ...	1145	365	1015
From the Creation of Adam to the Call of Abraham, . .	3387	2021	2322

* "Sem was a hundred years old when he begot Arphaxad, two years after the flood."—Genesis, xi. 10.

† This second Cainan does not appear in the Hebrew or the Samaritan version.

The Bible, then, does determine, though with some vagueness and uncertainty, the age of the Human Race. We have now to consider whether, in fixing the age of the Human Race, it fixes likewise the age of the World itself. For this purpose we must turn our attention to the first chapter of Genesis, in which is briefly set forth the origin and early history of our Globe from the Creation of the Heavens and the Earth in the beginning to the Creation of Man at the close of the Sixth Day. If it should appear that these two events were comprised within a very narrow limit of time, as is not unfrequently supposed, then indeed the age of the world must agree pretty nearly with the age of the Human Race. But if on the other hand, between these two events the Sacred Record allows us to suppose an interval of indefinite length, then it plainly follows that the age of the Human Race, as set forth in the Bible Genealogies, can afford no evidence against the Antiquity of the Earth. The question is thus brought within very narrow limits. We have simply to take up the First Chapter of Genesis, and inquire whether or no it is there conveyed that the Creation of Man, which is described toward the close of the chapter, followed after the lapse of only a few days upon the Creation of the Heavens and the Earth, which is recorded in the first verse.

For many centuries this question received but little attention from the readers of the Bible. It was commonly assumed that, as the various events of the Creation are traced out in rapid succession by the Inspired Writer, and strung together into one continuous narrative, so did they follow one another, in reality, with a corresponding rapidity, and in the same unbroken continuity. The progress of Physical Science had not yet shown any necessity for supposing a lengthened period of time to have elapsed between the Creation of the World and the Creation of Man: nor was there anything in the narrative itself to suggest such an idea. Thus it was generally taken for granted, almost without discussion, that when God had created the Heavens and the Earth in the beginning, He *at once* set about the work of arranging and furnishing the universe, and fitting it up for the use of man ; that He distributed this work over a period of six ordinary days, and at the close of the sixth day, introduced our First Parents upon the scene : and that, therefore, the beginning of the Human Race was but six days later than the beginning of the World.

These notions about the history of the Creation continued to prevail almost down to our own time. It is to be observed, however, that they were not founded on a close and scientific examination of the Sacred Text. The hypothesis of a long and eventful state of existence prior to the Creation of Man may be said rather to have been overlooked, than to have been rejected, by our Commentators. There was no good reasons for entertaining such a speculation, and so they said nothing about it. But now that the world is ringing with the wonderful discoveries of Geology, which seem to point more and more clearly every day to the extreme Antiquity of the Earth, it becomes an imperative duty to examine once again with all diligence and care the Inspired narrative of the Creation, and to consider well the relation in which it stands with this new dogma of Physical Science.

We are not the first to enter upon the inquiry. Already it has engaged the attention and stimulated the industry of Theological writers for more than half a century. Many eminent men, distinguished alike for their extensive acquirements and for their religious zeal, have protested warmly against the opinion of Geologists, concerning the Antiquity of the Earth, as one that cannot be reconciled with the historical accuracy of the Bible. But, on the other hand, there are writers no less illustrious, and no less sincerely attached to the cause of religion, who contend that there is nothing in the Sacred Text to exclude the supposition of a long and indefinite interval—an interval if necessary of many millions of years—between the first creation of matter and the creation of man. Thirty years ago this opinion was defended by Cardinal Wiseman with great learning, and with great felicity of illustration, in his famous Lectures on the Connection between Science and Revealed Religion. The eminent Roman Jesuit, Father Perrone, has followed the same line of argument in his Prælectiones Theologicæ, which, as every one knows, has long since become a classic work in schools of Theology. It has been yet more fully discussed, and supported by more elaborate reasoning, in a work entitled Cosmogonia Naturale Comparata col Genesi, lately published in Rome at the press of the Civiltà Cattolica, by another distinguished Jesuit, John Baptist Pianciani. Amongst Protestant writers, too, this view of the Mosaic narrative has found no inconsiderable number of able advocates. It is defended by Doctor Buckland, the eminent Geologist, in his celebrated Bridgewater Treatise, by Doctor Chalmers in his Evidences of the Christian Revelation, by Doctor Pye Smith in his dissertations on Geology and Scripture, by the eloquent and original Hugh Miller in his interesting work on the Testimony of the Rocks; and by a host of others scarcely less distinguished than these.

But these learned writers are not altogether of one accord as to the precise point in the First Chapter of Genesis, at which we may suppose a long interval of time to have intervened. Some, with Doctor Buckland, Doctor Pye Smith, and Doctor Chalmers, consider that this interval may best be introduced between the beginning of all time, when God created the Heavens and the Earth, and the beginning of the First Day, when He set about preparing the world as a dwelling-place for man. Sacred Scripture, they say, simply records these two events, (1) that "In the beginning God created the Heavens and the Earth," and (2) that, at some subsequent time, "God said: Let there be light: and light was made." But Sacred Scripture does not tell us what length of time elapsed between these two great acts of Divine Omnipotence. For aught we know from Revelation, it may have been but a single day, or it may have been a million of years. Others again, as for instance Pianciani, prefer to suppose that each one of the Six Days may have been itself a period of indefinite, nay of almost inconceivable duration. So that, between the beginning of the world and the creation of man six great ages of the Earth's history may have rolled by, each one distinguished by a new manifestation of God's power, and the introduction of new forms of life. These writers even fancy that they can discover a close analogy between the successive acts of creation recorded in Genesis, and the gradual development of organic life exhibited in the great Epochs of Geology.

To us it seems that either one or the other of these two systems, or both together, may be fairly admitted without any undue violence to the text of the Inspired narrative: and this, we would observe in passing, is the opinion to which Cardinal Wiseman appears to have inclined, thirty years ago, in his Lectures on the Connection between Science and Religion. We maintain, then, in the first place, that there is nothing in the Mosaic narrative, when carefully examined, at variance with the hypothesis of an indefinite interval between the creation of the world and the work of the Six Days. And, in the second place, we contend that it is quite consistent with the usage of Sacred Scripture to explain these Days of Creation as long periods of time.

It may appear, perhaps, to some of our readers that this is dangerous ground on which we are about to venture. They may have been accustomed all their lives to view the history of Creation through the medium of those notions that commonly prevailed before the discoveries of Geology:

and from the influence of long association they may have come, in the end, to regard their own interpretation with scarcely less veneration than the Inspired Text itself. Such persons will naturally be disposed to look upon our undertaking with disfavor and suspicion. They will think us guilty of irreverence toward Holy Scripture when we seek to modify our views about its meaning, in deference to the conclusions of Physical Science; and they may be tempted even to charge us with putting the idle interpretations of men into the balance against the Inspired Word of God.

To this line of objection we would answer, that we cannot be guilty of irreverence to the Holy Scripture, when we are only striving, with due submission to the authority of the Church, to discover the true meaning of an obscure and difficult passage, on which the Church has pronounced no definite judgment. Nor can we be said to make light of the Word of God, when we are but attempting to defend its unerring veracity from the assaults of infidel writers. Furthermore we would add, that, if it is a dangerous thing to modify the received interpretation of certain parts of Scripture, when the progress of science enables us to see physical phenomena under a new light, it is a far more dangerous thing to persist in imputing to Scripture a doctrine that, in a very short time, may be proved to be false, beyond the possibility of contradiction.

These sentiments are not altogether our own. They have come to us, in great part, from an illustrious Doctor of the Church; and we are glad, at this early stage of our discussion, to be able to shelter our humble efforts under the authority of his venerable name. It is now more than fourteen centuries and a half since Saint Augustine set about the literal interpretation of Genesis, which he accomplished in a Treatise of twelve books. Toward the close of the first book he expatiates at some length on the difficulty of his undertaking, and on the variety of diverse interpretations, which prevailed even in his time. From this he takes occasion to warn his readers that, "if we find anything in Divine Scripture that may be variously explained without any injury to faith, we should not rush headlong by positive assertion either to one opinion or the other; lest, if perchance the opinion we have adopted should afterward turn out to be false, our faith should fall with it; and we should be found contending, not so much for the doctrine of the Sacred Scriptures as for our own; endeavoring to make our doctrine to be that of the Scriptures, instead of taking the doctrine of the Scriptures to be ours."* And a little further on he again exposes the imprudence of such a proceeding, in words that cannot but be considered peculiarly applicable to our present subject:—

"It often happens that one who is not a Christian hath some knowledge derived from the clearest arguments or from the evidence of his senses about the earth, about the heavens, about the other elements of this world, about the movements and revolutions, or about the size and distances of the stars, about certain eclipses of the sun and moon, about the course of the years and the seasons, about the nature of animals, plants, and minerals, and about other things of a like kind. Now it is an unseemly and mischievous thing, and greatly to be avoided, that a Christian man speaking on such matters, as if according to the authority of Christian Scripture, should talk so foolishly that the unbeliever, on hearing him, and observing the extravagance of his error, should hardly be able to refrain from laughing. And the great mischief is, not so much that the man himself is laughed at for his errors, but that our authors are believed by people without the Church to have taught such things, and so are condemned as unlearned, and cast aside, to the great loss of those for whose salvation we are so much concerned. For, when they find

* Appendix (1).

one belonging to the Christian body falling into error on a subject with which they themselves are thoroughly conversant, and when they see him, moreover, enforcing his groundless opinion by the authority of our Sacred Books, how are they likely to put trust in these Books about the resurrection of the dead, and the hope of eternal life, and the kingdom of heaven, having already come to regard them as fallacious about those things they had themselves learned from observation or from unquestionable evidence? And, indeed, it were not easy to tell what trouble and sorrow some rash and presumptuous men bring upon their prudent brethren, who, when they are charged with a perverse and false opinion by those who do not accept the authority of our Books, attempt to put forward these same Holy Books in defence of that which they have lightly and falsely asserted; sometimes even quoting from memory what they think will suit their purpose, and putting forth many words, without well understanding either what they say, or what they are talking about." *

And many ages after, Saint Thomas, the great luminary of the schools, appeals to this wise admonition of Saint Augustine, and applies it to the circumstances of his own times. Writing about the work of the Second Day, he says that "in questions of this sort there are two things to be observed. First, that the truth of Scripture be inviolably maintained. Secondly, since Scripture doth admit of diverse interpretations, that we must not cling to any particular exposition with such pertinacity, that if what we supposed to be the teaching of Scripture should afterward turn out to be clearly false, we should nevertheless still presume to put it forward; lest thereby we should expose the Inspired Word of God to the derision of unbelievers, and shut them out from the way of salvation." †

Under the sanction of two such illustrious Saints and

* Appendix (2). † Appendix (3).

Doctors we need not hesitate to proceed in our attempt to reconcile the Inspired narrative of the Creation with the doctrine of the Antiquity of the Earth, as set forth by the advocates of Geology. Let it be remembered, however, that we do not undertake to prove the extreme Antiquity of the Earth from the language of Scripture; but simply to show that the language of Scripture leaves the Antiquity of the Earth an open question. The Geologist holds that this Globe of ours has been in existence for hundreds of thousands, perhaps for millions of years; and our object is to show that, while maintaining this opinion, he may, nevertheless, accept the historical truth of the Bible narrative.

As before explained, two points arise for discussion: first, can we suppose an interval of indefinite length to have elapsed between the Creation of the World, and the work of the Six Days? and secondly, is it lawful to explain these Days in the sense of long periods? We shall take these two questions in succession, dealing with each upon its own merits; and if we fail to enforce conviction, we hope, at least, to vindicate our right to toleration.

CHAPTER XIX.

FIRST HYPOTHESIS ;—AN INTERVAL OF INDEFINITE DURATION BETWEEN THE CREATION OF THE WORLD AND THE FIRST MOSAIC DAY.

The heavens and the earth were created before the first Mosaic day—Objection from Exodus, xx. 9-11—Answer—Interpretation of the author supported by the best commentators—Confirmed by the Hebrew text—The early fathers commonly held the existence of created matter prior to the work of the Six Days—Saint Basil, Saint Chrysostom, Saint Ambrose, Venerable Bede—The most eminent doctors in the schools concurred in this opinion—Peter Lombard, Hugh of Saint Victor, Saint Thomas—Also commentators and theologians—Perrerius, Petavius—Distinguished names on the other side, A Lapide, Tostatus, Saint Augustine—The opinion is at least not at variance with the voice of tradition—This period of created existence may have been of indefinite length—And the earth may have been furnished then as now with countless tribes of plants and animals—Objections to this hypothesis proposed and explained.

HE opening verses of the Mosaic history may be renderd thus literally from the Hebrew Text :—

(1) "In the beginning God created the Heavens and the Earth.

(2) "And the Earth was waste and empty ; and darkness was upon the face of the deep ; and the spirit of God moved upon the face of the waters.

(3) "And God said, Let there be light; and there was light.

(4) "And God saw the light that it was good; and God divided the light from the darkness.

(5) "And God called the light Day, and the darkness he called Night. And the evening was, and the morning was, the first day."

Now it appears to us that the great event with which this narrative begins, the creation of the Heavens and the Earth, is not represented as a part of the work that was accomplished within the Six Days. It is not said that *on the first day* God created the Heavens and the Earth, but *in the beginning.* Besides, the Sacred writer, uniformly throughout the chapter, employs one and the same peculiar phrase to introduce the work of each successive day. In describing the operations of God on the second day, he begins: "*And God said,* Let there be a firmament in the midst of the waters:" on the third day, "*And God said,* Let the waters that are under the Heavens be gathered together into one place:" on the fourth, "*And God said,* Let there be lights in the firmament of the Heavens to divide the day from the night:" on the fifth, "*And God said,* Let the waters bring forth the creeping thing having life:" on the sixth, "*And God said,* Let the earth bring forth the living creature after its kind." Hence, when we meet this same phrase for the first time in the third verse, "*And God said,* Let there be light," we may reasonably suppose that the work of the first day began with the decree which is set forth in these words. If so it plainly follows that we may allow the existence of created matter before that particular epoch of time which, in the language of Moses, is styled the First Day: for, before the creation of light, the Heavens and the Earth were already in existence, and the Earth was waste and empty, and darkness was upon the face of the deep, and the spirit of God moved upon the face of the waters.

An objection is sometimes raised from the words of God in the promulgation of the third commandment;—"Six days shalt thou labor and do all thy work. But the seventh day is the sabbath of the Lord thy God ; thou shalt do no work on it. . . . . . . For *in six days the Lord made the Heavens and the Earth* and the sea, and all that is in them, and resteth the seventh day."* It is argued that the creation of the Heavens and the Earth is here set forth as a part of the work accomplished within the Six Days ; which is directly against our opinion. This difficulty would be simply insurmountable, if it could be proved that the text refers to that *first act of creation* by which the Heavens and the Earth were brought into existence out of nothing. We think, however, that the phrase may fairly be understood to mean, in six days the Lord *fashioned* the Heavens and the Earth ; that is to say, gave to them that form and shape and outward character which they now possess. In this sense the words would apply, not to the first act of creation out of nothing, but rather to that subsequent series of operations by which the Earth was fitted up and furnished for the use of man.

And this interpretation is supported by the authority of our best Commentators. Perrerius formally discusses the point, and maintains that God may truly be said to have made the Heavens and the Earth in Six Days, although the Heavens and the Earth, as far as regards their substantial matter, had been created before the First Day : for it was only within the Six Days that they were adorned and completed and perfected. Tostatus is not less explicit. In this passage, he says, the word *made* is very properly employed ; for the Heavens and the Earth which are here referred to, and the other things that are included under this general designation, were all *made from matter already existing*, but this matter itself was not *made*, it was *created.* Petavius also adopts this view in his remarks upon the fourth verse of the second chapter of Genesis.†

*Exodus, xx. 9-11.

† Appendix (4), (5), (6).

We may add that this mode of explaining the passage receives no small support from the Hebrew text. When it is said, in the first chapter of Genesis, that "In the beginning God *created* the Heavens and the Earth," the word used by the Sacred writer is ברא (*Bara*), which strictly means to create out of nothing; whereas, in describing the operations of the Six Days, he commonly uses the word עשה (*Hasah*), which means to *form* and *fashion*, or to produce something out of pre-existing materials.* Now, in the text of Exodus we find the word עשה (*Hasah*), to *fashion* or *produce*, and not the word ברא (*Bara*), to *create*. We do not want to insist very rigorously upon this distinction between the two words ברא (*Bara*) and עשׂה (*Hasah*), nor would we deny that they are sometimes interchanged as regards their meaning. We think they are related to one another pretty nearly as the corresponding words to *create* and to *make* in English, and we know that the distinction between these two words is not always strictly observed. Thus, we sometimes say that God *made* the world, meaning that he brought it forth from nothing, and we speak of the *creation* of peers; and Shakspeare says:—

> "Now is the time of help; your eye in Scotland
> Would *create* soldiers, make our women fight
> To doff their dire distresses."—*Macbeth*, Act iv., Sc. iii.

Nevertheless, when we compare two such passages as these:—"In the beginning God *created* the Heavens and the Earth," and "In Six Days the Lord *made* the Heavens and the Earth and the sea, and all that in them is," we think the studied contrast of expression is a fair ground for supposing that, while the one refers to the Divine decree by which matter was first brought into existence out of nothing, the other may be understood of those subsequent operations by which it received its present form and shape.

* See Gesenius, sub vocibus.

We see no difficulty, then, as far as the Sacred Text is concerned, in supposing a condition of created existence prior to the period of the Six Days. But since this opinion is the foundation on which our whole argument rests, we should wish to show, moreover, even at the risk of being tedious, that it has been put forward and defended by the most eminent writers in every age of the Church. Amongst the early Fathers, Saint Basil reasons after this manner when commenting upon the passage, "There was evening and there was morning the first day:"—"The evening is the common term of day and night; and, in like manner, the morning is the point of union between night and day. Wherefore, in order to signify that to the day belonged the prerogative of being the first begotten, the sacred writer first commemorates the close of day, and afterward the close of night; implying thereby that *the day was followed by the night.* As to the condition of the world *before the formation of light,* that is not called Night, but simply Darkness; whereas that period which is distinguished from day and opposed to it, is called night." * This great Doctor, therefore, teaches that the First Day began with a period of light which is called day, and ended with a period of darkness which is called night; and he recognizes a previous state of existence which was no part of the First Day. So, too, Saint Chrysostom, in his third Homily upon Genesis, lays down that the Earth was first created a rude and shapeless mass, without form or ornament; that *afterward* light was made, and that, *with the creation of light, the First Day began.* †

In the Western Church, Saint Ambrose adopts the same line of interpretation. He sets forth that God first created the world, in the beginning; and afterward during the Six Days furnished and adorned it; just as a skilful workman first lays the foundation of a building, and afterward

* Appendix (7). † Appendix (8).

raises the superstructure, and superadds the ornament. And elsewhere, he says that, when the voice of God went forth, "Let light be made," in the same moment the First Day began. It follows, therefore, that the world existed before the beginning of the First Day. In another place he gives a new turn to the same idea, telling us that in the beginning God made the world; and with the world, time began. But not with time did the First Day begin : for the First Day is not the beginning of time, it is rather an epoch of time.*

Passing on to the middle ages, we find our view supported by the authority of Venerable Bede, in several parts of his writings. His notion is that, during the Six Days, God formed and fashioned the world out of shapeless matter ; but, before the Six Days began, He had made this shapeless matter itself out of nothing. "Two things," he says, "did God make before all days, the angelical nature, and shapeless matter. And again, he dresses up this opinion in the form of a dialogue :—"*Disciple.* Tell me the order in which things were made throughout the Six Days? *Master.* First, in the very beginning of created existence, were made heaven and earth, the angels, air, and water. *Disciple.* Continue the order of creation? *Master. In the beginning of the First Day* light was made ; on the second was made the firmament," etc.† Nothing can be more plain than the distinction here set up between the beginning of all time, when the Heavens and the Earth were made, and the beginning of the First Day, when light was made.

And when we come to still more recent times, we find this interpretation was taken up and defended by the great masters in the schools of Theology. Peter Lombard, the famous Magister Sententiarum, referring to the first verse of Genesis, says that "in the beginning God created

* Appendix (9). † Appendix (10).

Heaven, which means the Angels, and the Earth, which means confused and unshapely matter, the same that is called Chaos by the Greeks; *and this was before any day.*" Not less clearly speaks out Hugh of Saint Victor, who for his profound and varied erudition, was called the second Augustine. In explaining the history of the Six Days, he says: "The first of the Divine operations was the creation of light. But the light was not then created from nothing, it was formed from pre-existing matter. This was the work that was accomplished on the First Day: but the material of this work had been created *before the First Day.* Directly with the light the day began; for before the light it was neither night or day, though time already existed." *

Later still, St. Thomas himself clearly leans to this view when he says: "It is better to maintain that the creation was before any day." And Perrerius, the most learned, perhaps, of all our commentators on Genesis, argues with us that the world was created before the production of light, and before the commencement of the First Day. Nay, he adds that he cannot tell how long that primeval state of existence may have endured before the Six Days began; nor does he think it can be known except by a special revelation. Petavius, too, is with us. He does not indeed accept our interpretation of the first verse. When it is said, "In the beginning God created the Heavens and the Earth," he holds that these words do not describe any one particular act of God, but represent, as it were in a brief summary, the whole work of creation. Thus we are informed, at the outset, that the Heavens and the Earth as we see them now are the work of God; and afterward, the various parts that make up this great whole are described, and the order in which they were accomplished is set forth. According to Patavius, then, the creation of the Heavens and the Earth, recorded in the first verse, was not a distinct

* Appendix (11) (12).

act from the operations of the Six Days, but rather includes them all. Nevertheless, he maintains, as we do, that the earth, at least, and water, were in existence before the creation of light; and that, therefore, some period of time must have elapsed before the beginning of the Six Days. Furthermore, he says in the same spirit as Perrerius, that it is beyond our power to conjecture how long that period may have lasted.*

Our opinion, then, is not open, in the slightest degree, to the imputation of novelty or singularity. On the contrary, it would seem rather to reflect the prevailing tradition of the Church. We think it right, however, to add that there are great names against us. A Lapide, for instance, who considers that the Heavens and the Earth were created at the beginning of the First Day.† And Tostatus, who incidentally notices our view, and contents himself with saying that it is unreasonable. For himself he seems to waver between two opinions. He thinks the primeval darkness, described in the second verse, may have been the night belonging to the First Day; and that during that night, which probably lasted about twelve hours, we may suppose the Heavens and the Earth to have been created. Or else, he says, we may allow that the First Day of the Mosaic narrative began with the creation of light; but in that case we must hold that the Heavens and the Earth were created at the same time with light.‡

Saint Augustine, too, we must reluctantly give up; or, at least, we must be content to regard him as neutral. If he is not a decided opponent, he is certainly not a consistent advocate, of our opinion. No doubt he is often quoted in its favor; and it would be easy to select passages from his works which seem to enforce it in the plainest terms. As for example: "In the beginning, O my God, *before*

* Appendix (13) (14) (15). † Appendix (16). ‡ In Genes. cap. i. Quæst. xiv.

any day, Thou didst make the Heavens and the Earth."* But, in truth, this opinion is utterly irreconcilable with the well known and very singular teaching of Saint Augustine concerning the creation of the world. He held that all the great works recounted in the first chapter of Genesis were, in fact, accomplished in a single instant. There was no real succession, according to him, in the order of time, between the production of the Heavens and the Earth, of light and the firmament, of the sun, moon, and stars, of plants, trees, and animals. In one and the same instant of time all these came into existence together. As to the description given by Moses, it is accommodated to the capacity of a rude people; and the succession there set forth is intended only to exhibit the several parts of a great whole, in the manner best suited to the conceptions of human intelligence.†

This view of the creation is repeated again and again by Saint Augustine in his numerous works upon Genesis, and illustrated in diverse ways, so as to leave no doubt that he held it deliberately and persistently. With regard to such passages as that quoted above, in which he says that God created the Heavens and the Earth *before any day*, it may be maintained that Saint Augustine was not always consistent with himself, and that he held different opinions at different times; or even that he put forward opposite opinions at the same time, not setting them forth as true, but only as possible and legitimate.‡

We think, however, that his consistency, in this case at least, can be defended, and that he has himself sufficiently

* Appendix (17).

† See his various works upon Genesis, passim; in particular de Genesi ad Literam, Lib. i. cap. xv., Lib. iv. cap. xxxiii.; De Genesi Liber Imperfectus, cap. vii. and cap. ix.

‡ This latter view might be fairly maintained in conformity with the principles which Saint Augustine professes to follow in the interpretation of Genesis. See De Genesi ad Literam, Lib. i. cap. xxi. and cap. xxii.

explained in what sense he wished these passages to be understood. He tells us that we must distinguish two kinds of succession: succession in the order of time, and succession in the order of our conceptions. Thus, for example, in the order of time there is no succession between the sound of the voice in singing and the musical note that is sung: the sound is, in fact, the note, and the note is the sound. But in the order of our conceptions we first apprehend a thing according to its substance, and then according to its qualities. We first conceive the sound itself, as a sound, and then we conceive it as having that peculiar quality which makes it a musical note. Such as this is the succession Saint Augustine seems to admit in the order of the creation. He tells us, no doubt, that God first created shapeless matter, and afterward gave to it form and beauty: and certainly this statement, if standing alone, would, according to the ordinary use of language, imply a real succession in the order of time. But then, a little further on, he expressly repudiates the idea of a succession in point of time, and says that the priority he ascribes to shapeless matter is only a priority in the order of our conceptions. We must first conceive matter to exist before we can conceive it to have this or that particular form; and the Inspired Writer follows the order of our conceptions, in order to adapt his narrative to the mental feebleness of our present condition.*

With the truth or falsehood of these views we are not concerned just now. We have dwelt upon them rather from an honest desire of showing that Saint Augustine is not so clearly on our side in this question, as might be supposed from some isolated passages of his writings. He says indeed that the world was created before light, and before the beginning of the First Day; but then again he

* See De Genesi ad Literam, Lib. i. cap. xv.; De Genesi Liber Imperfectus, cap. vii.; Confess., Lib. xii. cap. xxix.

tells us that this is only a way of speaking, and that, in reality, all things were created together.

But although these high authorities—A Lapide, Tostatus, Saint Augustine—and some others less illustrious than these, are unfavorable to our interpretation, we think it is supported by a preponderance of the best interpreters, both in ancient and modern times. At all events, with such an array of venerable names as we have been able to bring forward in its behalf,—and they are but a few chosen out of many,—no one can deny that we are fairly entitled to hold it without any note of censure, without any suspicion of Theological error. Setting out, then, from this point, that there was a state of created existence prior to the Six Days of the Mosaic history, the question naturally arises, how long did that state of existence endure? Was it for an hour? a day? a week? a month? a century? a million of years? We cannot tell. To these questions the Sacred Text gives no reply. It simply records that in the beginning God created the Heavens and the Earth, and that, at some subsequent epoch of time, His decree again went forth, Let there be light, and light there was. One thing, however, is plain, that, if this period existed at all, it might just as well have lasted a hundred millions of years as a hundred seconds. It would be folly to attempt to measure the succession of God's acts, when he does please to produce effects in succession, according to our petty standards of time. "One day with the Lord is as a thousand years, and a thousand years as one day."*

And it is not a little remarkable that, long before the discoveries of Geology had suggested any necessity for allowing the lapse of many ages between the first creation of the world and the creation of man, the sagacity of our commentators led them to observe that the duration of this interval is left undefined in the Sacred Record. "How

* 2 Peter, iii. 8.

long that interval may have lasted," says Petavius, "it is absolutely impossible to conjecture." And Pererius, as we have seen, declared that it could not be known except by a special revelation. And five centuries earlier, at the very dawn of Scholastic Theology, Hugh of Saint Victor raised the same question, and expressed his opinion that it could not be solved from Scripture. Citing the passage, In the beginning God created the Heavens and the Earth, he says, "From these words it is plain that in the beginning of time, or rather with time itself, the original matter of all things came into existence. But how long it remained in this confused and unshapely condition the Scripture clearly does not tell us." *

We may go further still. If we are at liberty to admit an interval of indefinite length between the creation of the world and the work of the Six Days, there is certainly nothing which forbids us to suppose that, during this period, the earth should have undergone many revolutions, and have been peopled by countless tribes of plants and animals, which, as age rolled on after age, came into existence, and died out, and were succeeded by new creations. We cannot, perhaps, see the use of all this, nor can we penetrate the motives the Great Creator might have had in bringing into existence such a boundless profusion of organic life. Granted: but then we have studied the Sacred Text to little purpose if we have not yet realized the solemn truth that, to our poor and feeble intellects, His judgments are incomprehensible, and his ways unsearchable. Did He not set His stars in the remotest regions of space, far beyond the reach of unaided human vision, and did they not shine there for ages, though man could see them not? And for ages, too, did not the wild flowers spring up, and bloom, and decay, in many a fair and favored spot of this beautiful Earth, where there was none to

* Appendix (18) (19) (20).

admire their splendor, none to inhale their sweetness? Then again, look at that marvellous kingdom of minute animalcules, in number almost infinite, which only within the last few years the microscope has revealed to our wondering eyes. They swarm around us in the air, in the earth, in the water. Millions of them would fit in the hollow of your hand; many hundreds might swim side by side, without crowding, through the eye of a cambric needle. And they too, we can hardly doubt, must have flourished for centuries in countless myriads, unseen and unknown by man. It is impossible for us, in our present imperfect state, to understand the motives of an All-wise Creator in this profuse expenditure of his goodness, this lavish display of His power. How then can we presume to say that He may not have good reasons, though inscrutable to us, for peopling this Earth with many tribes of plants and animals, through a long cycle of ages, before it pleased Him to fit it up for the habitation of man? "Who is he among men that can know the counsel of God? or who can find out His designs? For the judgments of mortal men are hesitating, and uncertain are our thoughts. For the corruptible body is a load upon the soul, and the earthly dwelling presseth down the mind that museth upon many things. And hardly do we guess aright at things that are upon earth: and with labor do we find the things that are before us. But the things that are in heaven who shall search out?"*

We have heard it sometimes objected that plants and animals could not have existed without light; and that light was not created until the beginning of the First Mosaic Day. Many curious and interesting facts are adduced in support of this argument. For example, we are reminded that certain Fossil animals belonging to the earliest

* Wisdom, ix. 13–16.

Geological Periods, are shown by the clearest evidence, to have had eyes constructed on the same optical principles, and accommodated to the same optical conditions, as the eyes of those animals that have flourished on the Earth during the period of history: and such eyes, it is contended, plainly import the existence of light. The answer to this objection may be stated in a very few words. We freely admit that the hypothesis we have been defending would be of little use to account for Geological phenomena, if it did not include the existence of light, during that Period of indefinite duration which we suppose to have elapsed between the first creation of the world and the work of the Six Days. But in truth there is no difficulty in supposing that, during such an interval, light may have prevailed upon the earth, and air, and all the other conditions of organic life, pretty much as they do at the present day. Afterward, at the close of the period, when, perhaps, ages innumerable had rolled by, this planet of ours would have appeared in that condition which is described in the second verse of Genesis: "And the earth was waste and empty, and darkness was upon the face of the deep." Then the command of God would have gone forth, "Let there be light:" and at once the darkness would have been dispelled, a new era of existence would have commenced, and the Earth would forthwith have been set in order and furnished, in a special manner, for the habitation of man.

Even as regards the Sun, Moon, and Stars, they too may have existed before the work of the Six Days began. We read, no doubt, that on the Fourth Day, God said, "Let there be lights in the firmament of the heavens to divide the day from the night:" and a little farther on it is added that "God made two great lights; the greater light to rule the day, and the lesser light to rule the night; and the stars." But then it must be remembered that some of our best

Commentators, without any reference to Geology, have taught that, before this command was given, the heavenly bodies were already in existence for three days, and were already discharging the office of dividing day and night. They explain the passage by saying that the Sun, Moon, and Stars, are represented as having been made on the Fourth Day, not because they were then produced for the first time out of nothing, but because the vapors by which they had been obscured were, on that Day, dissipated, and they began to shine visibly in the Firmament of Heaven. If this line of interpretation is admissible, and it seems to us not unreasonable, then we are certainly at liberty to hold, consistently with the Mosaic narrative, that the Heavenly bodies may have been created with the Heavens and the Earth in the beginning of all time; and that on the Fourth Day they were made manifest in the Firmament to rule over the day and the night, and to regulate the course of the years and the seasons.*

Again it is urged against our hypothesis that Moses could not have passed over in complete silence such a long and eventful era in the history of the world. Certainly not, we admit, if he professed to write a complete history of the Earth and all its revolutions. But this was not his purpose. Every book, whether sacred or profane, must be examined and interpreted according to the end for which it was designed. Now the end and scope of the Book of Genesis was not to instruct mankind about the movements of the heavenly bodies, or the physical changes of the Earth's surface, or the laws which govern the material universe. It was, first of all, to impress on the minds of the Jewish people that this world of ours is the work of one only God, distinct from all creatures, and Himself the

* See Pianciani, Cosmogonia, pp. 384–90.

Creator of sun, moon, and stars, and of every other object which pagan nations were wont to worship: and in the next place, to set forth, briefly and simply, the story of God's dealings with man in the first ages of the human race. Whatever we may hold, therefore, about the revolutions and changes of the Earth's surface previous to the work of the Six Days, it is plain that the history of these phenomena did not appertain to the object which the Sacred writer had in view. Consequently he cannot be said, by the omission of these events, to lead his readers into error; he simply allows them to remain in ignorance. What it was his purpose to tell, he tells truly: what did not belong to his purpose, he passes by in silence.

But it is further argued that this long interval of time we have been contending for, is incompatible with the use of the copulative conjunction, by which the several clauses of the narrative are connected together. The Sacred text runs thus:—"In the beginning God created the Heavens and the Earth. *And* the Earth was waste and empty: and darkness was upon the face of the deep; and the spirit of God moved upon the face of the waters. *And* God said, Let there be light; and there was light." Is it possible, we are asked, to admit a period of indefinite length between events thus closely linked together? Our answer is that, according to the idiom of the Hebrew language, the conjunction וְ or וָ (*ve* or *va*), which is here employed, while it serves to connect together the clauses of a narrative, does not of necessity imply the immediate succession of the events recorded. The very wide and indefinite signification which belongs to this little particle is well known to all who are familiar with the Hebrew text. It is sometimes copulative, sometimes adversative, sometimes disjunctive, sometimes causal. Very frequently it is used simply for the purpose of *continuing the discourse*;* and this we believe is the true force of the word in the passage under discussion.

An example very much to the point occurs in the Book of Numbers, twentieth chapter and first verse:—"*And* the children of Isarel, the whole congregation came into the desert of Sin." Here the narrative opens with the connecting particle ו:—ויבאו בני־ישראל כל־העדה. And yet the reader will find, if he carefully examine the passage, that the event thus introduced by the sacred writer was separated by a period of eight-and-thirty years from those which had been related in the preceding chapter. This conjunction, therefore, does not exclude an interval of eight-and-thirty years between the events which it links together in history. And that being so, there is no good reason for supposing that it should, of necessity, exclude an interval of indefinite length.

The Weakness of this objection may be made even more strikingly manifest by an inspection of the opening words in the first chapter of Ezechiel:—ויהי בשלשים שנה. So little did the notion prevail that the conjunction ו (*ve*) could be used only to connect together events closely associated in point of time, that here it actually *begins* the narrative, and is, in fact, the first word of the whole book. In the Douay version the passage is not inaptly rendered after this manner: "Now it came to pass in the thirtieth year, in the fourth month, on the fifth day of the month, when I was in the midst of the captives by the River Chobar, the heavens were opened, and I saw the visions of God."

We have now brought to a conclusion the first part of our inquiry. We have endeavored to show that there is

* See Gesenius, Hebrew and Chaldee Lexicon to the Old Testament Scriptures; in voce. He thus explains the first meaning of this word: "*copulative*, and serves to connect both words and sentences, especially in *continuing a discourse*."

nothing in Scripture or Tradition which forbids us to admit a long interval of time between the Creation of the world and the work of the Six Days. It remains to examine what was the nature of these Six Days themselves. Were they, as Saint Augustine maintained, one single indivisible instant of time? or were they days of twenty-four hours, as is more commonly supposed? or were they simply periods of time of which the duration is left wholly undetermined in the Sacred Text?

CHAPTER XX.

SECOND HYPOTHESIS ;—THE DAYS OF CREATION LONG PERIODS OF TIME.

Diversity of opinion among the early fathers regarding the days of creation—Saint Augustine, Philo Judæus, Clement of Alexandria, Origen, Saint Athanasius, Saint Eucherius, Procopius—Albertus Magnus, Saint Thomas, Cardinal Caietan—Inference from these testimonies—First argument in favor of the popular interpretation; a day, in the literal sense, means a period of twenty-four hours—Answer—This word often used in Scripture for an indefinite period—Examples from the Old and New Testament—Second argument; the days of creation have an evening and a morning—Answer—Interpretation of Saint Augustine, Venerable Bede, and other fathers of the church—Third argument; the reason alleged for the institution of the Sabbath-day—Answer—The law of the Sabbath extended to every seventh year as well as to every seventh day—The seventh day of God's rest a long period of indefinite duration.

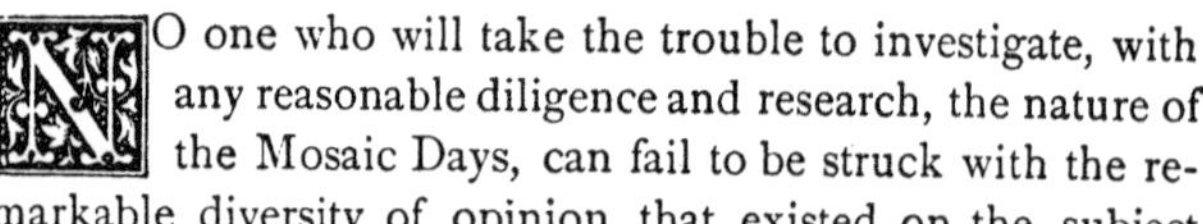

NO one who will take the trouble to investigate, with any reasonable diligence and research, the nature of the Mosaic Days, can fail to be struck with the remarkable diversity of opinion that existed on the subject among the early Fathers of the Church. Yet this diversity of opinion is often overlooked by modern writers. They fancy that the meaning of the word Day is so plain as to leave no room for doubt or controversy; that a day can be nothing else than a period of twenty-four hours, marked by the succession of light and darkness; and that in this sense the

Mosaic narrative was universally understood until quite recently, when a new explanation was invented, to meet the requirements of modern science. All this is far from true. The meaning of the Mosaic Days has been, in point of fact, a subject of controversy from the earliest times. And Saint Augustine tells us that the question appeared to him so difficult that he could pronounce no decisive judgment upon it. "As to these Days," he says, "what kind they were, it is very difficult, nay, it is impossible to imagine, and much more so to explain."*

Nevertheless, this great Doctor, having long pondered over the subject, and considered it on many sides, does not hesitate to express his own opinion. And he departs very widely, indeed, from the literal and obvious interpretation. He maintains, at great length,† as we had before occasion to observe, that God created all things in a single instant of time, according to the words of Ecclesiasticus, "He who liveth forever created all things at once."‡ Thus he is led to infer that the Six Days commemorated by Moses were, in reality, but one day; and this not such a day as those which are now measured by the revolution of the sun, for we find three successive days recorded by Moses before the sun appeared in the Heavens. It was, in fact, nothing else than that one single instant of time in which all things were created together.§

Nor was this opinion peculiar to Saint Augustine. At the very dawn of the Christian Era it was set forth by Philo the Jew; and afterward it was maintained by Clement of Alexandria, and by Origen. The great Saint Athanasius seems to throw the weight of his authority in the same

* Appendix (21).

† See De Genesi ad Literam, Lib. iv. capp. xxvi.–xxxv., Lib. v. cap. i, n. 3, and cap. iii. n. 6.

‡ Ecclesiasticus, xviii. 1.

§ Appendix (22).

direction, when he says, speaking of the Creation, that "no one thing was made before another, but all things were produced at once together by the self-same command." And after the time of Saint Augustine this figurative interpretation was defended by Saint Eucherius, Bishop of Lyons, in the course of the fifth century, and by Procopius of Gaza in the sixth. In the days of the schools we find it approved by Albertus Magnus, and treated respectfully by Saint Thomas; and later still, adopted by Cardinal Cajetan, in his commentary on the Book of Genesis.*

It will be said, perhaps, that we are here arguing against ourselves: these eminent writers are in favor of reducing the days of Creation to one single point of time; whereas it is our purpose to stretch them out to periods of indefinite length. But no: our object just now is not precisely to establish our own hypothesis, but rather to prepare the way for its discussion. We want to show that we are quite free to abandon the popular view of the Mosaic Days if there be good reason for our doing so. And it seems to us that we have abundantly established this point by a long list of eminent ecclesiastical writers, who, without any note of censure, have diverged very widely from the common interpretation. No doubt they have shortened the time, and we want to lengthen it. But in this they agree with us, that the days of Creation are not of necessity days in the ordinary sense of the word. Nay, Saint Augustine goes farther, and maintains, from the evidence of the Sacred Text itself, that they cannot be understood in this sense.†

Having thus cleared away a serious difficulty that seemed to obstruct our path, we may proceed without hesitation to the direct object of our inquiry. The burden of proof, let

* Appendix (23) (24) (25) (26) (27) (28) (29) (30) (31).

† See De Genesi ad Literam, Lib. iv. capp. xxvi., xxvii.; also Lib. i. capp. x., xi., xii.

it be remembered, is not with us, but rather with those who contend for Days of twenty-four hours. They must prove that this word Day in the first chapter of Genesis means a period of twenty-four hours, and *can mean nothing else.* If it *may* be understood in a wider sense, consistently with the usage of Scripture, that is quite enough for us. We are perfectly at liberty to adopt an interpretation which, on the one hand, the Sacred Text fairly admits, and on the other, the discoveries of Natural Science would seem to demand. Let us examine, then, the arguments that are usually adduced in favor of the popular interpretation.

Throughout the first chapter of Genesis the Hebrew word יוֹם (*yom*) is everywhere employed by Moses to designate the Days of Creation. And many writers contend that the use of this word is, in itself, evidence enough that he spoke of days in the common sense of the term. It is plain, they say, from the usage of Scripture, that the word יוֹם (*yom*) had a fixed and certain meaning in the Hebrew language; the same precisely as that which we now attach to the English word Day. Sometimes, when contradistinguished from night, it was applied to the period of light, from sunrise to sunset; otherwise, it meant the civil day of twenty-four hours, measured by the revolution of the Sun. Moreover, it had unquestionably attained this meaning at the time when Moses wrote, and therefore it could not have been employed by him in any other sense.

This argument rests upon a false foundation. It is true, no doubt, that the word יוֹם (*yom*) was more usually employed in one or other of the two senses just explained;—that is to say, (1) for the period of light from sunrise to sunset, or (2) for the period of twenty-four hours corresponding to a complete revolution of the Sun. But, for the validity of the argument, it would be necessary to show that, beside these two senses, there is no other in which the word may be fairly understood, conformably to the usage of the Hebrew language. Now this has never yet been proved. On the contrary, the Scripture affords abundant evidence that the word יוֹם (*yom*) had a third meaning quite different from the other two; that it was freely used to designate a period of time much longer than a common day, and generally of uncertain and indefinite duration. A few examples will be interesting, we hope, to our readers.

In the second chapter of Genesis, Moses, having completed his account of the Creation, says (v. 4): "These are the generations of the Heavens and the Earth when they were created, in the *Day* (יוֹם, *yom*) that the Lord God created the Earth and the Heavens: (v. 5), and every plant of the field before it was in the earth, and every herb of the field before it grew." There is a good deal of controversy about the precise meaning of this passage. But one thing at least appears to be plain, that the word יוֹם (*yom*), is not used to designate a day of twenty-four hours; nor yet the period of light from sunrise to sunset; but rather the whole period of the Creation.

On this point almost all our best commentators are agreed. "It is manifest," says Venerable Bede, "that in this place the sacred writer has put the word Day for all that time during which the primeval creation was brought into existence. For it was not upon any one of the Six Days that the sky was made and adorned with stars, and the dry land was separated from the waters, and furnished with trees and plants. But, *according to its accustomed practice*, Scripture here uses the word day in the sense of time." Saint Augustine gives even a wider expansion to the word when he writes: "Seven Days are enumerated above, and now that is called one Day in which God made the Heavens and the Earth, and every green thing of the field; by which term we may well suppose that *all time is meant*. For God then made all time when He made creatures that live in time; and these creatures are here signified by the Heavens and the Earth." Molina on the same passage says: "Learned writers tell us commonly that Moses in this place puts the word Day in the sense of Time, just as in the passage of Deuteronomy, 'The day of perdition is at hand.' . . . And elsewhere in Scripture Day is often used for Time." Bannez, too, concurs in this opinion. "The word Day," he says, "can be understood *for any duration whatsoever.*" Perrerius, answering an objection taken from this text, says that "Day is put for Time, as is *frequently done in Scripture.*" And Patavius not only adopts this interpretation, but contends that it is conformable to the usage even of the Greek and Latin writers. He gives an example from Cicero against Verres: "Itaque cum ego *diem* in Siciliam perexiguam postulavissem, invenit iste qui sibi in Achaiam *biduo breviorem diem* postularet."* Here, then, is an instance in which Moses himself uses the word Day (יוֹם, *yom*) not in the ordinary sense, but for a long period of time;—for all that time, whatever it may have been, which elapsed from the first act of creation to the close of the Six Days.

Another striking example occurs in the prophet Amos. "Behold, the days are coming, saith the Lord God, and I will send forth a famine into the land: not a famine of bread, nor a thirst of water, but of hearing the word of the Lord. And they shall wander from sea to sea and from the north to the east; they shall go about seeking the word of the Lord, and shall not find it. In that *day* (יוֹם, *yom*) shall the fair virgins and the young men faint for thirst."† Every one will see at a glance that the word Day in the latter part of this passage does not mean a day of twenty-four hours. It evidently refers to the whole period during which the calamities here foretold were to be inflicted on the Jewish people. What that period was may be a

* Appendix (32) (33) (34) (35) (36) (37).

† Amos, viii. 11, 12.

question of dispute. By some it is taken for the time of the Babylonian captivity; by others, for the present age of the world, in which the Jews are wanderers on the face of the earth, without a prophet and without a pastor, thirsting for the word of God, and seeking it in vain. But, in any case, it is clear from the opening words: "Behold, the days are coming," that it was a period not of one day only, but of many.

Then we have those well known words addressed by God the Father to His Eternal Son: "Thou art my Son, this *day* (יוֹם, *yom*) have I begotten thee."* The Son of God was begotten of the Father before all ages; and the *day*, therefore, on which he was begotten, cannot be a common day of twenty-four hours, but must rather be the long day of Eternity, without beginning and without end.

This text, we know, is sometimes applied to the day of our Lord's Resurrection; and sometimes, too, to the day of His Incarnation: nor do we want to deny that it may be thus rightly explained in a secondary and mystical sense. But in its literal sense we think it plainly refers to the Eternal Generation of the Son. This meaning is sufficiently implied by the word *begotten*, which cannot be understood with propriety, except of that Generation by virtue of which our Divine Lord was from Eternity the natural Son of God. Moreover, this is the sense in which the passage is adopted by Saint Paul in his Epistle to the Hebrews. Wishing to show that Our Lord has received by inheritance a name more excellent than any given to the Angels, he argues thus: "For to which of the Angels hath he said at any time, Thou art my Son, this day have I begotten thee?"† Now it seems to us that, unless we understand these words of the Eternal Generation, the point of the Apostle's argument is completely lost. The Angels are sometimes called in Scripture the sons of God; but they

* Psalm ii. 7. † Heb. i. 5.

were only the *adopted sons,* whereas Our Lord was the *natural Son* in virtue of His Eternal Generation. Consequently it was no other than the Eternal Generation which made the name of Son more excellent when applied to Christ than the same name when applied to the angels.

Again, it is quite a common thing, with the prophets generally, to use the word יוֹם (*yom*) for the season of tribulation and affliction, though the same may have extended over a period of many days or even many years. Jeremias employs it in this sense when he describes so vividly the manifold calamities that were impending over the ill-fated Babylon. "I have caused thee to fall into a snare, and thou art taken, O Babylon, and thou wast not aware of it: thou art found and caught because thou hast provoked the Lord. The Lord hath opened His armory, and hath brought forth the weapons of his wrath: for the Lord the God of hosts hath a work to be done in the land of the Chaldeans. Come ye against her from the uttermost borders: open, that they may go forth that shall tread her down: take the stones out of the way, and make heaps, and destroy her: and let nothing of her be left. Destroy all her valiant men, let them go down to the slaughter: woe to them, for their *day* (יוֹם, *yom*) is come, *the time* of their visitation. The voice of them that flee, and of them that have escaped out of the land of Babylon: to declare in Sion the revenge of the Lord our God, the revenge of His temple. Declare to many against Babylon, to all that bend the bow: stand together against her round about, and let none escape; pay her according to her work: according to all that she hath done, do ye to her: for she hath lifted up herself against the Lord, against the Holy One of Israel. Therefore shall her young men fall in her streets: and all her men of war shall hold their peace in that *day* (יוֹם, *yom*), saith the Lord. Behold I come against thee, O proud one, saith the Lord the God of hosts: for the *day* (יוֹם, *yom*) is come, the *time* of thy visitation. And the proud one shall fall, he shall fall down, and there shall be none to lift him up: and I will kindle a fire in his cities, and it shall devour all round about him."* And in the following chapter:—"Thus saith the Lord: Behold, I will raise up as it were a pestilential wind against Babylon, and against the inhabitants thereof who have lifted up their heart against me. And I will send to Babylon fanners, and they shall fan her, and shall destroy her land: for they are come upon her on every side in the *day* (יוֹם, *yom*) of her affliction."†

In another place the same prophet applies the word יוֹם (*yom*) to the whole duration of a long campaign carried on by Nabuchodonosor against Pharao Nechao, king of Egypt. "Prepare ye the shield and buckler, and go forth to battle. Harness the horses, and get up, ye horsemen: stand forth with helmets, furbish the spears, put on coats of mail. What then? I have seen them dismayed, and turning their backs, their valiant ones slain: they fled apace, they looked not back: terror was round about, saith the Lord. Let not the swift flee away, nor the strong think to escape: they are overthrown and fallen down, toward the north by the river Euphrates. Who is this that cometh up as a flood: and his streams swell like those of rivers? Egypt riseth up like a flood, and the waves thereof shall be moved as rivers, and he shall say: I will go up and will cover the earth: I will destroy the city and its inhabitants. Get ye up on horses, and glory in chariots, and let the valiant men come forth, the Ethiopians and the Lybians, that handle the shield, and the Lydians that handle and bend the bow. For this is the *day* (יוֹם, *yom*) of the Lord the God of hosts, a *day* of vengeance that He may revenge Himself of His enemies: the sword shall devour, and shall be filled, and shall be drunk with their

* Jeremias, cap. l. vv. 24-32. † Jeremias, li. 1, 2.

blood: for there is a sacrifice of the Lord God of hosts in the north country, by the river Euphrates. . . . Furnish thyself to go into captivity, thou daughter inhabitant of Egypt: for Memphis shall be made desolate, and shall be forsaken and uninhabited. Egypt is like a fair and beautiful heifer: there shall come from the north one that shall goad her. Her hirelings also that lived in the midst of her, like fatted calves are turned back, and are fled away together, and they could not stand: for the *day* (יוֹם, *yom*) of their slaughter is come upon them, the *time* of their visitation."*

The prophet Ezechiel, too, furnishes a forcible illustration when he thus foreshadows the course of a second expedition against Egypt undertaken by the same prince:—"Therefore thus saith the Lord God: Behold I will set Nabuchodonosor the king of Babylon in the land of Egypt: and he shall take her multitude, and take the booty thereof for a prey, and rifle the spoils thereof: and it shall be wages for his army; and for the service he hath done me against it: I have given him the land of Egypt, because he hath labored for me, saith the Lord God. In that *day* (יוֹם, *yom*) a horn shall bud forth for the house of Israel, and I will give thee an open mouth in the midst of them: and they shall know that I am the Lord."† And a little further on:—"For the *day* (יוֹם, *yom*) is near, yea the *day* of the Lord is near: a cloudy *day*, it shall be the *time* of the nations. And the sword shall come upon Egypt: and there shall be dread in Ethiopia, when the wounded shall fall in Egypt, and the multitude thereof shall be taken away, and the foundations thereof shall be destroyed. Ethiopia and Lybia, and Lydia, and all the rest of the crowd, and Chub, and the children of the land of the covenant, shall fall with them by the sword. . . . And they shall know that I am the Lord: when I shall have set a

* Jeremias, xlvi. 3–10, 19–21. † Ezechiel, xxix. 19–21.

fire in Egypt, and all the helpers thereof shall be destroyed. In that *day* (יוֹם, *yom*), shall messengers go forth from my face in ships to destroy the confidence of Ethiopia, and there shall be dread among them in that *day* (יוֹם, *yom*) of Egypt: because it shall certainly come." *

Once more, this word is applied to the period of Our Lord's life upon earth, and even to the whole duration of the Christain Church. Sophonias, for example, thus foretells the coming of the kingdom of Christ. "Wherefore expect me, saith the Lord, in the day of my resurrection that is to come, for my judgment is to assemble the Gentiles, and to gather the kingdoms. . . . . From beyond the rivers of Ethiopia shall my suppliants, the children of my dispersed people, bring me an offering. In that *day* (יוֹם, *yom*) thou shalt not be ashamed for all thy doings, wherein thou hast transgressed against me: for then I will take away out of the midst of thee thy proud boasters, and thou shalt no more be lifted up because of my holy mountain. . . . . Give praise, O daughter of Sion: shout, O Israel: be glad and rejoice with all thy heart, O daughter of Jerusalem. The Lord hath taken away thy judgment, he hath turned away thy enemies: the King of Israel the Lord is in the midst of thee, thou shalt fear evil no more. In that *day* (יוֹם, *yom*) it shall be said to Jerusalem: Fear not; to Sion: Let not thy hands be weakened. The Lord thy God in the midst of thee is mighty, He will save: He will rejoice over thee with gladness, He will be silent in His love, He will be joyful over thee in praise."†

And Isaias: "Is it not yet a very little while, and Libanon shall be turned into a charmel, and charmel shall be esteemed as a forest? And in that *day* (יוֹם, *yom*) the deaf shall hear the words of the book, and out of darkness and obscurity the eyes of the blind shall see. And the meek shall increase their joy in the Lord, and the poor men shall

* Ezechiel, xxx. 3–9. † Sophonias, v. 8-11, 14-17.

rejoice in the Holy One of Israel."* That this passage refers to the time of the Christain Church there can be no doubt; for our Lord himself appeals to it in proof of His divine mission: "Go and relate to John what you have heard and seen. The blind see, the lame walk, the lepers are cleansed, the deaf hear, the dead rise again, the poor have the Gospel preached to them."†

We may trace this use of the word even in the New Testament. Our Lord says, arguing with the Jews: "Abraham your father rejoiced that he might see my *day*: he saw it and was glad."‡ Saint Paul, too, though writing in the Greek language to the Corinthians, does not hesitate to adopt a passage from Isaias, in which the same meaning is conspicuously brought out: "And we helping do exhort you, that you receive not the grace of God in vain. For he saith: In an accepted time have I heard thee, and in the *day* of salvation have I helped thee. Behold, now is the *acceptable time*: behold, now is the *day of salvation*."§ And finally, Our Divine Lord, in His last touching address to the city of Jerusalem, applies the word *day* to the season of grace and mercy: "When he drew near, seeing the city, He wept over it, saying: If thou also hadst known, and that in this thy *day*, the things that are to thy peace: but now they are hidden from thy eyes. For the days shall come upon thee; and thy enemies shall cast a trench about thee, and compass thee round, and straiten thee on every side."||

So much, then, for the first argument. From the numerous examples we have given it is plain enough that the word יום (*yom*), in Scripture language, was often used for a period of many days, and even many years; nay sometimes for a period of many centuries. If so, Moses was free to use it in this sense. And consequently, as far as the word itself is concerned, it affords no conclusive proof that

* Isaias, xxix. 17-19. † Matth. xi. 4, 5.
‡ John, viii. 56. § 2 Cor. vii. 1, 2. || Luke, xix. 41-43.

the Days of Creation were days of twenty-four hours only: we may hold them to be long and indefinite periods of time, without departing in any degree from the established usage of Scripture.

But it is urged—and this is the second argument,—that, whatever may be the meaning of the word יוֹם (*yom*) elsewhere, in the first chapter of Genesis it must mean a day of twenty-four hours. For we are not merely told that there was a First Day, and a Second Day, and a Third Day; but each day is in a manner analyzed by the sacred writer, and its component parts set forth for our instruction. *There was evening and there was morning*, he says, the First Day; *there was evening and there was morning* the Second Day; *there was evening and there was morning* the Third Day; and so on. Now if the word were understood of those indefinite periods we have been speaking about, there would be no meaning in this analysis: for it could hardly be maintained that each of those periods had but one evening and one morning like an ordinary day. Furthermore, it is argued that there is a peculiar appropriateness in this phrase, which goes far to confirm the common interpretation. Amongst the Jews it was usual to compute the civil day from sunset to sunset. The civil day began then with the evening. And accordingly Moses, in describing the Days of Creation, puts the evening first, and says: There was evening and there was morning the First Day; there was evening and there was morning the Second Day; and so for the rest.

All this reasoning seems to us unsatisfactory and inconclusive. In the first place, it is not a fact, as would seem to be supposed, that the civil day is made up of evening and morning. The evening and the morning do not make the whole day; they are only certain periods of the day. Neither do they mark the limits of the day: for, though it is quite true that, in the computation of the Jews, the civil day began with the evening, it certainly did not end with the morning. If, then, by the word Day, Moses here meant the civil day of twenty-four hours, how is this clause to be understood, There was evening and there was morning the First Day? It cannot mean that the evening and the morning put together made up the First Day: for this is not a fact. It cannot mean that the evening marked the beginning of the day, and the morning marked its close: for the period included between the evening and the morning is not the day but the night. What does it mean, then?

Many writers seem to suppose that the evening and the morning are intended by Moses to designate the night and the day;—that is to say, the whole period of darkness and the whole period of light, which put together make up the civil day of twenty-four hours. If the text could be explained in this way, it would fit in, no doubt, much more appropriately with the theory of ordinary days than with the theory of indefinite periods. But the text *cannot* be explained in this way. The evening is *not* the whole period of darkness, and the morning is *not* the whole period of light. No English writer could say, with propriety, that the Day is made up of the evening and the morning. Neither could Moses have meant to say this in the first chapter of Genesis: for the Hebrew words ערב (*Ghereb*) *and* בקר (*Boker*) which are found in the original text, have a meaning not less fixed and definite than the corresponding words Evening and the Morning in the English language.

To prove the truth of this assertion by an investigation of all the passages in the Hebrew Bible, in which these words are found, would be a tedious and uninteresting task. But it may be easily tested in another way. If the words ערב (*Ghereb*) and בקר (*Boker*) were ever used to mean, not strictly the evening and morning, but the whole period of night and the whole period of day, this fact would surely have become known in the course of time to some of the many eminent and accomplished Hebrew lexicographers.

We ask, then, is there one Hebrew lexicon of note which assigns the sense of *night* to the word ערב (*Ghereb*) and the sense of *day* to the word בקר (*Boker*). For ourselves, we have searched several of the best of them, and we have not found a single one that even hints at such an explanation.

Perhaps, however, some of our readers might be unwilling to accept the authority of lexicons as conclusive on a point of this kind; seeing that lexicons very often represent but imperfectly the full power of a language. Well, then, there is another process, and a simple one enough, by which they may demonstrate the inaccuracy of our statement, if inaccurate it be. Let them produce any passage from the Hebrew Bible in which the words ערב (*Ghereb*) and בקר (*Boker*) are employed to designate the whole night and the whole day. If they fail to do so,—and as far as we are aware, no such passage has yet been discovered,—then surely we may fairly contend that the interpretation which thus explains the words in the first chapter of Genesis cannot be regarded as certain: nor can the argument founded on that interpretation be received as conclusive.

There is a text in the eighth chapter of the prophet Daniel which might, perhaps, appear at first sight to militate against our opinion. The prophet had a vision in which it was foreshadowed that Antiochus Epiphanes should come and prevail against the Jews, and should profane the temple of God, and should abolish the daily sacrifice. One of the Angels in the vision is heard asking of another, for how long should the daily sacrifice cease, and the sanctuary remain desolate. And the answer is given in these words: "Unto *evening-morning* (ער עדב בקד, *ghad ghereb boker*) two thousand three hundred; then shall the sanctuary be cleansed."* Now, this is commonly understood to mean that the daily sacrifice should be abolished for two thousand three hundred *days*. And therefore, it

* Dan. viii. 14.

would seem that, in this passage, the *evening and morning* are used to signify the *whole civil day* of twenty-four hours.

We will not dispute the correctness of the interpretation which is here set forth, although the words of the Angel are explained in a very different sense by many eminent commentators. But we think that the passage, even when understood according to this interpretation, cannot fairly be brought in evidence against us. The evening and the morning do not make up the whole day: but they occur once, and only once, in each day. Therefore a period of many days may be properly signified by noting the recurrence of the evening and morning a certain number of times. And in point of fact, a usage of this kind seems to prevail in most languages. The common word *fortnight*, in English, affords a good illustration. It signifies a period of fourteen nights and days: yet it does not specify the recurrence of fourteen days, but only the recurrence of fourteen nights. Again, the poet says:

"Fair was she to behold, that maiden of seventeen *summers*."

Nobody would argue from these examples that the word *summer* means a period of twelve months; or that the word *night* means a period of twenty-four hours. And so, in the case before us, the recurrence of the evening and morning two thousand three hundred times may be pointed out to mark a period of two thousand three hundred days, although the evening and morning are not the whole day, but only certain parts of the day. Nay, more; we fancy we can see a good reason why the Angel in the vision should single out the evening and the morning for special notice. He had been asked about the profanation of the sanctuary, and the abolition of the daily sacrifice. Now it was in the evening and the morning that the daily sacrifice was wont to be offered. And the Angel seems to answer: The evening and the morning shall return two thousand three hundred times; and there shall be no evening and morning sacrifice: but, after that time, the sanctuary shall be cleansed and sacrifice restored.

So far we have been arguing from the common usage of Scripture that the evening and the morning mentioned in the history of the Creation cannot mean the whole night and the whole day. But there is a special objection against this interpretation from the history of the Creation itself. The fifth verse in the first chapter of Genesis runs thus: "And God called the light Day, and the darkness he called Night. And there was evening and there was morning the First Day." In the first sentence it is recorded that God, having divided the light from the darkness, gave to each its proper name: He called the light, Day; and the darkness, Night. Is it not highly improbable that, after this announcement, the sacred writer would himself, in the very next sentence, employ names altogether different, if he wished to designate the period of light and the period of darkness?

We are not maintaining that the phrase under consideration—"there was evening and there was morning the First Day"—cannot be explained on the hypothesis that the Days of Creation were days of twenty-four hours. But we do contend that it affords no conclusive proof in favor of that hypothesis; because even in that hypothesis the meaning of the phrase is still doubtful and obscure. For ourselves, we candidly confess we can offer no explanation that seems to us, in any system of interpretation, altogether satisfactory. We may be allowed, however, to call attention to an opinion put forward by Saint Augustine, which fits in very appropriately with the doctrine that the Days of Creation were long periods of time. The distinctions of evening and morning, he says, are not to be understood in reference to the rising and setting of the Sun, which, in point of fact, was not created until the Fourth Day; but rather in reference to the works themselves that are recorded to have been produced. In this way the evening will naturally represent the bringing to an end of the work that had been accomplished; and the morning, on the other hand, the coming in of the work that was to be. This opinion was afterward adopted by Saint Eucherius, Bishop of Lyons, who seems almost to borrow the very words of Saint Augustine; and also by Venerable Bede, who says: "What is the evening, but the completion of each work? and the morning, but the beginning of the next?" In the twelfth century we find it again set forth by Saint Hildegarde, who was considered by Saint Bernard, as well as by Pope Eugenius the Third, to have been gifted with the spirit of prophecy.* This interpretation, it is true, does not explain the words *evening* and *morning* according to their literal signification: but then the metaphorical sense it ascribes to them is both simple and appropriate; more especially if we understand the word Day in the sense of a long and indefinite period. As the morning literally means the break of day, and the evening its decline, the Sacred Writer might, not inaptly, have employed these words to represent metaphorically the opening and the close of the various works which are ascribed to each successive period in the history of the Creation.

It may be observed, moreover, that this explanation seems quite in accord with the etymolgy of the Hebrew words עֶרֶב (*Ghereb*), and בֹּקֶר (*Boker*). The latter is formed from the root בָּקַר (*Bakar*), *to lay open*, and used to signify the morning, because in the morning the light of the sun is, as it were, unveiled, and *laid open* to the earth. Hence, the word might be applied with much propriety, in a metaphorical sense, to the unfolding of the various works of God, as each new period was, in its turn, ushered in with a new act of Creation. On the other hand, עֶרֶב (*Ghereb*) seems to be derived from ערב (*Gharab*), *to mingle*, and has probably come to signify the evening, as the famous Hebrew scholar,

* Appendix (38) (39) (40) (41).

Aben Ezra, suggests, because, in the uncertain light of evening, the forms of external objects lose their distinctness of outline, and become, in a manner, blended together. And so this word might have been employed, not unfitly, to represent the close of each period in the creation, which was marked, as Geologists tell us, by the gradual dying out or extinction of the various forms of life peculiar to that period. Anyhow, in following the opinion of so ancient and so venerable an authority as Saint Augustine, we cannot be charged with unduly straining the Sacred Text to meet the exigencies of modern science.

The next argument is founded on a passage in Exodus, to which we have already had occasion to refer: "Six days shalt thou labor, and do all thy work. But the seventh day is the Sabbath of the Lord thy God: thou shalt do no work on it, thou, nor thy son, nor thy daughter, nor thy man-servant, nor thy maid-servant, nor thy beast, nor the stranger that is within thy gates. For in six days the Lord made the Heavens and the Earth, and the sea, and all that in them is, and rested the seventh day; therefore the Lord blessed the seventh day and sanctified it."* We are to work upon six days, and to rest upon the seventh; *because* in six days God accomplished all the works of the creation, and rested on the seventh. There can be no mistake as to the meaning of this commandment. The six days on which it is lawful to labor are, beyond all doubt, six days in the common sense of the word; six days of twenty-four hours each: and the seventh day, on which it is forbidden to work, is a day of the same kind. But the example of God's labor and God's rest is set forth, in the text, as the pattern after which this law of the Sabbath was framed. And therefore, the six days in which God furnished and embellished the earth must have been likewise six days of twenty-four

Exodus, xx. 9-11.

hours each. This argument is regarded by many writers as decisive.

To us, on the contrary, it seems by no means necessary to understand the days on which God labored and rested, in precisely the same sense as the days on which it is enjoined that we should labor and rest. The examples of God is, no doubt, represented in the Sacred Text as the reason for the Jewish Sabbath : "Six days shalt thou labor, and rest upon the seventh ; *for* in six days the Lord made the Heavens and the Earth, and rested on the seventh." But, suppose for a moment that the days of creation were long periods of time, will not the significance of this reason remain unchanged? As God, in the great work of the creation, labored for six successive periods, and then rested for a seventh, so shall you likewise do all your work during six of those successive periods into which your time is divided, and rest upon the seventh.

In support of this view, we may observe that the Jews were commanded to abstain from work, not only every seventh *day*, but also every seventh *year*. "Six years thou shalt sow thy ground, and shalt gather the corn thereof; but the seventh year thou shalt let it alone, and suffer it to rest, that the poor of thy people may eat, and whatsoever shall be left, let the beasts of the field eat it : in like manner shalt thou do with thy vineyard and thy oliveyard. Six days shalt thou work : the seventh day thou shalt cease, that thy ox and thy ass may rest; and the son of thy handmaid and the stranger may be refreshed."* And in another place we read: "When you shall have entered into the land which I will give you, observe the rest of the Sabbath to the Lord. Six years thou shalt sow thy field, and six years thou shalt prune thy vineyard, and shalt gather the fruits thereof ; but in the seventh year there shall be a Sabbath to the land, of the resting of the Lord ; thou shalt not sow thy field, nor prune

* Exodus, xxiii, 10–12.

thy vineyard. What the ground shall bring forth of itself thou shalt not reap: neither shalt thou gather the grapes of the first fruits as a vintage; for it is a year of rest to the land: But they shall be unto you for meat; to thee, and to thy man-servant, and to thy maid-servant, and to thy hireling, and to the strangers that sojourn with thee, to thy beasts of burden, and to thy cattle, all things that grow shall be for meat."* The seventh year, then, according to Divine command, was a year of rest among the Jews, just as the seventh day was a day of rest; and it is evident that the one precept, no less than the other, was founded on the great example of God's rest when He had finished the work of Creation. We are satisfied, therefore, that whatever may have been the length of those six days in which God labored, and of the seventh day on which He rested, His example might still be properly set forth as the model on which the law of the Sabbath was founded.

It is urged, however, that in this passage of Exodus, we have the same word יוֹם (*yom*) applied in the very same context to the six days of the Creation and to the six days of the week; and it can hardly be supposed that the inspired writer would pass thus suddenly from one meaning of the word to another, and a very different meaning, without giving any intimation to his readers of such a transition. If this argument is a good one, we can only say that it completely oversets the opinion of those against whom we are contending. In the fifth verse of the first chapter of Genesis we read: "And God called the *light Day*, and the *darkness* he called *Night*. And there was evening and there was morning the first *Day*." Now, those who reject the theory of long periods, maintain that by the word Day in the latter part of this verse, is meant the whole civil day of twenty-four hours; while it is plain that, in the earlier part of the verse, the same word Day is em-

* Leviticus, xxv. 2-7.

phatically applied to only a part of that period—that is, to the time of light as distinguished from the time of darkness. Therefore, they are themselves, in fact, upholding an interpretation which supposes the inspired writer to pass from one meaning of the word Day to another, without any intimation of a change of meaning.

But we do not want to shrink from dealing with this argument on its merits. The principle on which it is founded seems to us unsound and inconsistent with the evidence of the Sacred Books themselves. It is quite a common thing, we contend, in Scripture, for the writer to pass from one meaning of a word to another without any explicit indication of such a transition, when, as in the case before us, the two senses, though different, are analogous: the one being, as it were, the figure, or the symbol, or the pattern, of the other. A few examples will make this clear. In the Second Epistle of St. Paul to the Corinthians, we read as follows: "For the charity of Christ presseth us: judging this, that if one *died* for all, then all were *dead;* and Christ *died* for all."* Here, when it is said that "all were *dead,*" the meaning is, that all men were *dead spiritually* by sin; whereas, in the clause immediately preceding, and in the clause immediately following, the same word is used in its literal sense for the death of Christ upon the cross. And yet the Apostle, though he thus passed from the literal to the metaphorical sense of the word, and then back again from the metaphorical sense to the literal, gives no express indication of these transitions.

Again, in the Gospel, when a certain man, being called by our Lord, said: "Lord, suffer me first to go and bury my father," Jesus reproved him in these words: "Let the *dead* bury their *dead;* but go thou and preach the kingdom of God."† There is some difference of opinion amongst commentators as to the exact meaning of this

* 2 Cor. v. 14, 15. † Matt. viii. 22; Luke, ix. 60.

phrase. But whatever interpretation be adopted, it seems evident from the context that the *dead to be buried* were those who were literally dead; whereas, the *dead* who were to *bury them* were manifestly *not* those who were literally dead, but those who were dead in some analogous or metaphorical sense. Another example occurs in the twentieth chapter of Saint John. Christ says to His Apostles: "I ascend to my Father and your Father, to my God and your God."* When He says, "I ascend to my Father," the meaning is, "to Him who has begotten me from all eternity." When He adds, "and your Father," the meaning is, "to Him who has *adopted* you for His children." Here, then, the word Father is first used in the sense of a natural father, and immediately after in the sense of a father by adoption, without any explicit declaration of a change in meaning.

The Epistle of Saint Paul to the Romans furnishes an instance in which the transition from one meaning to another occurs in the case of the word Day itself: "The night is passed, and the *day* is at hand. Let us, therefore, cast off the works of darkness, and put on the armor of light. Let us walk honestly as in the *day*."† The word Day, in the earlier part of this passage, is used by Saint Paul for the Day of Eternity which is to follow the darkness of this life; while, in the next sentence, it means clearly the period of light between sunrise and sunset. Another illustration of the same kind occurs in the first Epistle to the Thessalonians. "But you, brethren, are not in darkness that that *day* should overtake you as a thief; for you are all the children of light and the children of the *day*."‡ No one familiar with the language of Scripture can doubt that the first *day* here is the Day of Judgment; and it is quite plain that the second *day* is *not* the Day of Judgment.

Our next example, and one most appropriate to our

* John, xx. 17. † Rom. xiii. 12, 13. ‡ I. Thessal. v. 4, 5.

purpose, is taken from the prophet Amos: "And it shall come to pass in that *day*, saith the Lord God, that I will make the sun go down at noon, and I will darken the earth in the clear *day*."* This prophecy is commonly referred by the Fathers to the time of our Lord, when the earth was darkened in the clear day on the occasion of His crucifixion; but some eminent authorities, with Saint Jerome at their head, explain it of the Captivity in Babylon. Either interpretation will suit our argument. The sacred writer first employs the word Day for a long period of time, and afterward proceeds to use it in its more ordinary sense, without giving his readers any express intimation of such a transition.

We hope it is now pretty clear that neither the reason assigned for the institution of the Sabbath Day, nor the particular form of words in which that ordinance is set forth, offers any insurmountable obstacle to the opinion we are defending. And this is quite enough for our purpose. For we would again remind our readers that we are not attempting to prove from the Sacred Text that this opinion *must* be true, but only that it *may* be true. Our object has been sufficiently attained if we have succeeded in showing that the hypothesis which makes the Days of Creation long periods, is not inconsistent with the language of Scripture.

We are tempted, however, in the case of this objection, to go somewhat further than the scope of our argument strictly demands. The text we have just been discussing brings before us, in fact, a consideration of great weight in favor of the system of long periods. "In six days the Lord made the Heavens and the Earth and the sea, and all that in them is, and rested on the seventh day." Now, what was this Seventh Day on which God rested? Was it a common day of twenty-four hours? or was it not rather a long and

* Amos, viii. 9.

undefined period of time? Saint Augustine answers plainly enough: "The seventh day," he says, "is without an evening, and has no setting." And Venerable Bede, asking why the sacred writer had assigned no evening to the seventh day, gives this answer: "Because it has no end, and is shut in by no limit."*

The common sentiment of Theologians, as far as we know, seems to point in the same direction. They tell us that God is said to have rested, inasmuch as He ceased from the creation of new species; and they hold that since the close of the Sixth Day no new species have been brought into existence. But whether this be true or not, it would be very difficult, we think, to point out any sense in which God can be said to have rested after the work of the Six Days, and in which He is not resting at the present moment. If so, the day of His rest is still going on; and it is not a period of twenty-four hours only, but a period of many thousand years. Now, if the Seventh Day on which God rested is a period of many thousand years, are we not fully justified in supposing that the Six Days on which He formed and furnished the Heavens and the Earth were likewise periods of many ages?

* Appendix (42) (43).

CHAPTER XXI.

APPLICATION OF THE SECOND HYPOTHESIS TO THE MOSAIC HISTORY OF CREATION—CONCLUSION.

Summary of the argument—Striking coincidence between the order of creation as set forth in the narrative of Moses and in the records of Geology—Comparison illustrated and developed—Scheme of adjustment between the periods of Geology and the days of Genesis—Tabular view of this scheme—Objections considered—It is not to be regarded as an established theory, but as an admissible hypothesis—Either the first hypothesis or the second is sufficient to meet the demands of Geology as regards the antiquity of the earth—Not necessary to suppose that the sacred writer was made acquainted with the long ages of geological time—He simply records faithfully that which was committed to his charge—The Mosaic history of creation stands alone, without rivals or competitors.

HE results at which we have arrived by the long, and we fear tedious, line of argument pursued in the last Chapter, may be briefly summed up. First, many illustrious Fathers of the Church—Saint Augustine, Origen, Clement of Alexandria, Saint Athanasius, and others—plainly declared against the opinion that the Days of Creation were days in the ordinary sense of the word; and, therefore, it is a mistake to suppose that this opinion is supported by the unanimous voice of Christian tradition. Secondly, the word Day is frequently used in Scripture for a long period of time, and sometimes for a period of indefinite

duration. Thirdly, there is nothing in the language of Moses that forbids us to explain the word according to this sense, in the first chapter of Genesis. And fourthly, there is, at least, one grave consideration, derived from Holy Scripture itself, which distinctly points to such an interpretation. The Six Days of Creation are contrasted with the Seventh Day of God's rest; and this Seventh Day of God's rest is unquestionably a long period of undefined duration. From all this it is obvious to conclude, that we may fairly adopt this mode of interpreting the Mosaic Days, if it will assist us in reconciling the received conclusions of science with the truths of Revelation.

Now, there is a striking resemblance, in some important respects, between the order of Creation as exhibited in the successive days of the Sacred Record, and the order of Creation as manifested in the successive periods of Geological time. Three days are specially marked out by the Inspired Historian as distinguished by the creation of vegetable and animal life—the Third, the Fifth, and the Sixth. On the Third Day were created plants and trees; on the Fifth, reptiles, fish, and birds; on the Sixth, cattle, and the beasts of the earth, and, toward the end, man himself. Geologists, on the other hand, not influenced in the least degree by the Scripture narrative, but guided chiefly by the remains of animal and vegetable life which are preserved in the Crust of the Earth, have established three leading divisions of Geological time; the Palæozoic, or first age of organic life, the Mesozoic, or second great age of organic life, and the Kainozoic, or third great age of organic life. Here, no doubt, is a remarkable coincidence.

But it would be still more remarkable if we could recognize, in the three epochs of Geology, the same general characteristics of organic life as we find ascribed by Moses to the three successive days of the Bible narrative. And so we may, it is said, if we will only take the pains to examine for ourselves the organic remains of these geological epochs as they lie dispersed through the Crust of the Earth, or even as they are to be found collected and arranged for exhibition in our museums. The first great age of Geology is eminently distinguished for its plants and trees; the second, for its huge reptiles and great sea-monsters; the third, for its vast herds of noble quadrupeds. Nay, to complete the harmony between the two Records, as man is represented by the Inspired Writer to have been created toward the close of the last day, so, toward the close of the last Geological age, the remains of man and of his works are found, for the first time, laid by in the archives of the Earth.

Such is the coincidence which some ingenious writers fancy they can trace between the history that is set forth in the written Word of God, and the history that is so curiously inscribed upon His works. Our readers, perhaps, will not be unwilling to consider it a little more in detail. We read in the first chapter of Genesis, that on the Third Day God said: "Let the earth bring forth the green herb, and such as may seed, and the fruit-tree yielding fruit after its kind, which may have seed in itself upon the earth. And it was so done. And the earth brought forth the green herb, and such as yieldeth seed according to its kind, and the tree that beareth fruit, having seed each one according to its kind. And God saw that it was good."* Let us now turn to the Carboniferous Period of Geology, which occupies a large space in the great Palæozoic age. All writers agree that it was specially marked by a gorgeous and luxuriant vegetation: and as we contemplate the multitudinous remains of plants and trees which have been gathered so abundantly in our coal measures, and ranged with such striking effect along the walls of our museums, we can scarcely help thinking that we have before us a practical commentary on the text of Moses. The gifted Hugh Miller, who is universally

* Gen. i. 11, 12.

allowed to have been one of the most practical and experienced Geologists of the modern school, gives a very picturesque and graphic sketch of the Carboniferous flora. "In no other age," he says, "did the world ever witness such a flora: the youth of the earth was peculiarly a green and umbrageous youth,—a youth of dusk and tangled forests,—of huge pines and stately araucarians,—of the reed-like calamite, the tall tree-fern, the sculptured sigillaria, and the hirsute lepidodendron. Wherever dry land, or shallow lake or running stream appeared, from where Melville Island now spreads out its ice-wastes under the star of the pole, to where the arid plains of Australia lie solitary beneath the bright cross of the south, a rank and luxuriant herbage cumbered every footbreadth of the dank and steaming soil; and even to distant planets our earth must have shown, through the enveloping cloud, with a green and delicate ray."* Such an age as this might well be described in history as the age in which the earth brought forth the green herb, and the fruit-tree yielding seed according to its kind.

Again, the work of the Fifth Day is thus described in the Sacred Narrative:—"God also said: Let the waters bring forth the creeping creature having life, and the fowl that may fly over the earth under the firmament of Heaven. And God created the great whales, and every living and moving creature which the waters brought forth, according to their kinds, and every winged fowl according to its kind. And God saw that it was good."† And in this case, as in the former, we may find the counterpart of the Bible story in the records of Geology. "The secondary age of the geologist," says the eminent writer from whom we have already quoted, "possessed, like the earlier one, its herbs and plants, but they were of a greatly less luxuriant and conspicuous character than their predecessors, and no longer formed the prominent trait or feature of the creation to which they be-

* The Testimony of the Rocks, p. 125.

† Genesis, i. 20, 21.

long. The period had also its corals, its crustaceans, its molluscs, its fishes, and, in some one or two exceptional instances, its dwarf mammals. But the grand existences of the age,—the existences in which it excelled every other creation, earlier or later,—were its huge creeping things,—its enormous monsters of the deep,—and, as shown by the impressions of their footprints stamped upon the rocks, its gigantic birds. It was peculiarly the age of egg-bearing animals, winged and wingless. Its wonderful *whales*, not however as now, of the mammalian, but of the reptilian class—ichthyosaurs, plesiosaurs, and cetiosaurs—must have tempested the deep; its creeping lizards and crocodiles, such as the teliosaurus, megalosaurus, and iguanodon,—creatures some of which more than rival the existing elephant in height, and greatly more than rivalled him in bulk,—must have crowded the plains, or haunted by myriads the rivers of the period; and we know that the foot-prints of, at least, one of its many birds, are fully twice the size of those made by the horse or camel. We are thus prepared to demonstrate that the second period of the geologist was peculiarly and characteristically a period of whale-like reptiles of the sea, of enormous creeping reptiles of the land, and of numerous birds, some of them of gigantic size."*

Once more, it is written that, on the Sixth Day, "God said: Let the earth bring forth the living creature in its kind, cattle and creeping things, and beasts of the earth, according to their kinds. And it was so done. And God made the beasts of the earth according to their kinds, and cattle and every thing that creepeth on the earth after its kind. And God saw that it was good."† And again Geology seems to confirm the truth of the Inspired narrative, and to fill up the details of the picture. "The Tertiary period," continues Hugh Miller, "had also its prominent class of existences.

* Testimony of the Rocks, p. 126. † Genesis, i. 24, 25.

Its flora seems to have been no more conspicuous than that of the present time; its reptiles occupy a very subordinate place; but its beasts of the field were by far the most wonderfully developed, both in size and numbers, that ever appeared upon the earth. Its mammoths and its mastodons, its rhinoceri and its hippopotami, its enormous dimotherium and colossal megatherium, greatly more than equalled in bulk the greatest mammals of the present time, and vastly exceeded them in number. The remains of one of its elephants (Elephas primigenius) are still so abundant amid the frozen wastes of Siberia, that what have been not inappropriately termed 'ivory quarries' have been wrought among their bones for more than a hundred years. Even in our own country, of which, as I have already shown, this elephant was for long ages a native, so abundant are the skeletons and tusks, that there is scarcely a local museum in the kingdom that has not its specimens, dug out of the Pleistocene deposits of the neighborhood. And with this ancient elephant there were meetly associated in Britain, as on the northern continents generally all around the globe, many other mammals of corresponding magnitude. 'Grand indeed,' says an English naturalist, 'was the fauna of the British islands in those early days. Tigers as large again as the biggest Asiatic species lurked in the ancient thickets; elephants nearly twice the size of the largest individuals that now exist in Africa or Ceylon roamed in herds: at least two species of the rhinoceros forced their way through the primeval forests; and the lakes and rivers were tenanted by hippopotami as bulky, and with as great tusks, as those of Africa.' The massive cave-bear and large cave-hyæna belong to the same formidable group, with at least two species of great oxen, with a horse of smaller size, and an elk that stood ten feet four inches in height. Truly this Tertiary age—this third and last of the geologic periods—was peculiarly the age of great 'beasts of the earth after their kind, and of cattle after their kind.'"*

We shall be told, perhaps, that there are Six Days assigned to the work of creation in the Mosaic narrative, and that we have accounted but for three. Let it be remembered, however, that Geology does not profess to give a complete history of our Globe. It can set before us those events only which have left their impress indelibly stamped upon the rocks that compose the Crust of the Earth. These events Geologists have attempted to reduce to the order of a chronological system; and in prosecuting this task they have been guided almost exclusively by the evidence of Organic Remains. Hence it was not to be expected that, in Geological Chronology, we should find a Period specially set apart as the Period in which Light was made; or another as the Period in which the Firmament was spread out over the Earth; or a Third as the Period in which the sun and moon and stars shone forth in the expanse of Heaven. Such phenomena had, indeed, a very important influence on the physical condition of our globe. But they must occupy a very secondary place, if indeed they are distinctly chronicled at all in the records of Geology. It is the formation of rocks and the embedding therein of Fossil Remains that constitute the main study of the Geologist, and that guide him in the distribution of Geological time.

Furthermore, we would observe that the scheme of Chronology which Geologists put before us, affords abundant room for each and all of the Mosaic Days. Let it be assumed for a moment that the Carboniferous Period corresponds with the Third Day of the Sacred narrative. The earlier Periods of the Palæozoic Age will then fit in with the First and Second Days of Scripture; and the Permian, which intervenes between the Carboniferous Period and the

* Testimony of the Rocks, pp. 127, 128.

Secondary Age, may be supposed to correspond with the Fourth Day of Scripture. This adjustment between the Mosaic Days and the Periods of Geology will probably be made more intelligible to the general reader by the Table that appears on the following page.

The reader must not think it amiss, in this distribution of the Mosaic Days, that four out of six are crowded together into one Geological Age, while each of the other two has an entire Age assigned to itself. If the Days of Creation were indefinite periods, there is no incongruity in supposing that one may have corresponded to a longer, another to a shorter interval in the history of our planet. But, in truth, our scheme of distribution does not of necessity imply that the Mosaic Days were periods of unequal length. Geologists do not pretend that there is even a remote approximation to equality between the several divisions of Geological time. The three great Epochs are distinguished from each other by reason of the very marked difference in the character of their Fossil Remains. And the multiplication of Periods in each Epoch seems to depend rather upon the degree of completeness with which the strata of that Age have been examined, than upon any conjecture as to the probable length of its duration. Thus, for example, Sir Charles Lyell thinks that, as far as the present condition of Science affords the means of forming an opinion, almost any one of the Periods in the Palæozoic Age was as long as all the Periods of the Tertiary Age taken together.*

But there is another and a more serious objection against our hypothesis. It has been observed more than once that the periods of Geology are out of harmony with the Days of Genesis, even as regards the history of Organic life. According to the Scripture narrative no Organic life appeared upon the Earth previous to the Third Day. Now

* Elements of Geology, p. 100.

the Third Day of Scripture corresponds, in our scheme, with the Carboniferous Period of Geology. And yet there is abundant evidence in the Fossil Remains of the Devonian, the Silurian, and the Cambrian Formations, that

DAYS.	PERIODS.	EPOCHS.
DAY OF GOD'S REST.	RECENT.	HISTORIC AGE.
SIXTH MOSAIC DAY.	POST-PLIOCENE. PLIOCENE. MIOCENE. EOCENE.	TERTIARY OR KAINOZOIC AGE.
FIFTH MOSAIC DAY.	CRETACEOUS. JURASSIC. TRIASSIC.	SECONDARY OR MESOZOIC AGE.
FOURTH MOSAIC DAY. THIRD MOSAIC DAY. FIRST AND SECOND MOSAIC DAYS.	PERMIAN. CARBONIFEROUS. { DEVONIAN. SILURIAN. CAMBRIAN. LAURENTIAN. }	PRIMARY OR PALÆOZOIC AGE.

Organic life—both plants and animals—prevailed upon the Earth for many ages before the Carboniferous Period began. Nay, it is now commonly held, since the discovery of the famous *Eozoon Canadense*, the oldest known Fossil, that life already existed during the deposition of the Laurentian Rocks, the earliest of all the Stratified Formations. Furthermore, in the Mosaic account, Fish are represented as having been created only on the Fifth Day, which we have fitted in with the Secondary Age of Geology: whereas in the Geological Record we find Fish as early as the Silurian Period, which is far back in the Primary Age. These considerations, and divers others of a like nature, have been regarded by some eminent writers as altogether fatal tc the hypothesis for which we are contending.

To us, however, it appears that such points of discrepancy involve no contradiction between the two Records. The Sacred Writer tells us, no doubt, that on the Third Day God created plants and trees: but he does not say, either expressly or otherwise, that previous to the Third Day the Earth was devoid of vegetation. Again, we read that reptiles, fish, and birds were created on the Fifth Day. But there is nothing in the language of the Inspired narrative from which it can be inferred that these several classes of animal life may not have been represented before that time, by many and various species: though probably, it was only on the Fifth Day that they were developed in such vast numbers, and assumed such gigantic proportions, as to become the most conspicuous objects of creation.

The first chapter of Genesis is but a brief summary of an inconceivably vast series of events. It is nothing more than a rapid sketch, exhibiting, as it were, to the eye the prominent features in the history of Creation. Moreover, we should remember that it was written with a specific end in view. The purpose of the Sacred Writer was plainly to impress upon the Hebrew people, naturally prone to idolatry, the existence of One Supreme Being, who has made all things. Hence we should naturally expect that, amid the boundless variety of God's works, he would make choice of those that were most calculated to strike the mind with wonder and awe, and to bring home to a rude and uncultivated race of men the Almighty Power and Supreme Dominion of the Great Creator. Now the Zoophytes, and Graptolites, and Tribolites, of the Devonian and Silurian Periods, however curious and interesting they may be to men of science, would have had but little significance for the Jewish people. Let us suppose that these more humble forms of animal life had, in fact, existed during the First and Second Days of the Mosaic narrative, and where is the wonder that the Inspired Historian, under the guidance of the Holy Spirit, should pass them by in silence, and choose rather to commemorate the more striking and impressive facts, that, at the bidding of God, Light shone forth from the midst of darkness, and the blue firmament of Heaven was expanded above the waste of waters?

We say, then, that events which are simply left unrecorded by the Sacred Writer are not, on that account, untrue:* that he describes to us, not all the works of Creation, which would have been an endless task, but only the more conspicuous objects in each successive stage; and that he sketches them, most probably, as they would have appeared to the eye of a human observer, if a human observer at the time had existed on the Earth. If this view be admitted, then it is not inconsistent with the Scripture narrative to suppose that plants may have existed before the Third Day, and fish before the Fifth. Each Day in its turn would have been rendered conspicuous to an observing spectator by those events which are recorded by Moses. But each Day, too, would have witnessed many other events, unnoticed by Moses, of which the memorials have been preserved, even to our time, in the Crust of the Earth.

We should observe, however, that though this scheme of adapting the Periods of Geology to the Days of Moses, may be defended as a legitimate hypothesis, it cannot be upheld as an established truth. The geological records that have hitherto been brought to light represent but the merest fragment of the Earth's past history. Each year that passes over our heads is adding largely to the store of facts already accumulated. And it needs but little reflection to perceive that an hypothesis may be quite consistent with the knowledge we possess to-day, and yet may be found altogether inconsistent with the knowledge we shall possess to-morrow. We must be content, therefore, to suspend our judgment,

* "Aliquid esse a Deo conditum, de quo sileat liber Genesis, nihil re pugnat." Saint Augustine, Confess. Lib. xii., cap. xxii.

and to await the progress of events. It may be that future discoveries shall bring to light new points of harmony between the Days of Genesis and the Periods of Geology; it may be they shall demonstrate that no such harmony exists. For us it is enough to have shown that this hypothesis is consistent, on the one hand, with the story of Genesis—on the other, with the actual discoveries of Geology; and, therefore, that it may be adopted, in the present condition of our knowledge, as a legitimate means of reconciling the established conclusions of that science with the truths of Revelation.

Conclusion.—We have, then, two distinct systems of interpretation, according to which the vast Antiquity of the Earth, asserted by Geology, may be fairly brought into harmony with the history of creation, recorded in Scripture. The one allows an interval of incalculable duration between the creation of the Heavens and the Earth, and the work of the Six Days: the other supposes each one of these Six Days to have been itself an indefinite period of time. We cannot, indeed, prove that either of these two systems is true in point of fact; but we have attempted to show that neither is at variance with the language of the Sacred Text. On the other hand, when we look to the evidence of geological facts, we see no decisive reason for preferring one to the other. Either mode of interpretation seems in itself quite sufficient to meet all the present requirements of Geology; for, according to either interpretation, the Bible narrative would allow time without limit for the past history of our Globe; and time without limit is just what Geology demands. We may say, then, on this point, what Saint Augustine said long ago, in speaking of the diverse interpretations which the text of Genesis admits: "Let each one choose according to the best of his power: only let him not rashly put forward as known that which is unknown; and let him not fail to remember that he is but a man searching, as far as may be, into the works of God."*

It must not be supposed that, according to our view, the Sacred Writer, in composing his account of the Creation, had before his mind those vast Geological Periods about which we have said so much in the course of this volume. Such an opinion is no part of our system. We see no good reason for believing that the author of Genesis was specially enlightened from Heaven on the subject of Stratified Rocks and Fossil Remains, of Upheaval and Denudation, of Volcanic Action and Subterranean Heat. These are matters of Physical, not of Religious Science. And it seems to be the order of Providence to leave the discovery of such things to the industry and ingenuity of man: "Cuncta fecit bona in tempore suo, et mundum tradidit disputationi eorum."†

What we maintain, then, is simply this: that the Sacred Writer recorded faithfully, in language fitted to the ideas of his time, that portion of Revelation which was committed to him; and, in the accomplishment of this task, made such a choice of words and phrases, under the guidance of the Holy Spirit, to whom all truth is present, as to set forth plainly those facts that were unfolded to him, without introducing any error about those facts of which he was ignorant. The language is the language of men, but the voice that speaks therein is the voice of God. And thus it comes to pass that this Mosaic story, when fairly examined according to the ordinary laws of human speech, is found in every age to accommodate itself, with quite an unexpected simplicity, to those new and wonderful views of God's manifold power which each human science in its turn brings to light.

Before taking leave of the subject, we would venture to bring under the notice of our readers one very obvious reflection, which is sometimes lost sight of in the heat of con-

* Appendix (44). † Ecclesiastes, iii. 2.

troversy. The Mosaic history of the Creation absolutely stands alone. It has no rivals, no competitors. Every other attempt that has been made to explain the origin of the world, and of the human race, is refuted by its own intrinsic extravagance and absurdity. The wisest nations of antiquity failed to discover that great fundamental truth, which stands out so boldly on the first page of Genesis, that there is One God who hath made all things. The philosophers of Chaldæa were familiar with the course of the Heavens, and could predict the eclipses of the sun and moon. But the philosophers of Chaldæa could not rise from the contemplation of creatures to the knowledge of the Creator: the creatures themselves were the gods that Chaldæa worshipped. Egypt had greatness of mind to conceive the idea of the Pyramids, and skill to devise the plan of their construction, and strength of arms to lift up the huge stones on these stupendous piles. But Egypt raised up temples to the river that waters its plain, and offered sacrifice to the reptile that crawls upon the earth, and the beast that grazes in the field. In Greece the human mind soared to its highest flight, and ranged over the widest and most beautiful fields of thought. Peerless is she among the nations, the mistress of the arts, the fountain source of refined taste, the storehouse of intellectual power, the great nurse of human genius. Her schools of philosophy have influenced and guided to a marvellous extent the thoughts and speculations of all subsequent times. The song of her immortal bard has kindled the imagination of the poet in every generation, and enriched his mind with glowing images. Orators and statesmen still love to copy the lofty sentiments, the graceful diction, the flowing periods, of her golden eloquence. And students from every clime stand enraptured before the beauty and the majesty of her sculptured marble. But Greece, Imperial Greece, knew not the One God, the giver of all good gifts, by whom she was so highly endowed. She fashioned for herself gods and goddesses after her own fancy, and portioned out the universe between them. Jupiter hurled his thunderbolts from the clouds: Neptune ruled the sea: Pluto swayed the sceptre of the infernal regions: Minerva was the goddess of wisdom: Vulcan the god of fire: Apollo the god of music. Nay, the very infirmities and vices of human nature were personified under the names of divinities, and worshipped in the Pantheon of the gods. Rome, too, the conqueror of the world, had its philosophers and its orators, its poets and its sculptors, whose productions still charm and instruct mankind. Yet was Rome no exception to the common lot of the gentile world. For Rome, like Greece, had its long array of gods and goddesses, with their petty jealousies, their vindictive malice, their shameless passions. Alone, amidst all the Mythologies and Cosmogonies of ancient nations, the story of the Hebrew Legislator rises superior to the gross and silly speculations of mortal men. It alone proclaims to mankind what Philosophy and Science, when left to themselves, have never been able to teach, that, In the beginning God created the Heavens and the Earth; that the plants and the animals, the ocean and the elements, the sun and moon and stars, man himself, and all that delights the eye and charms the ear and fills the mind, are His creatures; and that besides Him there is no other God. Away, then, with the idea that this Sacred Narrative, stamped as it plainly is with the imprint of its Divine Author, should ever be found at variance with the truths of science,—or rather, we should say, with those scanty fragments of truth, those crumbs of knowledge, falling from the table of our Heavenly Father, which it is given to man here below to gather up with laborious care, and which, however they may excite his longings, cannot satisfy his hunger.

Here, for the present, we must stop. At some future time, perhaps, if our opportunities permit, we shall return to this subject, and, taking up the second branch of the controversy, investigate the recent discoveries of Geology in reference to the teaching of the Bible as regards the Antiquity of the Human Race.

APPENDIX.

EXTRACTS FROM THE FATHERS AND THEOLOGIANS.

REFERRED TO IN THIS VOLUME.

(1.) SAINT AUGUSTINE.—P. 297.

"Et in rebus obscuris atque a nostris oculis remotissimis, si qua inde scripta etiam divina legerimus, quae possunt salva fida qua imbuimur, alias atque alias parere sententias; in nullam earum nos praecipiti affirmatione ita projiciamus, ut si forte diligentius discussa veritas eam recte labefactaverit, corruamus: non pro sententia divinarum Scripturarum, sed pro nostra ita dimicantes, ut eam velimus Scripturarum esse, quae nostra est; cum potius eam quae Scripturarum est, nostram esse velle debeamus."—De Genesi ad Litteram, lib. i. cap. 18, n. 37.

(2.) IDEM.—P. 298,

"Plerumque enim accidit ut aliquid de terra, de coelo, de caeteris hujus mundi elementis, de motu et conversione vel etiam de magnitudine et intervallis siderum, de certis defectibus solis ac lunae, de circuitibus annorum et temporum, de naturis animalium, fruticum, lapidum atque hujusmodi caeteris, etiam non christianus ita noverit, ut certissima ratione vel experientia teneat. Turpe est autem nimis et perniciosum ac maxime cavendum, ut christianum de his rebus quasi secundum christianas Litteras loquentem, ita delirare quilibet infidelis audiat, ut, quemadmodum dicitur, toto coelo errare conspiciens, risum tenere vix possit. Et non tam molestum est, quod errans homo deridetur, sed quod auctores nostri ab eis qui foris sunt, talia sensisse creduntur, et cum magnc eorum exitio de quorum salute satagimus, tanquam indocti reprehenduntur atque respuuntur. Cum enim quemquam de numero christianorum in ea re quam optime norunt, errare deprehenderint, et vanam sententiam suam de nostris Libris asserere; quo pacto illis Libris credituri sunt, de resurrectione mortuorum, et de spe vitae aeternae, regnoque coelorum, quando de his rebus quas jam experiri, vel indubitatis numeris percipere potuerunt, fallaciter putaverint esse conscriptos? Quid enim molestiae tristitiaeque ingerant prudentibus fratribus temerarii praesumptores, satis dici non potest, cum si quando de prava et falsa opinione sua reprehendi, et convinci coeperint ab eis qui nostrorum Librorum auctoritate non tenentur, ad defendendum id quod levissima temeritate et apertissima falsitate dixerunt, eosdem Libros sanctos, unde id probent, proferre conantur, vel etiam memoriter, quae ad testimonium valere arbitrantur, multa inde verba pronuntiant, 'non intelligentes neque quae loquuntur, neque de quibus affirmant' (I. Tim., i. 7)."—Ibid., cap. 19, n. 39.

(3.) Saint Thomas.—p. 298.

"Dicendum quod, sicut Augustinus docet, in hujusmodi quaestionibus duo sunt observanda. Primo quidem, ut veritas Scripturae inconcusse teneatur. Secundo, cum Scriptura divina multipliciter exponi possit, quod nulli expositioni aliquis ita praecise inhaereat, ut si certa ratione constiterit hoc esse falsum quod aliquis sensum Scripturae esse credebat id nihilominus asserere praesumat; ne Scriptura ex hoc ab infidelibus derideatur, et ne eis via credendi praecludatur."—Summa Theologica, Pars Prima, Quaest. lxviii. art. primus.

(4.) Perrerius.—p. 302.

"Quod autem in xx. et xxxi. cap. Exod. dictum est, Deum sex diebus fecisse coelum et terram, et omnia quae in eis sunt, non est huic opinioni contrarium: illud enim spatium temporis ante primum diem annumeratur sex diebus, quia fuit quam brevissimum, et fuit continuata Dei operatio: nec sane plures dies naturales consumpti sunt quam sex: ac licet ante primum diem, coelum et elementa facta sint secundum substantiam, tamen non fuerunt perfecta et omnino consummata, nisi spatio illorum sex dierum; tunc enim datus est illis ornatus, complementum, et perfectio."—Comment. in Genes., cap. 1, v. 4, n. 80.

(5.) TOSTATUS.—P. 302.

"*Sex diebus fecit Dominus coelum et terram.* Recte dicitur hic *facere*, quia coelum et terra, quae hic nominantur, et omnia alia, quae nomine eorum subintelliguntur, ista quidem omnia de materia prima facta sunt: materia autem non *facta* sed *creata* est."—Comment. in Exod., cap. 20, quaest. 15.

(6.) PETAVIUS.—P. 302.

Writing on the phrase *In die quo fecit Dominus Deus coelum et terram*, he says, "hoc est, perpolitum et elaboratum esse sex continuis diebus, id enim *faceindi* vox Hebraeis ipsis interpretibus significare videtur."—De Opificio Sex Dierum, lib. cap. 14, sect. 1.

(7.) SAINT BASIL.—P. 304.

"*Et facta est vespera, et factum est mane, dies unus.* Vespera igitur diei ac noctis est communis terminus: et similiter mane, est noctis cum die vicinitas. Itaque ut *prioris generationis praerogativam diei tribueret*, prius commemoravit finem diei, deinde noctis, velut insequente diem nocte. Nam qui status in mundo fuit ante lucis generationem, is non erat nox, sed tenebrae: quod autem a die distinguebatur, eique opponebatur, id nox appellatum est."—Homilia ii. in Hexaemeron; Edit. Bened. p. 20; Edit. Migne, Patr. Graec. Cursus Completus, tom. 29, p. 47.

(8.) SAINT CHRYSOSTOM.—P. 304.

"Ostendimus enim heri, ut meministis, quomodo beatus Moses enarrans nobis horum visibilium elementorum creationem et opificium, dixerit: *In principio fecit Deus coelum et terram: terra autem erat invisibilis et incomposita:* et vos causam docuimus, quare Deus terram informen et nullis figuris expolitam creaverit; quae, opinor, omnia mente tenetis; necessarium est igitur nos ad ea quae sequuntur hodie progredi.

Nam postquam dixit, *Terra autem erat invisibilis et incomposita*, nos accurate docet, unde invisibilis erat et inculta, dicens: *Et tenebrae erant super abyssum, et Spiritus Dei superferebatur super aquam.* . . . Quandoquidem igitur diffusa erat magna universi visibilis informitas, praecepto suo Deus, optimus ille artifex, deformitatem illam depulit, et immensa lucis visibilis pulchritudo producta tenebras fugavit sensibiles, illustravitque omnia."—In Cap. i. Genes. Homil. iii.; Edit. Migne, Patr. Graec. Cursus Completus, tom. 53, p. 33. Here Saint Chrysostom plainly teaches that the world existed before the creation of light. In his Fifth Homily he is equally clear that the First Day of the Mosaic narrative began with a period of light, and not with a period of darkness: "Vide quomodo de singulis diebus sic dicat: *Et factum est vespere, et factum est mane, dies tertius:* non simpliciter nec absque causa: sed ne ordinem confundamus neque putemus vespera ingruente finem accepisse diem; sed sciamus vesperam finem esse lucis, et principium noctis: mane autem finem noctis, et complementum diei. Hoc enim nos docere vult beatus Moses, dicens: *Et factum est vespere, et factum est mane, dies tertius.*"—Edit. Migne, p. 52.

(9.) SAINT AMBROSE.—P. 305.

"*Terra autem erat invisibilis et incomposita.* Bonus artifex prius fundamentum ponit: postea, fundamento posito, aedificationis membra distinguit, et adjungit ornatum. Posito igitur fundamento terrae, et confirmata coeli substantia, duo enim ista sunt velut cardines rerum, subtexuit: *Terra autem erat inanis et incomposita.*"—Hexaemeron, Lib. i. cap. 7; Edit. Bened. p. 13; Edit. Migne, Patr. Lat. Cursus Completus, tom. 14, p. 135.

"Principium ergo diei, vox Dei est: *fiat lux; et facta est lux.*"—Lib. i. cap. 10; Edit. Bened. p 21; Edit. Migne, p. 144.

"In principio itaque temporis coelum et terram Deus fecit. Tempus enim ab hoc mundo, non ante mundum: dies autem temporis portio est, non principium."—Lib. i. cap. 6; Edit. Bened. p. 10; Edit. Migne, p. 132.

(10.) VENERABLE BEDE.—P. 305.

"Scriptura ait: *Qui fecisti mundum de materia informi.*

Sed materia facta est de nihilo, mundi vero species de informi materia. Proinde duas res ante omnem diem et ante omne tempus condidit Deus angelicam videlicet creaturam et informem materiam."—In Pentateuch. Comment.; sub. cap. 1: Edit. Migne, Patr. Lat. Cursus Completus, tom. 91, p. 191. In another place, citing the words of Ecclesiasticus, *Qui vivit in aeternum creavit omnia simul*, he says, "hoc utique ante omnem diem hujus saeculi fecit, cum in principio coelum creavit et terram."—Hexaemeron, Lib. i. in Genes. ii. 4; Edit. Migne, tom. 91, p. 39.

"*Discipulus.* Da ordinem per sex dies factarum rerum? *Magister.* In ipso quidem principio conditionis facta sunt coelum, terra, aer, et aqua. . . . . *Discipulus.* Sequere ordinem generationis? *Magister.* In principio diei primae lux facta est; secunda vero factum firmamentum;" etc.—*Quaestiones super Genesim;* Edit. Migne, Patr. Lat. tom. 93, p. 236. This work is classed by Migne among the Dubia et Spuria of Bede. The critics, however, seem to be agreed that it belongs to a period not later than the tenth century. If it is not the genuine composition of Bede, which is considered more probable, then it only follows that we have, besides Bede, another ancient authority in favor of our opinion.

(11.) PETER LOMBARD.—P. 306.

"Cum Deus in sapientia sua angelicos condidit spiritus, alia etiam creavit, sicut ostendit supradicta Scriptura, quae dicit *in principio Deum creasse coelum*, id est, angelos, *et terram* scilicet, materiam quatuor elementorum adhuc confusam et informem, quae a Graecis dicta est chaos, *et hoc fuit ante omnem diem. Deinde* elementa distinguit Deus, et species proprias atque distinctas singulis rebus secundum genus suum dedit; quae non simul, ut quibusdam sanctorum Patrum placuit, sed per intervalla temporum ac sex volumina dierum, ut aliis visum est formavit."—Sentent. Lib. ii. Distinct. 12; Edit. Migne, Patr. Latin. Cursus Completus, tom. 192, p. 675.

(12.) HUGH OF SAINT VICTOR.—P. 306.

"Principium ergo divinorum operum fuit creatio lucis,

quando ipsa lux non materialiter de nihilo creata est; sed de praejacenti illa universitatis materia formaliter facta est ut lux esset, et vim ac proprietatem lucendi haberet. Hoc opus prima die factum est; sed hujus operis materia ante primam diem creata. Moxque cum ipsa luce dies cœpit; quia ante lucem nec nox fuit nec dies, *etiamsi tempus fuit.*"—De Sacram. Lib. i. Pars i. cap. 9: Edit. Migne, Patr. Lat. tom. 176, p. 193.

(13.) SAINT THOMAS.—P. 307.

"Sed melius videtur dicendum quod *creatio fuerit ante omnem diem.*" In II. Sentent. Distinct. xiii. Art. 3, *ad tertium:* see also ibidem *ad primum*, and *ad secundum.* And again in the Summa he says: "Coelum et terram fecit in prima die, *potius ante omnem diem.*"—Pars i. Quaest. lxxxiv. Art. 2.

(14.) PERRERIUS.—P. 307.

"Licet *ante primum diem*, coelum et elementa facta sint *secundum substantiam*, tamen non fuerint perfecta et omnino consummata, nisi spatio illorum sex dierum: tunc enim datus est illis ornatus, complementum, et perfectio. Quanto autem tempore status ille mundi tenebrosus duraverit, hoc est, utrum plus an minus quam unus dies continere solet, nec mihi compertum est, nec opinor cuiquam mortalium nisi cui divinitus id esset patefactum."—Comment. in Genesim, cap. 1, v. 4, n. 80.

(15.) PETAVIUS.—P. 307.

"Nostra itaque sententia haec est; prima illa Geneseos verba: *In principio creavit Deus coelum et terram;* non peculiare opus aliquod continere, quod initio, et ante dies sex molitus sit Deus: quasi ante lucem, ac reliquas deinceps opificii partes, qualecumque coelum ac terram creaverit. Sed esse generale quoddam effatum, quo omnia, quae sunt a Deo facta, complexus est. Etenim Moses, ut initio dicebam, Judaeos statim edocere voluit; totam illam aspectabilem rerum universitatem a Deo conditore profectam esse. Quare ita pronuntiavit, tanquam diceret: Quidquid videtis et quodcumque coeli ac terrae comprehendit ambitus, una cum coelo ipso, terrâque, id omne fabricatus est initio Deus. Postea vero per partes, ac singillatim, ut quaeque est elaborata, decripsit."—De Opificio Sex Dierum, Lib. i. cap. 2, sect. 10.

"Imprimis *ante dierum sex initium* solam cum aqua terram extitisse credimus: . . . . Habet haec opinio fidem ex Mosis narratione; qui ante coelum id est *firmamentum*, terram, et aquarum abyssum extitisse refert. . . . Nam illud Severiani valde probatur, prima die Deum omnia creasse: reliquis autem diebus, ex jam extantibus: Ubi primam diem non lucis tantum creatione circumscribit: sed quod ante illam factum est, id eidem tribuit. Quod intervallum quantum fuerit, nulla divinatio posset assequi. Neque vero mundi corpora illa, quae *prima omnium extitisse* docui, aquam et terram, arbitror *eodem, in quem lucis ortus incidit, fabricata esse die;* ut quibusdam placet, haud satis firma ratione."—Ibid., cap. 10, sect. 6.

(16.) A Lapide.—p. 307.

"S. Basilius et Beda putant coelum et terram non primo die, sed paulo ante primum diem, utpote ante lucem, create esse. Verum haec non ante, sed ipso primo die, puta initio primae diei, antequam lux produceretur, creata esse, patet Exodi xx. v. 11."—Comment. in Genes., cap. 1, v. 1.

(17.) Saint Augustine.—p. 308.

"Fecisti ante omnem diem in principio coelum et terram." —Confess. Lib. xii. cap. 12: see also Lib. xii. cap. 8. And again, De Genesi ad Litteram, Lib. i. cap. 9, he writes:— "Atque illud ante omnem diem fecisse intelligitur, quod dictum est, *In principio fecit Deus coelum et terram;* . . . Terrae autem nomine invisibilis et incompositae, ac tenebrosa abysso, imperfectio corporalis substantiae significata est, unde temporalia illa fierent, quorum prima esset lux."

(18.) Petavius.—p. 311.

"Quod intervallum quantum fuerit, nulla divinatio posset assequi."—De Opific. Sex Dierum, Lib. i. cap. 10, sec. 6.

(19.) Perrerius.—p. 311.

"Quanto autem tempore status ille mundi tenebrosus duraverit, hoc est, utrum plus an minus quam unus dies continere solet, nec mihi compertum est, nec opinor cuiquam mortalium, nisi cui divinitus id esset patefactum."—Comment. in Genes., cap. 1, v. 4.

(20.) HUGH OF SAINT VICTOR.—P. 311.

"Fortassis jam satis est de his hactenus disputasse, si hoc solum adjecerimus *quanto tempore* mundus in hac confusione, prius quam ejus dispositio inchoaretur, perstiterit. Nam quod illa prima rerum omnium materia, in principio temporis, vel potius cum ipso tempore exorta sit, sonstat ex eo quod dictum est: in principio creavit Deus coelum et terram. *Quamdiu* autem in hac informitate sive confusione permanserit, *Scriptura manifeste non ostendit.*"—De Sacram., Lib. i., pars i. cap. 6.

(21.) SAINT AUGUSTINE.—P. 319.

"Qui dies cujusmodi sint, aut perdifficile nobis, aut etiam impossibile est cogitare; quanto magis dicere."—De Civitate Dei, Lib. xi. cap. 6.

Again: "Arduum quidem et difficillimum est viribus intentionis nostrae, voluntatem scriptoris in istis sex diebus mentis vivacitate penetrare." — De Genesi ad Litteram, Lib. iv. cap. 1.

(22.) IDEM.—P. 319.

"Ac sic per *omnes illos dies unus est dies, non istorum dierum consuetudine intelligendus, quos videmus solis circuitu determinari atque numerari;* sed alio quodam modo, a quo et illi tres dies, qui ante conditionem istorum luminarium commemorati sunt, alieni esse non possunt. Is enim modus non usque ad diem quartum, ut inde jam istos usitatos cogitaremus, sed usque ad sextum septimumque perductus est; ut longe aliter accipiendus sit dies et nox, inter quae duo divisit Deus, et aliter iste dies et nox, inter quae dixit ut dividant luminaria quae creavit, cum ait, 'Et dividant inter diem et noctem.' Tunc enim hunc diem condidit, cum condidit solem, cujus praesentia eumdem exhibet diem: ille autem dies primitus conditus jam triduum peregerat cum haec luminaria illius diei quarta repetitione creata sunt."—De Genesi ad Litteram, Lib. iv. cap. 26. "De quo enim Creatore

Scriptura ista narravit, *quod sex diebus consummaverit omnia opera sua, de illo alibi non utique dissonanter scriptum est, quod creaverit omnia simul* (Eccles. xviii. 1). Ac per hoc et *istos dies sex vel septem vel potius unum sexies septiesve repetitum simul fecit* qui fecit omnia simul. Quid ergo opus erat sex dies tam distincte dispositeque narrari? Quia scilicet ii qui non possunt videre quod dictum est, 'Creavit omnia simul;' nisi cum eis sermo tardius incedat ad id quo eos ducit, pervenire non possunt."—Ib. cap. 33.

(23). PHILO JUDÆUS.—P. 320.

"Tum igitur omnia *simul* sunt condita. In quo quidem universali opificio necesse erat servari ordinem."—De Mundi Opificio; Edit. Francofurti, p. 14. This passage may, at first sight, appear somewhat obscure; but the meaning of it is made clear enough, when we read elsewhere in the same writer: "*Rusticanae simplicitatis est putare, sex diebus, aut utique certo tempore mundum conditum.* . . . . . . Ergo cum audis: 'Complevit sexto die opera, intelligere non debes de diebus aliquot, sed de senario perfecto numero."—De Legis Allegor.; Edit. Francofurti, p. 41.

(24). CLEMENT OF ALEXANDRIA.—P. 320.

Stromatum, Lib. vi. Edit. Benid. p. 291; Edit. Migne, Patrum Graec. Cursus Completus, vol. 9, pp. 370-5. See also Dissertatio de Libris Stromatum, by the learned Benedictine, Nicholas le Nourry, cap. viii. artic. 1.

(25). ORIGEN.—P. 320.

"Quod autem prima die lucem, secunda firmamentum creaverit, tertia aquae quae sub coelo erant, in suis fuerint collectae receptaculis, atque ita terra solius naturae administratione suos fructus protulerit; quod quarta creata fuerint luminaria et stellae, quinta vero natatilia, sexta demum terrestria et homo, haec omnia, pròut facultas tulit, in nostris in Genesim commentariis explicavimus. Quin et supra *contra eos qui obvio sensu Scripturam interpretantes asserunt sex dies ad creationem mundi insumptos fuisse*, adduximus hunc locum: 'Iste est liber generationis coeli et terrae quando creata sunt, in die quo fecit Deus coelum et terram,"—Contra Celsum, Lib. vi. Edit. Bened. pp. 678, 679; Edit. Migne, Patr. Graecor. Cursus Completus, vol. 11, p. 1390: for the passage referred to at the close of the extract see p. 1378. The Commentary upon Genesis of which Origen here speaks no longer exists, but the following passage has been preserved. "Aliqui jam absurdum existimantes Deum architecti more non aliter, quam plurium dierum, labore, fabricam valentis absolvere, intra multos dies mundum perfecisse *uno cuncta momento* ac simul extitisse aiunt, et hinc illud adstruunt; ordinis autem causa, et ut series constet, dierum et rerum quae in illis factae sunt, numerum dictum putant. Hi probabiliter sententiam stabiliunt ea auctoritate qua dictum est: 'Ipse dixit et facta sunt; ipse mandavit, et creata sunt.'"—Selecta in Genesim, Edit. Bened. p. 27; Edit. Migne, Patr. Graec. Cursus Completus, vol. 12, p. 98. Again, in his Treatise De Principiis, Lib. iv., he says: "Quis igitur sanae mentis existimaverit primam et secundam et tertiam diem, et vesperam, et mane, sine sole, luna, et stellis, et eam quae veluti prima erat, diem sine coelo fuisse?" Edit. Bened. p. 175; Edit. Migne, vol. 11, p. 378. See also P. Danielis Huetii Origeniana, Lib. ii. cap. 2, Quaest. 8, § 6; Edit. Migne, vol. 17, p. 979.

(26.) SAINT ATHANASIUS.—P. 320.

"Cum ex supra dictis constet, *nullam e rebus creatis prius altera factam esse*, sed res omnes factas uno eodemque mandato *simul* extitisse."—Oratio ii. Contra Arianos, n. 63. Edit. Bened. p. 418. New Edition, p. 528. Edit. Migne, Patr. Graecor. Cursus Completus, p. 275.

(27.) SAINT EUCHERIUS.—P. 320.

Speaking stricly we should rather say the author of a Commentary upon Genesis belonging to a very early period of the Church, ascribed by some to Saint Eucherius, and usually published with his works. This author says, no doubt, that God first, in the beginning, created the substance of all things, and afterward developed the various forms on succes sive days (Gen. ii. 4): but then he tells us expressly that the substance did not precede the forms by any priority of time, but only by priority of origin (Gen. i. 2). Thus his view coincides pretty nearly with that of Saint Augustine, whose words, indeed, he seems to borrow. "'Terra autem erat inanis et vacua.' Id est, adhuc informis erat ipsa materia: quia necdum ex ea coelum et terra, necdum omnia formata erant, quae formari restabant: haec enim materia, ex nihilo facta, praecessit tamen res ex se factas, *non quidem aeternitate vel tempore, sicut praecedit lignum arcam;* sed sola origine, *sicut praecedit vox verbum, vel sonus cantum:* nam 'qui vivit in aeternum creavit omnia simul.'"—Edit. Migne, Patr. Latin Cursus Completus, vol. 50, p. 894.

(28.) Procopius of Gaza.—P. 320.

We quote this writer on the authority of Perrerius, from whom the following passage is taken. "Idem censet hoc loco Procopius Gazæus: Mozen enim, inquit, in describendo mundi opificium, sex dierum distinctione usum esse docendi gratia ob tarditatem, videlicet, ruditatemque Judæorum, quibus hæc scribebat: qui quæ Deus *simul* fecerat, ob tantam eorum multitudinem atque varietatem simul et indiscrete capere et comprehendre, ut erant angustissimis ingeniis nequaquam potuissent."—In Genes., cap. 2, vers. 4, 5, 6, n. 179.

(29.) Albertus Magnus.—P. 320.

"Videtur mihi Augustino consentiendum."—Summa P. 1, Quæst. 12, art. 6. See Pianciani, Cosmogonia Naturale, p. 23.

(30.) Saint Thomas.—P. 320.

Summa Pars. 1. Quæst. 74, art. ii.; also in an earlier work, Super Libros Sententiarum Petri Lombardi Commentarius, Distinct. xii. art. i. and iii. Having explained the opinion of Saint Augustine that there was no real succession in the order of time between the various works of the creation, but that all were created together; and also the opinion of other Holy Fathers, that there was a real succession, he continues thus: "Prima ergo opinio [Sancti Augustini] *ma-*

gis convenit rationi, nec est contra Scripturam; quia ea quae in Scriptura ordinem temporis importare videntur, ad ordinem naturae Augustinus refert: secunda vero magis convenit Scripturae secundum suam superficiem. Quia ergo utraque a Sanctis patrocinium habet, utramque sustinendo, objectionibus hinc inde factis respondendum est."—Loco citato, art. i. Solutio.

(31.) CARDINAL CAJETAN.—P. 320.

We are again indebted to Perrerius for the views of Cardinal Cajetan. He writes thus: "Accedit huic sententiæ Cajet. in Comment. super i. cap. Genes., et distinctionem sex dierum putat in id positam a Mose, quo facilius declararet naturalem rerum ordinem, consequentiam et dependentiam. Sic enim res suaptè natura inter se aptæ et connexæ sunt, ut si mundum successivè voluisset Deus facere, non alio ordine vel successione, quàm ut hic narratur, facturus eum fuisset."—In Genes., cap. ii. vers 4, 5, 6, n. 179.

(32.) VENERABLE BEDE.—P. 323.

"Aperte intelligi quia *diem* hoc loco Scriptura *pro omni illo tempore ponit* quo primordialis natura formata est. Neque enim in unoquolibet sex dierum coelum factum est et sideribus illustratum, et terra est separata ab aquis, atque arboribus et herbis consita; sed *more sibi solito Scriptura diem pro tempore ponit;* quomodo Apostolus, cum ait, 'Ecce nunc dies salutis,' non unum specialiter diem, sed totum significat tempus hoc quo in praesenti vita pro aeterna salute laboramus."—Hexaemeron, Lib. i. in Gen. ii. 4; Edit. Migne, Patr. Lat. Cursus Completus, vol. 91, p. 39.

(33.) SAINT AUGUSTINE.—P. 323.

"Superius septem dies numerantur, nunc unus dicitur dies, quo die fecit Deus coelum et terram, et omne viride agri, et omne pabulum, *cujus diei nomine omne tempus significari bene intelligitur.* Fecit enim Deus omne tempus simul cum omnibus creaturis temporalibus, quae creaturae visibiles coeli et terrae nomine significantur."—De Genesi contra Manichaeos, Lib. ii. cap. 3, n. 4.

(34.) MOLINA.—P. 323.

"Dicunt Doctores communiter, Moysem eo loco sumpsisse *diem* pro *tempore* juxta illud Deuteronomii xxxii., juxta est dies perditionis, ... et alibi saepe, in Scriptura sumitur dies pro tempore."—In primam partem, De opere sex dierum, D. I. See Pianciani, Cosmogonia Naturale, p. 27.

(35.) BANNEZ.—P. 323.

"Dies potest accipi pro quacumque duratione et mensura." —In Summa, Pars 1. Quæst. 73.

(36.) PERRERIUS.—P. 323.

"Nec officit huic sententiae, quod paullo superius ex cap. ii. Geneseos prolatum est, 'In die quo fecit Dominus Deus coelum et terram.' Ibi enim *dies pro tempore, sicut crebro fit in Scriptura, positus est.*"—In Gen. cap. i. v. 4, n. 80; see also cap. ii., n. 186.

(37.) PETAVIUS.—P. 323.

"Postquam Moyses sex dierum opificium toto primo capite descripsit, mox in sequenti summatim universeque colligens, 'Istae sunt,' inquit, 'generationes coeli et terrae, quando creata sunt, in die quo fecit Dominus Deus coelum et terram.' Quae verba non unius diei mentionem faciunt, ut quibusdam videtur; qui primum diem designari putant, in quo factum illud est, praeter lucem, quod initio libri Moyses explicat, 'In principio creavit Deus coelum et terram.' Sed eam nos opinionem minime probamus, ac supra docuimus, *diei* nomen istic usurpari pro *tempore:* quod apud Graecos Latinosque, non minus quam Hebraeos, usitatem est. Exemplo sit Ciceronis illud ex libro secundo in Verrem: 'Itaque cum ego diem in Siciliam inquirendi prexiguam postulavissem, invenit iste, qui sibi in Achaiam *biduo breviorem diem* postularet.' Igitur cum dixisset, *in die*, id est tempore illo, factum esse coelum et terram, hoc est perpolitum et elaboratum esse sex continuis diebus," etc.—De Opificio Sex Dierum, Lib. i. cap. 14, sect. 1.

(38.) SAINT AUGUSTINE.—P. 335.

"Tres enim dies superiores quomodo esse sine sole potuerunt, cum videamus nunc solis ortu et occasu diem transigi, noctem vero fieri solis absentia, cum ab alia parte mundi ad orientem redit? Quibus respondemus, potuisse fieri ut tres superiores dies singuli per tantam moram temporis computarentur, per quantam moram circumit sol, ex quo procedit ab oriente quousque rursus ad orientem revertitur. Hanc enim moram et longitudinem temporis possent sentire homines etiamsi in speluncis habitarent, ubi orientem et occidentem solem videre non possent. Atque ita sentitur potuisse istam moram fieri etiam sine sole antequam sol factus esset, atque ipsam moram in illo triduo per dies singulos computatam. Hoc ergo responderemus, nisi nos revocaret, quod ibi dicitur, 'Et facta est vespera et factum est mane,' quod nunc sine solis cursu videmus fieri non posse. Restat ergo ut intelligamus, in ipsa quidem mora temporis *ipsas distinctiones operum sic appellatas, vesperam propter transactionem consummati operis, et mane propter inchoationem futuri operis;* de similitudine scilicet humanorum operum, quia plerumque a mane incipiunt, et ad vesperam desinunt. Habent enim consuetudinem Divinae Scripturae de rebus humanis ad divinas res verba transferre."—De Genesi contra Manichaeos, Lib. i. cap. 14, n. 20.

(39.) SAINT EUCHERIUS.—P. 335.

It is uncertain, as we before observed, if this commentary is the genuine work of Saint Eucherius; at all events it is the production of some learned and Catholic writer of the fifth or sixth century. His words run thus: "*Vespere conditae creaturae terminus; mane initium condendae creaturae alterius.*" —Comment. in Genes. cap. i. v. 4; Edit. Migne, Patr. Latin. Cursus Completus, vol. 50, p. 897. And again in v. 10 et seqq.:—"Si quarto die facta sunt luminaria, quomodo tres dies jam ante fuerunt? nisi ut intelligamus, in ipsa hora temporis ipsas operum distinctiones ita appellatas; *vesperam propter transactionem consummati operis; mane propter inchoationem* futuri diei; in similitudinem humanorum operum quod plerique mane incipiunt et in vesperam desinunt."—Ib. p. 899.

(40.) VENERABLE BEDE.—P. 335.

"Quid est *vespere* nisi *ipsa perfectio singulorum operum?* et *mane*, id est inchoatio sequentium?"—De Sex Dierum Creatione, De Prima Die; Edit. Migne, Patrum Lat. Cursus Completus, vol. 93, p. 210.

In another place he says: "Vespere autem in toto illo triduo, antequam luminaria essent, *consummati operis terminus* non absurde fortasse intelligitur; Mane autem *futuræ operationis significatio.*" In Pentateuchum Comment. Gen. cap. i.; Edit. Migne, vol. 91, p. 194.

(41.) SAINT HILDEGARDE.—P. 335.

"Sex enim dies, sex opera sunt; quia inceptio et completio singuli cujusque operis dies dicitur."—Epist. ad Colonienses. See Pianciani, Cosmogonia, p. 34.

(42.) SAINT AUGUSTINE.—P. 342.

"Dies autem septimus sine vespere est nec habet occasum." —Confess. Lib. xiii. cap. xxxvi.

(43.) VENERABLE BEDE.—P. 342.

"Quia finem non habet, neque ullo termino clauditur."—De Sex Dierum Creatione, De Die Septima; Edit. Migne, Patr. Lat. Cursus Completus, vol. 93, p. 218. And elsewhere he says: "Septimus dies coepit a mane et in nullo vespere terminatur."—In Pentateuch Comment., Gen. ii.; Edit. Migne, vol. 91, p. 203.

(44.) SAINT AUGUSTINE.—P. 355.

"Eligat quis quod potest: tantum ne aliquid temere atque incognitum pro cognito asserat; memineritque se hominem de divinis operibus quantum permittitur quærere."—De Genesi Liber Imperfectus, cap. ix., n. 80.

APPENDIX TO THE AMERICAN EDITION.

From Prof. J. D. Dana's Manual of Geology. [*8vo. Philadelphia: T. Bliss & Co.*] *By permission of the author.*

COSMOGONY.

THE science of cosmogony treats of the history of creation.

Geology comprises that later portion of the history which is within the range of direct investigation, beginning with the rock-covered globe, and gathering only a few hints as to a previous state of igneous fluidity.

Through Astronomy our knowledge of this earlier state becomes less doubtful, and we even discover evidence of a period still more remote. Ascertaining thence that the sun of our system is in intense ignition, that the moon, the earth's satellite, was once a globe of fire, but is now cooled and covered with extinct craters, and that space is filled with burning suns,—and learning also from physical science that all heated bodies in space must have been losing heat through past time, the smallest most rapidly,—we safely conclude that the earth has passed through a stage of igneous fluidity.

Again, as to the remoter period: the forms of the nebulæ and of other starry systems in the heavens, and the relations which subsist between the spheres in our own system, have been found to be such as would have resulted if the whole universe had been evolved from an original nebula or gaseous fluid. It is not necessary for the strength of this argument that any portion of the primal nebula should exist now at this late period in the history of the universe: it is only what might have been expected that the nebulæ of the present heavens should be turning out to be clusters of stars. If, then, this nebular theory be true, the universe has been developed from a primal unit, and the earth is one of the individual orbs produced in the course of its evolution. Its history is in kind like that which has been deciphered with regard to the earth: it only carries the action of physical forces, under a sustaining and directing hand, further back in time.

The science also of Chemistry is aiding in the study of the earth's earliest development, and is preparing itself to write a history of the various changes which should have taken place among the elements from the first commencement of combination to the formation of the solid crust of our globe.

It is not proposed to enter either into chemical or astronomical details in this place, but, supposing the nebular theory to be true, briefly to mention the great stages of progress in the history of the earth, or those successive periods which stand out prominently in time through the exhibition of some new idea in the grand system of progress. The views here offered, and the following on the cosmogony of the Bible, are essentially those brought out by Professor Guyot in his lectures.

Stages of progress.—These stages of progress are as follow:—

(1.) *The* BEGINNING OF ACTIVITY IN MATTER.—In such a beginning from matter in the state of a gaseous fluid the activity would be intense, and it would show itself at once by a manifestation of light, since light is a resultant of molecular activity. A flash of light through the universe would therefore be the first announcement of the work begun.

(2.) *The development of the* EARTH.—A dividing and subdividing of the original fluid going on would have evolved systems of various grades, and ultimately the orbs of space, among these the earth, an igneous sphere enveloped in vapors.

(3.) *The production of the* EARTH'S PHYSICAL FEATURES, —by the outlining of the continents and oceans. The condensible vapors would have gradually settled upon the earth as cooling progressed.

(4.) *The introduction of* LIFE *under its simplest forms,*—as in the lowest of plants, and perhaps, also of animals. As shown on page 396, the systems of structure characterizing the two kingdoms of nature, the *Radiate* of the Vegetable kingdom, and the *Radiate, Molluscan, Articulate,* and *Vertebrate* of the Animal, are not brought out in the simplest forms of life. The true *Zoic* era in history began later. As plants are primarily the food of animals, there is reason for believing that the idea of life was first expressed in a plant.

(5.) *The display of the* SYSTEMS *in the Kingdoms of Life,*—the exhibition of the four grand types under the Animal kingdom, being the predominant idea in this phase of progress.

(6.) *The introduction of the highest class of Vertebrates—that of the* MAMMALS (the class to which MAN belongs), viviparous species, which are eminent above all other Vertebrates for a quality prophetic of a high moral purpose,—that of suckling their young.

(7.) *The introduction of* Man,—the first being of moral and intellectual qualities, and one in whom the unity of nature has its full expression.

There is another great event in the Earth's history which has not yet been mentioned, because of a little uncertainty with regard to its exact place among the others. The event referred to is the first shining of the sun upon the earth, after the vapors which till then had shrouded the sphere were mostly condensed. This must have preceded the introduction of the Animal system, since the sun is the grand source of activity throughout nature on the earth, and is essential to the existence of life, excepting its lowest forms. In the history of the globe which has been given on page 196, it has been shown that the outlining of the continents was one of the earliest events, dating even from the Azoic age; and it is probable, from the facts stated, that it preceded that clearing of the atmosphere which opened the sky to the earth. This would place the event between numbers 3 and 5, and as the sun's light was not essential to the earliest of organisms, probably after number 4.

The order will, then, be—

(1.) Activity begun,—light an immediate result.

(2.) The earth made an independent sphere.

(3.) Outlining of the land and water, determining the earth's general configuration.

(4.) The idea of life expressed in the lowest plants, and afterward, if not cotemporaneously, in the lowest or systemless animals, or Protozoans.

(5.) The energizing light of the sun shining on the earth,—an essential preliminary to the display of the systems of life.

(6.) Introduction of the system of life.

(7.) Introduction of Mammals, the highest order of Vertebrates,—the class afterward to be dignified by including a being of moral and intellectual nature.

(8.) Introduction of Man.

Cosmogony of the Bible.—There is one ancient document on cosmogony—that of the opening page of the Bible—which is not only admired for its sublimity, but is very generally believed to be of divine origin, and which, therefore, demands at least a brief consideration in this place.

In the first place, it may be observed that *this document if true, is of divine origin.* For no human mind was witness of the events; and no such mind in the early age of the world, unless gifted with superhuman intelligence, could have contrived such a scheme;—would have placed the creation of the sun, the source of light to the earth, so long after the creation of light, even on the *fourth* day, and, what is equally singular, between the creation of plants and that of animals, when so important to both; and none could have reached to the depths of philosophy exhibited in the whole plan.

Again, *If divine, the account must bear marks of human imperfection, since it was communicated through man.* Ideas suggested to a human mind by the Deity would take shape in that mind according to its range of knowledge, modes of thought, and use of language, unless it were at the same time supernaturally gifted with the profound knowledge and wisdom adequate to their conception; and even then they could not be intelligibly expressed, for want of words to represent them.

The central thought of each step in the Scripture cosmogony —for example, Light,—the dividing of the fluid earth from the fluid around it, individualizing the earth,—the arrangement of its land and water,—vegetation,—and so on—is brought out in the simple and natural style of a sublime intellect, wise for its times, but unversed in the depths of science which the future was to reveal. The idea of vegetation to such a one would be vegetation as he knew it; and so it is described. The idea of dividing the earth from the fluid around it would take the form of a dividing from the fluid above, in the imperfect conceptions of a mind unacquainted with the earth's sphericity and the true nature of the firmament,—especially as the event was beyond the reach of all ordinary thought.

Objections are often made to the word "day,"—as if its use limited the time of each of the six periods to a day of twenty-four hours. But in the course of the document this word "day" has various significations, and, among them, all that are common to it in ordinary language. These are—(1.) The light,—"God called the light day," v. 5; (2) the "evening and the morning" before the appearance of the sun; (3) the "evening and the morning" after the appearance of the sun; (4) the hours of light in the twenty-four hours (as well as the whole twenty-four hours), in verse 14; and (5) in the following chapter, at the commencement of another record of creation, the whole period of creation is called a "day." The proper meaning of "evening and morning," in a history of creation, is *beginning and completion*; and, in this sense, darkness before light is but a common metaphor.

A Deity working in creation like a day-laborer by earth-days of twenty-four hours, resting at night, is a belittling conception, and one probably never in the mind of the sacred penman. In the plan of an infinite God, centuries are required for the maturing of some of the plants with which the earth is adorned.

The order of events in the Scripture cosmogony corresponds essentially with that which has been given. There was first a void and formless earth: this was literally true of the "heavens and the earth," if they were in a condition of a gaseous fluid. The succession is as follows:

(1.) Light.

(2.) The dividing of the waters below from the waters above the earth, (the word translated *waters* may mean *fluid.*)

(3.) The dividing of the land and water on the earth.

(4.) Vegetation; which Moses, appreciating the philosophical characteristic of the new creation distinguishing it from previous inorganic substances, defines as that "which has seed in itself."

(5.) The sun, moon, and stars.

(6.) The lower animals, those that swarm in the waters, and the creeping and flying species of the land.

(7.) Beasts of prey ("creeping" here meaning "prowling')—

(8.) Man.

In this succession, we observe not merely an order of events, like that deduced from science; there is a system in the arrangement, and a far-reaching prophecy, to which philosophy could not have attained, however instructed.

The account recognizes in creation two great eras of three days each,—an *Inorganic* and an *Organic.*

Each of these eras opens with the appearance of *light:* the *first,* light cosmical; the *second,* light from the sun for the special uses of the earth.

Each are ends in a "day" of two great works,—the two shown to be distinct by being severally pronounced "good." On the *third* "day," that closing the Inorganic era, there was first the *dividing of the land from the waters,* and afterward the *creation of vegetation,* or the institution of a kingdom of life,—a work widely diverse from all preceding it in the era. So on the *sixth* "day," terminating the Organic era, there was first *the creation of Mammals,* and then a second far greater work, totally new in its grandest element, *the creation of Man.*

The arrangement is, then, as follows:—

1. *The Inorganic Era.*

1st Day.—LIGHT cosmical.

2d Day.—The earth divided from the fluid around it, or individualized.

3d Day.— { 1. Outlining of the land and water.
2. Creation of vegetation.

2. *The Organic Era.*

4th Day.—LIGHT from the sun.

5th Day.—Creation of the lower orders of animals.

6th Day.— { 1. Creation of Mammals.
2. Creation of Man.

In addition, the last day of each era included one work typical of the era, and another related to it in essential points, but also prophetic of the future. Vegetation, while, for physical reasons, a part of the creation of the third day, was also prophetic of the future Organic era, in which the progress of life was the grand characteristic. The record thus accords with the fundamental principle in history that the characteristic of an age has its beginnings within the age preceding. So, again, Man, while like other Mammals in structure, even to the homologies of every bone and muscle, was endowed with a spiritual nature, which looked forward to another era, that of spiritual existence.—The *seventh* "day," the day of rest from the work of creation, is man's period of preparation for that new existence; and it is to promote this special end that—in strict parallelism—the Sabbath follows man's six days of work.

The record in the Bible is, therefore, profoundly philosophical in the scheme of creation which it pesents. It is both true and divine. It is a declaration of authorship, both of Creation and the Bible, on the first page of the sacred volume.

There can be no real conflict between the two Books of the GREAT AUTHOR. Both are revelations made by Him to man,—the *earlier* telling of God-made harmonies coming up from the deep past, and rising to their height when man appeared, the *later* teaching man's relations to his Maker, and speaking of loftier harmonies in the eternal future.

www.ingramcontent.com/pod-product-compliance
Lightning Source LLC
LaVergne TN
LVHW020127110826
845151LV00001B/293

9781425540548